The Art of Solution Focused Therapy

Elliott Connie, MA, LPC, lives in Arlington, Texas. He maintains private practices in Keller and Fort Worth, Texas, and is frequently a presenter and lecturer on topics related to solution focused therapy. Currently, he is pursuing a PhD in family therapy from Texas Woman's University.

Linda Metcalf, PhD, LPC, LMFT, is a former classroom teacher, licensed professional counselor and licensed marriage and family therapist. She is the author of several books on solution focused therapy including *Counseling Toward Solutions* (1995, 2008), *Parenting Toward Solutions* (1997), *Teaching Toward Solutions* (1999, 2005), *Solution Focused Group Therapy* (1999, 2005), and *The Miracle Question* (2005). She has also authored numerous articles on solution focused therapy. She has presented her work throughout the United States, Canada, Australia, Japan, Singapore, Norway, Germany, and the United Kingdom. She is a Professor in the Department of Education at Texas Wesleyan University, and coordinator of the school counseling program. She is also the president-elect of the American Association for Marriage and Family Therapy.

The Art of Solution Focused Therapy

ELLIOTT CONNIE, MA, LPC
LINDA METCALF, PhD, LPC, LMFT

Editors

SPRINGER PUBLISHING COMPANY
New York

Springer Publishing Company, LLC
11 West 42nd Street
New York, NY 10036
www.springerpub.com

Acquisitions Editor: Jennifer Perillo
Project Manager: Mark Frazier
Cover Design: Steven Pisano
Composition: Apex CoVantage, LLC

Ebook ISBN: 978–0–8261–1738–0

09 10 11 / 5 4 3 2 1

Library of Congress Cataloging-in-Publication Data

The art of solution focused therapy / [edited by]
Elliott Connie, Linda Metcalf.
p. cm.
Includes bibliographical references and index.
ISBN 978–0–8261–1737–3 (alk. paper)
1. Solution-focused therapy. I. Metcalf, Linda. II. Connie, Elliott.
RC489.S65A78 2009
616.89'14—dc22 2009014206

Printed in the United States of America by Hamilton Printing

To Annette Hellum, my family Matriarch, you truly taught me to pay attention to what I could do and not what I couldn't.

Also, to all of the SFTer's that came before us, this book is a testament to the groundwork you laid before us.

—E.C.

This book is dedicated to the students of solution focused therapy.

May the words inside inspire you. It is also dedicated to my family, who continues to be the exceptions in my life.

—L.M.

Contents

Contributors

Brian Cade
Registered Family Therapist,
United Kingdom Council
for Psychotherapy

Yvonne Dolan, MA
Private Practice
Denver, CO

Cynthia Franklin, PhD, LCSW, LMFT
University of Texas
Austin, TX

Rayya Ghul
Certificate of Qualification,
London School of
Occupational Therapy

Debbie Hogan, MS, BCPC
Academy of Solution Focused Training
Singapore

Chris Iveson BSc
Sociology, Certificate of Qualification
in Social Work, UK Council for
Psychotherapy Accreditation

Alison Johnson, PsyD
Private Practice
Pasadena, CA

Harry Korman, MD
Private Practice
Malmo, Sweden

Eve Lipchik, LMFT, LCSW
Private Practice
Milwaukee, WI

Alasdair Macdonald, MB, ChB, MRCPsych, FRCPsych, DPM
Private Practice
United Kingdom

Thorana Nelson, PhD
Utah State University
Logan, Utah

Sara Smock, PhD, LMFTA
Texas Tech University
Lubbock, Texas

Terese Steiner, MD
Private Practice
Switzerland

Tracy Todd, PhD
Association for Marriage
and Family Therapists
Washington, DC

Ron Warner, EdD
University of Toronto
Toronto, Canada

Preface

Many persons have a wrong idea of what constitutes true happiness. It is not attained through self-gratification but through fidelity to a worthy purpose.

—Helen Keller

The idea for this book actually began, for Linda Metcalf and for me, years before either of us was aware of it.

During the second semester of my graduate studies, our school announced that the codeveloper of the solution focused approach, Insoo Kim Berg, would be coming to our area (Fort Worth, Texas) to speak at another local university. This created quite a stir for students. By this time, we had been studying psychotherapy theories for almost two years and now there was an opportunity to meet one of the theorists we had been studying. I will never forget the excitement this created. Student groups made plans to go, professors offered extra credit for attending the event, and students hoped for a chance to meet the speaker to request an autograph. It was nothing short of amazing. However, despite all of this, I made no plans to attend.

At this point in my education I was still not sure which theory would be the best fit for me. I had only been introduced to solution focused therapy (SFT) in the previous semester during an introduction to theories course. I knew that SFT agreed with the way I viewed people, but I did not yet understand how the approach worked with clients. A profound event that occurred later that semester would change my understanding. So, I decided not to attend the workshop. My thinking was that if I attended, I would be impacted by what I heard from the speaker and biased toward SFT before I had the chance to explore any other theories. I was a passionate student and I wanted so much to have a theory that I believed in and could be effective with later on when I began seeing clients. Yet I did not want to be prematurely biased toward SFT by attending the event. I thought I would have plenty of chances to hear Insoo Berg speak if I later decided SFT was the model that best suited me. Sadly, this was not to be.

As my education went on, it became clear to me that SFT was indeed the model that was the best fit. I began to regret my decision to miss Insoo's speech. Throughout the rest of my studies, I would hear stories of how amazing the event was. Students remarked on the elegance of Insoo, along with her passion and her belief in the theory. I heard stories of the exercises she conducted with the audience and her humility when people met her. The stories increased my remorse for missing the event and simultaneously strengthened my resolve to attend one of her events once I graduated.

In January of 2007, just two months after my graduation, Insoo Kim Berg passed away suddenly. Upon hearing the news, I wept. I wept for a person I had not had the chance to meet because her work had impacted my life and my education so profoundly. I was further saddened because I would never be able to make up for my decision to miss her speaking engagement.

I would later learn that her husband and partner in the development of SFT, Steve de Shazer, had passed away just two years earlier while in Europe. Other key theorists associated with various family therapy approaches had either already passed away or would soon pass. They included Paul Watzlawick (the communications theorist associated with the Mental Research Institute in Palo Alto, California) and Jay Haley (developer of the strategic family therapy approach). With this knowledge came an acute awareness that if I was ever to have the opportunity to be in the presence of one of the influential people in the field of psychotherapy, specifically brief therapy due to my interests, then I needed to seize that chance. These theorists would not be around forever, and their presence should not be taken for granted.

My interest in meeting, and learning from, the developers was not just to be awe-stricken (though I admit to being in awe at times). It was to ask them a simple question that has been on my mind since my graduate studies. That question is: "How did you discover the way you work best with clients?"

I couldn't find the answer anywhere. It went unanswered in all the texts I read. They often went into great detail explaining the concepts of one particular theory or another, the techniques associated with the theory, and the key developer(s) of the theory. I would always want to know more. As I was going through my journey of discovery toward

SFT, I became very interested in the stories of others who utilized the model in their work. I have always been interested in stories of others; as I reflect on my education, it was not what my teachers taught me that I recall with ease, but rather the stories they told while teaching. I would always ask my professors, "How did you get interested in the field?" or "How did you discover your theoretical approach?" As my professors answered my questions, they taught me much more than I could learn from a textbook. They opened my eyes to a world of discovery that would later lay the groundwork for this book. I was able to notice passion as they each spoke about their theories and the way those theories had impacted the lives of their clients and themselves professionally.

The conversations I had were not just limited to the professors in my program. My fellow students and I often discussed what we liked about one theory or another and what it was like to practice at our practicum sites. Many trends became apparent to us during this period of discussion, some of them amazingly helpful, while others were a bit more confusing.

I noticed that the students that found themselves attracted to traditional psychotherapy models such as cognitive behavioral therapy (CBT), rational emotive behavior therapy (REBT), or theoretical intergrationism (eclectic) seemed to be more accepted by their peers and professors. They were excited about the way their supervisors responded to them at their sites, and often times were offered long-term therapy positions or positions as supervisors once their degree was completed. The students that were gravitating toward more postmodern theories such as SFT and narrative therapy had a different experience. There were stories of supervisors threatening jobs and removing once-promised promotions. We were all confused about this dynamic. This led me to ask the question, "What is different about therapists that use a postmodern theory? Why did they choose to work in this way as opposed to the more traditional approaches to working with clients?"

I read every book I could on solution focused therapy in an attempt to learn more, and not just learn about the model, but also about the people that called it their own. I read in Bill O'Hanlon's work that problem-focused assumptions never seemed to fit him. I read Peter De Jong and Insoo Kim Berg's description of the shift from the medical model (problem solving) to the new focus of solution building. Sometimes I noticed that the word *brief* would be included. I soon learned that both solution focused and brief were not synonymous. Yet I was still curious about more of the people that used the model and how they learned about SFT. I wanted to know what type of people they were and if I had anything in common with them. I also wondered if they had experienced some of the same things that I encountered once I discovered SFT—the increase of passion, the impact on my personal life, and indeed some of the more difficult experiences at my job. Did other solution focused practitioners have these things in common?

One day, I approached Linda Metcalf, who by this time was mentoring me in using SFT in my work, and I discussed with her my curiosity. I will never forget her response. Her eyes lit up as she proclaimed, "Elliott, I have always wondered that too!" We spoke for over an hour about how she had discovered SFT and what she had experienced as a result of that discovery. We brainstormed about what we would ask other solution focused practitioners if they were in the room with us at that moment. She made a list of each question. We went on to make a wish list of people we would like to contact and pose our questions to. At the end of this meeting, she said something that I was already thinking, but afraid to say: "This would make a good book." With that proclamation, the idea was born.

As we contacted each person on our list, we quickly realized it was true; we had a *great* book idea. The leaders in the field were all gracious enough to answer our questions. I will digress for a moment to remark on the wonderful people that responded to our requests. This project simply would not exist without their efforts. The responses we received from the practitioners touched us deeply on several levels. We remain both moved and humbled to this day. This collection of willing participants began to fill the void that existed from my decision to miss Insoo's presentation just a few short years before. I was now having my questions answered by the people that remained to carry the torch of the model, and this time, the answers would be immortalized on paper. Now everyone has an opportunity to read the answers from the remarkable people included in this book on how they discovered the model of solution focused therapy.

THE CONTENTS OF THIS BOOK

Since SFT takes such a different approach to therapy, we wanted to address several important components of the approach. Currently, there are several excellent books available on the how-to guidelines of this approach (we have provided a list of some of our favorites at the end of this book). However, this book serves a different purpose. We hope to address the art of SFT, focusing on being solution focused in session and in life. To accomplish this, we will begin with an overview of the solution focused model in chapter 1. We will review some of the questions associated with the model, as well as the history of its development at the Brief Family Therapy Center in Milwaukee, Wisconsin, by Steve de Shazer and Insoo Kim Berg. We will also review some of the important tenets and assumptions of the model and how they guide a practitioner working from the solution focused perspective. In chapter 2 there is a review of the different settings in which SFT has been utilized as well as different research that has been conducted on this approach. There will also be a review of the research body of SFT. Focusing on solutions often requires a different type of thinking and this type of review is needed before the true highlight of the book is unveiled.

The real spotlight of this book is, of course, the stories by the practitioners themselves. This book is a collection of the most published and experienced SFT practitioners in the world, how they each discovered the theory, and what that process was like for them. The practitioners included in this volume are a diverse collection of counselors, social workers, psychiatrists, and marriage and family therapists. They utilize the solution focused approach in settings ranging from psychiatric services, to not-for-profit agencies, to work with children, to building the research base of SFT. They hail from all over the world and come from remarkably diverse backgrounds. Considerable effort was made to leave each contributor's text as close to what they sent to preserve this diversity. This was the most respectful way we could handle their stories; in the same way we work to honor our clients, we desired to honor these amazing practitioners.

Two of the people that were key in founding this approach, Eve Lipchik and Yvonne Dolan, authored chapters 3 and 4. They offer the unique perspective of what it was like in the early days of searching for solutions. This early group influenced the chapter 5 contributor, Chris Iveson, who went on to found BRIEF Therapy in Europe.

The following three chapters illustrate the diversity of this approach as Alison Johnson, Tracy Todd, and Brian Cade discuss how, though they are widely different, they each migrated toward this approach.

Chapters 9 and 10, by Cynthia Franklin and Sara Smock, discuss the growing research base and what it is like to be a researcher interested in this approach.

The next five chapters offer vivid depictions of how SFT can work in a wide variety of settings. Rayya Ghul discusses how SFT works in her occupational therapy practice; Debbie Hogan talks about establishing SFT in Singapore; Harry Korman is noted for his work in substance abuse; Linda Metcalf discusses her pioneering work in the schools; and Terese Steiner and Alasdair Macdonald show how SFT can be integrated into psychiatric settings.

This section of the book is concluded by three chapters that offer insight into how SFT differs from other approaches as this author (Elliott Connie), Thorana Nelson, and Ron Warner discuss what it was like learning SFT after previously being trained in another approach.

To each practitioner, Linda and I posed certain open-ended questions:

INTRODUCTION TO THE SOLUTION FOCUSED THERAPY MODEL

- How did you first learn about solution focused therapy?
- How did you discover that solution focused therapy was the model that seemed to fit with your way of working with clients?
- What characteristics of the model drew you toward it?

WORKING WITH CLIENTS: THE PROFESSIONAL IMPACT OF SOLUTION FOCUSED THERAPY

- How has utilizing solution focused therapy impacted your work with clients? (Please mention if you utilized a previous model and the difference you noticed in clients and yourself after switching to solution focused therapy.)
- How would your clients describe your work with them? Have any of them who experienced another model of therapy commented on the difference (if any) that they perceived when working with you?
- What is it about SFT that makes it so effective?
- Describe one of your favorite cases and how it impacted your work as a therapist.

LIFE OUTSIDE THE THERAPY ROOM: PERSONAL EFFECTS OF SOLUTION FOCUSED THERAPY

- Has the use of solution focused therapy impacted you in your personal life?
- What are some key personality traits that you think are shared among solution focused practitioners?

TRAINING AND REFLECTION

- What are some common mistakes that therapists trying on the model make most often? If you had a chance to guide them differently, how would you do so?
- What are some things you notice students doing while trying on this model that lets you know this model may fit them?
- If you were training therapists in the solution focused therapy model, what strategies would you use to train them and how would you present the material?
- If you could pick a pioneer solution focused therapist who impacted your work, whom would you name and why?
- What developments would you like to see in the future of this model?

As we reviewed each of the chapters, Linda Metcalf and I realized that not only were our original questions answered in a way that had never been done before, but they were answered beyond our wildest dreams. What we learned went far beyond theory and practice, and touched that piece of the human experience that led each of us to enter the helping profession.

The book ends with chapter 20, a conclusion, describing what it was like for us to write this book. We want to share what we learned, what themes we identified, and what traits seemed to be common amongst the practitioners.

Lastly, we hope that we can address some of the myths of SFT . . . the myths that baffle others who don't seem to understand the model or criticize it. For example, statements such as, "SFT does not have a research base," or "SFT ignores too much," or "SFT only addresses superficial issues." We sincerely hope to address these, and many others, throughout this text.

So, as you begin reading this text, I would like to share with you a story that may be helpful. It is a story that a close friend and colleague named Cecilia once told me related to learning SFT. She had just graduated from a social work program where the emphasis was placed on CBT. Months before this story took place, Cecilia had approached me and expressed an interest in learning SFT. I informed her that I would be conducting an upcoming workshop on SFT. She attended the workshop and immediately began practicing using the model with the type of passion that every teacher hopes to see in their students.

One day while I was sitting in my office, Cecilia approached me and asked to talk. I could tell that she was looking to have a serious conversation, so I invited her in and closed the door. She was aware that I was working on this book and had a suggestion for me. She asked that I be sure to explain that people studying this model need to understand, above all else, that SFT represents a way of thinking and not just a collection of techniques. She asked me to express that to truly understand SFT, people have to observe it, read about it, think about it, and focus on solutions in their personal lives. I asked what led to her making these suggestions, as this was very out of character for her. She explained that since she began studying SFT, she had made many changes in her own life. She used to have so much anxiety that she experienced physical symptoms, usually stomachaches. The stomachaches had gone away and she was experiencing more rewarding experiences in her family, work, and personal life. My only response was to let her know that I would do my best.

So here it is: my best. On behalf of myself and Linda Metcalf, we hope you truly enjoy our effort to express what we think are important components of this approach, as well as enjoy, as we did, reading the work of the practitioners that so graciously added to this project.

Elliott Connie, MA, LPC

Acknowledgments

I would like to start off by thanking the person that introduced me to the world of solution focused therapy, Dr. Linda Metcalf. I will never forget the first time I heard you talking about this approach. It was clear that you were not just talking about a way of doing therapy but a way of being. Hour after hour, we discussed this way of being as you shared your experience and wisdom with me. It was this generosity that helped me grow from a passionate student to an author. Thank you.

To Jennifer Perillo, thank you for taking a chance on this project and supporting the idea for a different kind of book. Your feedback throughout this process was incredibly helpful and I will never forget getting an e-mail from you with "Good News" in the subject line.

To Rayya Ghul, who was so curious about how an SFT therapist knew his question would work that she was moved to tears. Thank you for being so skillful at describing your passion and curiosity about this approach. To Eve Lipchik, thank you for sharing what it was like in the early days of SFT. Your excitement was evident as you described the way the team at the Brief Family Therapy Center (BFTC) formed these ideas and pioneered a new way of thinking. To Yvonne Dolan, thank you for being supportive from the first time we contacted you about this project. Your stories about how SFT impacted your work with children and how being around SFT practitioners impacted your life were amazing. To Chris Iveson, thank you for contributing to this project. Your presence in this book truly allowed my best hopes to be realized. To Alison Johnson, thank you for working so hard and taking so much time each morning to put together such an inspirational chapter—it was so appreciated. To Thorana Nelson, thank you for sharing the story about working with the single mother. It is a wonderful illustration of how being curious about details of a solution can bring about change. To Sara Smock, thank you for sharing your passion for increasing the research base of SFT in this book. I feel so lucky that there is someone like you tenaciously working to demonstrate that this approach is effective through research. To Ron Warner, thank you for taking the time to have a conversation with an aspiring author about a book idea and for agreeing to help. I very much appreciated your generosity.

To my wife, Carmesia, your support and patience truly made this project possible. Thank you for seeing success in me long before I could see it in myself, you have changed my life in so many ways with your love. To my mother, Jeanette, watching your strength throughout my life allowed me to demonstrate my own; thank you for showing me how to be strong. To my aunt, Lynette, you carry a graceful confidence with you in everything that you do. Thank you for sharing that confidence with me. To my brothers, Adam and Issac, thank you for your understanding as I spent countless weekends away from each of you working on this project. I owe you. To my best friends, Kyle and Matt, thank you for believing in me! Without that belief this project would never have been completed. To my friend Cecilia, thank you for helping me fix my many grammatical errors. You really saved me.

Elliott Connie

I would like to express my gratitude to my coauthor, Elliott Connie, whose incredible enthusiasm about solution focused therapy has served to ignite my passion all over again for teaching and learning from those whose work I have always admired. The day I mentioned my query to you, Elliott, about the traits, personality, and talents that seemed to draw a person to solution focused therapy, you took the challenge and brought it to life, producing a proposal that won us this project. You have helped to fulfill a curiosity I have had for a long time and bring it to life through the marvelous answers provided by our colleagues inside these pages. Thank you. To Jennifer Perillo, thank you for believing in our project. Your enthusiasm was contagious and your editing, helpful. I appreciated your excitement about solution focused therapy and your willingness to bring Springer Publishing into its world.

To Tracy Todd, who was determined to give us his best, thank you for the lovely story of walking around the lake with de Shazer. It fits de Shazer's simplicity well, to think of him in such a peaceful surrounding, musing about therapy with a student full of curiosity. To Brian Cade, always the humorist and always ready with the right quotes, the right case, and the personal sharing that make you such an irresistible colleague to know and work with, thank you for the time you took out of your busy life to give us your words. To Harry Korman, Terese Steiner, and Alasdair Macdonald, you are physicians who take psychiatry to a higher level of understanding where patients become people with abilities and strengths, rather than numbers needing a diagnosis. Your patients are lucky. I admire your tenacity to integrate solution focused work into a medical model that has its own strengths, helping patients to flourish even more when combined with their strengths. Your heartwarming stories of patients, and your own professional and personal growth and gratification, give us all hope and inspiration with clients who only see their deficits. To Cynthia Franklin, I share with you the love of schools and schoolchildren and have huge hopes that the world of education will stop, look, listen, and pay attention to what's working, rather than what's not, with your work leading the pack. Thank you for your work at Garza High School, a school that has given a second and third chance to students who otherwise might have missed out on futures you helped them to create. I appreciate your research and your passion to make the model visible in education. To Debbie Hogan, such a wonderful host to me in Singapore and such a talented therapist, thank you for giving us your account of what helped you grow as a therapist, under the marvelous guidance and personality of Insoo Berg. We miss her so, and yet you carry on what she meant to continue. Your pursuits in Asia are met with excitement because you are excited.

To my husband, Roger, who is always ready to get one more take-out dinner while I finish one more chapter, thank you for your belief in me and reassurance that I can write one more book. To my two golden retrievers, Rex 1 and Rex 2, your need for exercise each day was a stress relief that gave me time to mentally write while I walked. To my grown children, Roger, Kelli, and Ryan, you are always acknowledged because your influence in my life makes me who I am.

Linda Metcalf

1 Overview of Solution Focused Therapy

ELLIOTT CONNIE

You have got to discover you, what you do, and trust it.

—Barbra Streisand

HOW DOES SOLUTION FOCUSED THERAPY WORK?

One of the creators of this approach, Steve de Shazer, often replied to this question by simply saying, "It is magic, I do not know how clients do it." The presence of magic is not limited to solution focused therapy (SFT). All therapy contains something magical. There is something unknowable that occurs in the relationship between the client and therapist that allows healing to take place. However, there is something very different about SFT as compared to traditional psychotherapy approaches. In my own attempts to answer this question, I admit to having significant difficulties. I have learned to answer the initial question when conducting trainings by providing three different types of information:

1. An explanation of the history and development of SFT
2. A review of the tenets and assumptions associated with the model
3. A review of the techniques and questions that SFT is known for

This chapter will be an explanation of the solution focused approach from that perspective. There is simply no other way to say it: A therapist utilizing SFT thinks differently than therapists using other approaches. Not better, just different. Yet understanding these differences can be a key component to becoming an effective solution focused therapist.

HISTORY OF SOLUTION FOCUSED THERAPY

The solution focused approach was developed in the late 1970s by Steve de Shazer and his wife, Insoo Kim Berg, while working at the Brief Family Therapy Center in Milwaukee, Wisconsin, following the example set in Palo Alto, California, at the Mental Research Institute (MRI). After studying brief therapy at MRI, Steve de Shazer developed an interest in what makes brief therapy work. Intent on establishing the "MRI of the Midwest," de Shazer teamed up with wife and other practitioners such as Eve Lipchik, Jim Derks, Elam Nunnally, and Marilyn LaCourt. Later, others were added, such as John Walter, Jane Peller, Alex Molnar, Kate Kowalski, and Michelle Weiner-Davis (Lipchik, 2002).

This group built on the work of those at the MRI, especially Milton Erickson and John Weakland. They routinely conducted therapy in front of a team observing from a one-way mirror. Many conversations and ideas came from these early observations that ultimately led to the development of SFT and the innovative process associated with the approach. From my perspective, an amazing facet of those observations and conversations is the diversity of the group involved. This diversity has led to the widespread utilization of SFT in settings ranging from schools (Metcalf, 2008) to working to overcome addictions (Berg & Miller, 1992) and from Child Protective Services (Berg & Kelly, 2000) to domestic violence (Lee, Unken, & Sebold, 2004).

The diversity may also have led to widespread misunderstandings of SFT (Lipchik, 2002). The current emphasis on evidence-based approaches in the field of psychotherapy requires approaches to specialize for the purposes of research and demonstrated efficacy. There are approaches that specialize in treating one diagnosis or another, one age group or another, one type of family problem or another. SFT is different in that there is no *one* area where this approach has been effective. Rather, there have been many. These studies will be further discussed in chapters 9 and 10, among others.

Recently, while doing some work for a local social service agency, I was told that the agency would be implementing a plan to only utilize evidence-based programs. They were going to utilize one program for clients with "externalizing disorders," another program for "internalizing disorders," and so on. From then on, this would be how treatment decisions would be made at the agency. Each service offered had to match up to the client's presenting problem or situation.

In my work for the agency, I had been utilizing SFT exclusively and experiencing success (the agency measured success by use of treatment plans and tracking missed appointments). So, I decided I would raise the possibility of using SFT as a part of their evidence-based programs. I will never forget being told that SFT did not fit into their plans because there was no research to support SFT as an evidence-based approach.

This statement came as a shock to me. I had been exposed to a mountain of research on the approach and had not heard anyone say this before (although I have heard it since). How could someone say there was no research to support the approach? The research base of SFT seemed so obvious to me.

SFT is an approach that is rooted in research both at MRI, then later in Milwaukee at the Brief Family Therapy Center, and now all over the world. Each new development in the theory was researched by asking clients about the helpfulness of the approach. The team examined several session hours to determine which questions seemed to be linked to the client having effective conceptualizations that led to sustainable solutions (de Shazer et al., 2007). This early research focused on the helpfulness of the model and the questions being asked in therapy. The team only kept those aspects that were helpful and led toward the client's solutions. Later, the effective techniques and questions were published both in books and in journal articles. Also, in later years, this approach would be researched in more scientific studies where SFT was compared to other more widely accepted evidenced approaches. In these studies SFT has continued to achieve outcomes that either match or surpass these other approaches (Macdonald, 2007).

There have also been research studies comparing SFT to other therapeutic approaches. In the largest outcome study ever done, helpfulness of the therapeutic approach was not linked to the problem type the client was experiencing (Seligman, 1995). This led me to wonder why so many mental health organizations and funding sources make treatment decisions that match therapeutic approaches with client problems when there is minimal research to suggest that such a practice is helpful.

As I contemplated why professionals do not accept the research, I came to a few conclusions. The first is related to the thinking of solution focused practitioners. In preparing to write this book, I had the pleasure of corresponding with several practitioners that utilize this approach from all over the world. One thing that many of them shared was that when they discovered SFT, they realized it was something that they already were doing (or thinking) as they worked with clients. They realized that SFT was more than just a way of working. It is a way of thinking: a way of thinking about people, a way of thinking in session, and a way of thinking about research. If someone only has an understanding of the process and questions used in the approach, then they may only be looking for research to support the effectiveness of those questions and techniques with specific problems. This is drastically different than reviewing the research to determine the efficacy of the approach as a whole. People cannot evaluate the overall efficacy of SFT (its assumptions, tenets, and questions) if all they have been exposed to are the techniques.

Another reason may be the language and stance of the solution focused practitioners themselves. To make this point, I will share two different stories to show the difference in how someone from a solution focused perspective and someone from a more traditional perspective answered the same question.

The first was a therapist that utilized cognitive behavioral therapy (CBT) in her work. A mother of a young child asked the therapist if she treated children that have experienced trauma. The therapist answered by explaining that she had recently learned to do trauma-focused cognitive behavioral therapy (TFCBT). She explained that this was an approach that was effective for treating trauma in children and she believed that since she had tried other treatments, this is what "should be tried next." The mother agreed to allow the therapist to see her daughter.

I do not mean to imply that there is anything wrong with her answer. It is just very different from the way a solution focused practitioner would respond. In a training video, Steve de Shazer explained that he is often asked if he believes SFT is effective with one diagnosis or another and his answer was always the same: "50–50." The differences in the responses are astounding and have wide-ranging ramifications. A therapist working from a solution focused perspective believes that the client has the answer and thus should be the expert himself/herself. The therapist that believes he or she is the expert must also believe that he or she knows something that the client does not know and needs to learn. This is opposite from the assumptions of SFT.

Additionally, a solution focused therapist would not consider the diagnosis as a necessary component for treatment. This makes it impossible for the solution focused therapist to respond the way the CBT therapist did. Answers like the one given by Steve de Shazer may lead people to believe that perhaps the SFT approach is not as effective because the therapist does respond with a "yes, I treat X diagnosis." It is not that the diagnosis is not treated, rather, the therapist thinks past the diagnosis, toward the client's competencies, rather than pathology. Perhaps this kind of explanation has led people to believe SFT is not as effective as other approaches in certain therapeutic settings, when the contrary is true.

The history of SFT is rich with stories of practitioners that thought, talked, and worked differently. It was not just people using different techniques in a session; it was people with a different way of thinking that led to the revolutionary techniques. This new way of thinking is illogical. Logic leads us to believe that if there is a problem someone needs solved, we must first learn as much about the problem as possible in order to cure it. Logic also leads us to believe that if we have an intense problem, then an intense solution is required. This original group of SFT developers did not follow this logic. In fact, they went to the opposite end of the spectrum as they created what became known throughout the world as solution focused therapy.

TENETS OF SFT

I will utilize the tenets offered by Steve de Shazer and his colleagues in *More Than Miracles* (2007, pp. 1–3) to point out the differences between SFT and other problem-focused approaches, as well as demonstrate how these tenets can be followed in session. SFT is not theoretically based but instead is based on practicality. Coming from a minimalist perspective, these are the tenets that are key to solution focused therapy.

If It Is Not Broken, Don't Fix It

This tenet is crucial and perhaps the single most important tenet underlying this approach. If the client is not reporting something as a problem, then they have already fixed it or are currently fixing it, making any therapeutic interventions irrelevant.

Stephanie and Seth were a couple in their late 20s that came to my office to attempt to repair their relationship, which had recently become so difficult that she had to move out of their apartment. The couple expressed a strong desire to reconnect and we began to have conversations about the type of relationship they would like to have.

After three sessions, which occurred over the course of six weeks, the couple reported that they had experienced significant progress in their relationship and were now beginning to dream about the future together again. This reported progress included elimination of arguments, living in the same residence, increased intimacy, and increased trust.

However, none of this is why I have included this story in this book. Something fascinating happened before and during the fourth session. I received a phone call from Stephanie prior to that session. She explained to me that this session would be a "doozy" due to what she was "ready to admit." This statement was made through tears and I began to imagine the worst. When the couple arrived at my office, I could tell Stephanie had been crying and Seth was unusually quiet. As the session began, the couple explained just what this "doozy" was. Stephanie said that she had a serious drinking problem and consumed approximately a pint of vodka per day. As she described the extent of her drinking, Seth sat quietly, occasionally nodding in agreement. Stephanie went on to say that her family had tried to get her to go to rehab but she had refused and was still not willing to go. Then, she made a statement that shocked me. She explained that she had found the work we had been doing to improve their relationship helpful and thus felt hopeful that if we began to address the drinking, the outcome would also be positive. Seth then explained that prior to the first session, Stephanie made him promise not to talk about the drinking at all. So, prior to that moment, it never came up.

Throughout the same session, Stephanie remarked about how important it was to know that therapy would be helpful before she began to discuss this issue and that is why she only focused on the relationship first, which she called "a test." As the session went on, and we had discussions about her desire to reduce her drinking and have a happier life, Stephanie still refused to enter treatment but did agree to make some other changes. Some examples included allowing Seth to hold her check card while he was at work and to have only a minimal amount of alcohol in the home, managed by Seth. The couple agreed to schedule another session, then left.

I received another call prior to the next session, but this time it was Seth. He explained that they would be unable to attend the session because Stephanie had agreed to enter a residential treatment center. He informed me that one day, "out of the blue," she called him at work and stated she was ready. He knew exactly what she was referring to, so he headed home immediately and together they found a place for her to safely detox and then a subsequent location to receive treatment. Seth was tearful, stating he could not believe she was actually going to treatment. They had been together for almost 5 years and the drinking had been an issue for most of that time.

After several months with no contact, I met with the couple at their request. Stephanie looked like a new person, and in fact, so did Seth. Physically, they looked as though they had been made over. They were smiling, laughing, and had a certain glow about them. I began the session with a usual question, "What has been different since our previous meeting?" They replied that Stephanie had over 90 days clean. Seth had stopped drinking in support of Stephanie, familial relationships had improved, and the couple was happier than ever before.

When I sit back and reflect on this remarkable couple, I am reminded that they came to the first session needing to "test" me. I admit that during the second session, I smelled alcohol on Stephanie's breath, but decided not to mention it because she was clearly not intoxicated and in no danger. I chose to not fix the drinking because the couple did not tell me it was broken, or, that they wanted to discuss it. The couple stated that the relationship was what they wanted to work on so that is where we focused our conversation. I sincerely believe if I had mentioned the drinking when I first noticed it, I would have failed Stephanie's test and she would not have returned to therapy. This may seem obvious, but just a few short years prior, I would have done something completely different. In my original training, I was taught to identify all of the factors that contribute to the problem, even if the client did not desire to fix them. As a solution focused therapist today, I let my clients identify the problem.

If Something Is Found to Be Working, Do More of It

Central in practicing from an SF perspective is the belief that all people come to counseling already doing something to resolve the problem (or at least preventing the problem from getting worse). According to de Shazer et al. (2007), this tenet amplifies the hands-off perspective of this approach. If a client is already doing something that is effective, then the task is for the therapist to get out of the way and encourage the client to more of that behavior. The task is to be tenacious about seeking to locate these things and respectful in inviting the client to do more of these things.

While facilitating a group for parents, I observed this tenet in action. One of the attendees explained that she was having a difficult time getting her children to respect her and her rules. She had three teenage children and all of them violated curfew, did not do chores, and experimented with risky behaviors, such as drugs and sexual activity. I later learned that the mother was a schoolteacher, and not just any type of teacher. She was responsible for the behavior intervention classroom for her school and she *loved* it. Wow! This meant that she spent her day working with, and enjoying, the school's most difficult students.

When I asked her how her students behaved in her class, she explained they behaved well for her—so much so that other teachers often asked her how she was able to elicit such responses from the kids when they themselves had such struggles. She then explained to the group what she did in her classroom. She had a chart on the wall so that each student knew their expectations for the day, she made sure she was pleasant, because the students deserved a pleasant teacher, and she never ever raised her voice at a student. As she spoke, other parents began taking notes and one of them said, "Is that how you are at home?" The mother simply shook her head in silence. She then stated that she would start treating her home the same way she treated her classroom.

Each week thereafter, the mother updated the group on something different she was doing with her children and the progress the children were making as a result of her changes. It was amazing. After the final group, the mother expressed how thankful she was that the group members encouraged her to "treat her home the way she treats her classroom."

This mother did not need to be taught how to be a parent or to learn something new about parenting. She simply needed to be encouraged and reminded that she already knew how to manage teenage behaviors. Once this occurred, the children rapidly began to respond to her in a very desirable way, just as the kids in the school did. She already had the solution; she just needed to do more of it.

If Something Is Found to Not Be Working, Do Something Different

There is a human tendency to repeat a solution that has not worked in the past. This is true for therapists and clients alike. As therapists, we often justify the repetition by thinking, "Maybe the client isn't ready for change, but this is what needs to happen." This tenet highlights the fact that a solution is not a solution unless it works; if something does not work it must not be a solution (de Shazer et al., 2007). Many approaches in therapy believe that if something does not work it must be the client's fault, but in SFT, if the task developed in session is not effective for the client, then a different solution is developed. To illustrate the difference, I will share an experience I had while working at a social service agency.

A few years ago, one of my duties was to attend weekly supervision meetings with an agency treatment team. The purpose of this meeting was a noble one: to provide support for the staff with their most difficult clients. However, many members of the treatment team dreaded this meeting more than any other requirement associated with their job and so did I. Each treatment provider was mandated to discuss their most difficult cases by explaining what they were currently doing with the client. The conversation was focused on the interventions being used by the therapist. If they weren't working (and they often weren't), the client was labeled as resistant or not ready for change. The supervisor would then make suggestions about how the practitioner could prepare the client for the intervention. Below are a few common suggestions from those meetings:

- Increasing engagement by doing something for the client/family
- Returning to the initial assessment data to review the client's problem
- Developing new ways to present the same intervention so that the client could accept it

I noticed that each week practitioners were talking about the same clients without much progress. The same solutions were suggested, with few results. I often wondered why the intervention itself wasn't discarded—or why clients were never asked what *they* thought would be helpful. Perhaps that conversation would have led to a meeting that the staff would not have dreaded.

This tenet is also true for clients. People often attempt the most logical solution to resolve a problem, but it may not always be the most effective. Once, a mother I was working with explained that she had tried "everything" in her attempts to elicit desirable behaviors from her children. She had been consistent and firm throughout their lives and as they continued to misbehave, she became more strict and more firm.

This pattern persisted for years. In session, she was able to realize that this approach, though it made logical sense, was not highly effective, allowing for more effective parental strategies to be developed.

Small Steps Can Lead to Big Changes

Recognizing that small steps lead to big changes is one of the most important tenets of SFT. SFT is a minimalist and systemic approach; the task for the therapist is to understand that all that is required is for the client to do one small thing differently in order to solve the problem (de Shazer, 1985). The belief is that that one different behavior will escalate into other changes, until the problem no longer exists.

A social worker friend of mine, who works in an agency setting, once shared a story that illustrates this point. She was visiting with a woman in her mid-40s who desired to focus on herself more. The woman explained that she was the primary caregiver to her father, who was struggling with the early stages of Alzheimer's disease, and her children. She was spending all of her time caring for her father and children and had forgotten to take care of herself. Due to her father's illness, he was frequently verbally and physically aggressive, giving her one more troubling thing to deal with.

During the first session, the woman explained that she wanted to focus on herself more. She had dreams of going back to school and completing her degree, spending more time with her extended family, and becoming more socially active. From most traditional therapeutic approaches, this would require a lot of work for the therapist and client alike. Instead, while working from a solution focused perspective, the social worker remembered that all that is required is for the client to do one small thing differently and she encouraged the client to do so. The client then came up with a great idea: She decided that instead of serving her family dinner as she normally would, that week she would simply prepare the meal and require the family members to serve themselves.

When the client returned the following week, she reported that the entire family were now feeding themselves, which allowed her more time for herself. By the end of treatment (five sessions), this amazing woman had returned to school and had begun spending time with her friends. Yet neither of these changes were the most remarkable that she experienced. She reported that the Alzheimer's symptoms in her father began to change. Her father was no longer being aggressive, which allowed her to leave him in the care of a nurse while she was in class or spending time with friends. This story illustrates the ripple effect of SFT. Once the client did something different, in this situation allowing the family to feed themselves, she was able to experience her own independence and impact the independence of her family. This ripple effect included her father; once he was able to feel trusted by the client, then he was able to gain further control of the symptoms associated with the illness that was troubling him.

The Solution Is Not Necessarily Related to the Problem

Because there is limited or even no time spent examining the situation that led someone into counseling in SFT, oftentimes the solution is not related to the problem. Instead, the solution is related to the client's desired future. In this way SFT therapists work backwards as the client's real life is carefully examined, searching for the presence of this desired future (de Shazer et al., 2007).

Steve and Jane were a couple in their early 30s that attended therapy because their marriage was struggling. After years of difficulty, Jane had an affair with a man she met on the Internet and was now confused about what she wanted for her future. She had feelings for this other man but was not sure that she wanted to end her marriage. Almost every other therapeutic approach would have examined a number of problems:

- What led to Jane searching for something else?
- What was she looking for?
- What risk factors have been present in the marriage that allowed for trouble to occur?

These questions, and others like them, are common *problem-focused questions*. The therapist could also have chosen to teach the couple what a healthy marriage looks like, according to research. These are all therapeutically appropriate approaches and would have led to a solution that is very much related to the problem.

However, SFT utilizes a different approach and leads to a different type of solution. Instead of asking any of the problem-focused questions referenced above, or teaching the couple how to have a healthy marriage, the couple was asked to describe what their marriage would be like without the problems that led them to therapy. The answer was nothing short of amazing. Jane began to smile and described a sensation that became the catalyst to their new marriage, a catalyst that had nothing at all to do with their problem. She explained that she really enjoyed the feeling of having the bed made up while she was lying in it. The soft pleasant sensation of the sheets gently falling on her was what she would like to see occurring in their future. For an hour other details were discussed: passion would be present, trust would reemerge, and chores would be shared. At the end of the hour when asked what changes the couple would be making first, it was the bed making that Jane requested. Steve agreed to do this for a week and the session ended.

At their second and final session, the couple reported that their marriage had completely changed and that this one act had led to many other changes such as the other details discussed in the first session. That small change allowed each spouse to feel important to the other, allowing them to meet the other spouse's needs more consistently. Almost two years after their last session the couple contacted me and reported they were still happily married and that Steve was continuing to make the bed with Jane in it.

The Language for Solution Development Is Different From Language Needed to Describe a Problem

Albert Einstein once said that you cannot solve a problem with the same thinking that created it. SFT adds to this that the language must be different as well. For example, take the difference in these two statements:

> I have to go to work tomorrow.
>
> I get to go to work tomorrow.

The conversation surrounding the first statement is negative; the second is positive. Ironically, we use such negative language every day without giving much thought to its impact.

People come to therapy making hopeless, negative statements such as the one listed above. They say things like, "I am depressed." Our task is to insert a bit of hope into that statement, such as, "So, you struggle with depression" or "You are depressed right now." These slight changes in the language invite hopefulness into the room and this hope elicits other language changes. In her book *Solution Focused Group Therapy* (1998, p. 9), Linda Metcalf illustrates this point by using a table comparing problem descriptions and solution perceptions. Table 1.1 offers a similar comparison.

Table 1.1

REDESCRIPTIONS

PROBLEM DESCRIPTION	SOLUTION PERCEPTION
Defiant child	A child that enjoys thinking independently.
Relationship discord	An undesirable pattern of interactions has developed based on differences as opposed to the previous desirable interactional pattern based upon similarities.
Depression	A feeling of sadness that, at times, interferes with your ability to experience happiness.
Addictions	A habit of continuing a behavior that is not working for you.

By talking in a solution focused perspective, we invite our clients to begin to think of solutions instead of allowing the problem to become who they are. We also inject hope into a situation that may not have had any for some time.

No Problem Happens All of the Time; There Are Always Exceptions

This tenet builds on the previous one. One of the most important aspects of the SFT approach is the search for exceptions and the utilization of exceptions once found. The exceptions are often small and may occur outside a person's awareness of the problem, but once located and amplified, can grow and become more powerful. Also, these times lead to the discovery of hidden talents that can, and often do, lead toward solutions.

I once heard a story about how basketball star Michael Jordan discovered his hidden talents. As a collegiate star, and later while playing for the Chicago Bulls, Jordan earned a reputation as a tremendous scorer but not much of a defender. Jordan, a master of turning his perceived weaknesses into real strengths, met with his coach before one season to discuss his defensive abilities. His coach asked him to list the skills and attributes he possessed that made him a prolific scorer. Jordan stated that he was competitive and possessed quick hands and feet, aggression, leaping ability, and so forth. The coach then asked Jordan what he thought it would take to be a strong defender. Jordan realized that the same skills he used to score at a record's pace could be used to excel as a defender. With this new perspective he went on to win the NBA Defensive Player of the Year Award that season and made the NBA all-defensive team nine times. There are always times when the problem is either not present at all or present in a less severe way. These are the times that should be explored and amplified.

The Future Is Creatable

This is the optimistic part of SFT. When people are not viewed as trapped, but instead are seen as stuck and possessing all of the tools they will need one day in the future to become unstuck, the future is seen as a hopeful place (de Shazer et al., 2007).

While recruiting practitioners for this book, I had the pleasure of talking to Ron Warner, a social work professor at the University of Toronto and founder of the SFT certification program at the same school (see chapter 19). I told him that Linda Metcalf and I hoped to identify common themes that exist among people that utilize the SFT approach. Without hesitating, Dr. Warner said that in his opinion, SFT practitioners have an undying belief in a person's ability to have a new future. This optimistic view of clients, and the world, leads practitioners to continue to follow the client as they describe their future without the problem, with the hope that the future can be created.

KEY POINTS IN SFT

From my own studies and practice, are a few points that I believe are key to effectively using the SFT approach:

Use the Phrases "Let's Suppose" and "Instead of That Problem" to Open Possibilities

I once watched a tape of Insoo Kim Berg conducting a workshop and she made this statement: By saying "suppose," we are inviting the client to imagine. Since SFT is a future-focused approach, imagination is crucial. Clients begin to imagine the future without the problem when asked questions that begin with "suppose." Also, SFT focuses on the presence of the solution and not the absence of the problem, which is often new to our clients. By asking someone what they would like to feel instead of the problem, we invite the client to think about the presence of the solution, opening the door for the solution focused questions to be effective.

The Client Is the Expert

This is not always easy to remember. I once attended a conference where Michael White, the codeveloper of narrative therapy, explained how important he felt it was to allow the client to be the expert. During one of his workshops, he showed a tape of his work with a young woman. One of the attendees asked Michael why he did not compliment the client despite many opportunities to do so. I will never forget watching Michael think for a moment and respond by explaining that if he compliments, then he assumes the expert role, hindering the therapeutic process. Instead, he compliments with curiosity and questions.

Do Not Hypothesize

Steve de Shazer frequently referred to the act of hypothesizing as a disease. Due to the nonexpert role of this approach, once we begin to think we know something about the client then we must work hard to not know something, as it will get in our way of hearing what the client wants to change. The SFT approach is about cooperating with the client's reality, not attempting to understand it. This allows the therapist to follow the client where the client would like to go instead of following the therapist's hypothesis about the client.

Be Tenacious When Searching for Details About the Client's Desired Future and Exceptions to the Problem

Whenever I watch a session conducted by one of the gurus of the SFT approach, I am struck by their tenacity. This is an approach that gets as much detail as possible about the client's goals through questions such as, "What else would you notice?" or "Who else will notice?" Until these details are explored thoroughly, the therapist does not proceed.

Go Slow

This is true in the actual session, as well as in treatment as a whole. Asking clients to describe their lives when things are "slightly" better instead of when the problem is completely solved is a helpful way to accomplish this. Also, because so much of SFT's effectiveness can be attributed to clients beginning to think about things they either have not thought about before or have not thought about in a while, silence is often important. This visualization of the future on the client's part requires the therapist to wait for the client to think and answer the questions about the key details of the solution instead of rushing toward a solution.

Maintain a Respectful and Curious Stance

The solution focused therapist will gently invite the client to think differently about his or her situation by being curious about the client. Respecting the client's situation is crucial; clients typically come to treatment when their problem is at its worst. By respecting that and saying, "That sounds so difficult. What would you like to be experiencing instead?" the therapist conveys to the client that the therapist has a genuine curiosity about the client's solution.

When Discussing the Client's Desired Future, Use Presuppositional Language

There is a big difference between saying "if your miracle occurs" and "*when* your miracle occurs." There is a big difference between saying "Has anything gotten better?" or "What has gotten better?" When using the SF approach, presupposing a positive future through the use of language is a useful tool for helping the client discover his or her exceptions.

Simplify

When she was asked what she was most proud of in regard to SFT, Insoo Kim Berg often replied, "Its simplicity." When attempting to examine and understand a problem, things rapidly get worse and more complicated. Once you begin to focus on solutions and ask the client what he or she would like to accomplish, the opposite occurs. This approach simplifies everything.

SOLUTION FOCUSED TECHNIQUES/PROCESSES

Whenever I am at a workshop on SFT, either as an attendee or as the presenter, there are always questions related to the techniques. Attendees want to know when to use them and how to use them effectively. I honestly feel that these are questions that cannot be answered, because therapy is such a subjective process based on a relationship between two people. These are difficult questions since solution focused therapists don't see SFT as having *techniques* that they use on people. Instead, SFT is a way of thinking and being curious with clients. It is the process of SFT that is flexible and applicable to what the client wants to talk about and explore. The questions follow where the client takes the therapist. However, in an effort to answer questions about techniques, I have found it helpful to place the techniques/processes into the several categories that follow.

Future-Focused Questions

These questions invite the client to imagine a future without the problem. This is key in practicing SFT, as the goal for therapy is developed as the future is envisioned. The most famous future-focused question is the miracle question, which appears below, but this is not the only future-focused question used in the approach. Here is the miracle question and some further examples:

> Suppose while you were sleeping tonight, a miracle occurred that completely removed the problem that led you to therapy. Since this miracle occurred while you were sleeping, you don't know that it happened. What would be your first, smallest clue that something miraculous occurred while you were asleep?
>
> What are your best hopes for this therapy?
>
> Suppose when you woke up tomorrow, your marriage was back to the way it was when you both were at your happiest. What would you be able to do that is not happening now?

Exception-Finding Questions

These questions are used to identify times when the problem is either solved or not as severe. These types of questions are key to practicing SFT. Once an exception is identified, the client has the opportunity to learn more about when and how the exception occurs.

> When are the times when a small piece of your miracle is already happening?

When are the times when your confidence is high and you feel you will accomplish what you wish?

When is your marriage at its happiest?

Assessment Questions

The most popular question of this type is known as the scaling question. The scaling question allows for the client and therapist to have a conversation based upon the client's assessment of progress. Also, this allows the client to track progress between sessions.

On a scale of 0 to 10, with 10 being the day after the miracle occurs and 0 being the worst it has ever been, where would you say you are today?

On that same scale, where would you like to be at the end of successful treatment?

What things could you do between now and the next time we meet that would move you up the scale just a half of a point?

Attribution Questions

These types of questions are often referred to as coping questions but I prefer to call them attribution questions. This is because I hope to learn more than just how the client coped with the problem: I hope to identify what attributes the client possesses that will be helpful in accomplishing their goals.

How have you been able to survive the problem for this long?

So, you were able to move up your scale this week two points? Wow, how did you do that?

What attributes do you have that allowed you to move up the scale this week?

SUMMARY

SFT is a model that is very different from almost all other psychotherapy models due to the focus on the presence of the solution and not just the absence of the problem. To be effective with this approach, a therapist must have an understanding of much more than just the techniques. The practitioner must understand the key tenets so as to see if it is an approach that fits the practitioner. Once it is determined that this approach does fit the therapist's personality and theoretical beliefs about the therapy process, then all that remains is for the therapist to trust the model and allow the client to guide them both through the therapy process. By utilizing SFT questions and ideas along the way, the journey of therapy together becomes full of possibilities.

REFERENCES

Berg, I. K., & Kelly, S. (2000). *Building solutions in Child Protective Services.* New York: Norton.

Berg, I. K., & Miller, S. (1992). *Working with the problem drinker.* New York: Norton.

de Shazer, S., Dolan, Y., Korman, H., Trepper, T., McCollum, E., & Berg, I. K. (2007). *More than miracles: The state of the art of solution-focused brief therapy.* Binghamton, NY: Haworth Press.

de Shazer, S. (1985). *Keys to solution in brief therapy* New York: W.W. Norton & Company.

Lee, M. Y., Unken, A., & Sebold, J. (2004). Accountability for change: Solution-focused treatment with domestic violence offenders. *Families in Society, 85*(4), 463–476.

Lipchik, E. (2002). *Beyond technique in solution focused therapy.* New York: Guilford Press.

Macdonald, A. (2007). *Solution-focused therapy: Theory, research, & practice.* London: Sage.

Metcalf, L. (1998). *Solution focused group therapy: Ideas for groups in private practice, schools, agencies, and treatment programs.* New York: Free Press.

Metcalf, L. (2008). *Counseling toward solutions: A practical solution-focused program for working with students, teachers, and parents* (2nd ed.). San Francisco: Jossey-Bass.

Seligman, M. (1995). The effectiveness of psychotherapy. *American Psychologist, 50,* 965–974.

2

Solution Focused Therapy: Its Applications and Opportunities

LINDA METCALF

It's Monday morning, and the adolescent group gets together to discuss its members' weekends. One by one, they answer the question that their facilitator asks: "What went slightly better?" They are used to this question. It is asked every Monday morning and every evening before they leave their outpatient program for substance abuse. A few of the adolescents who are new to the program have not completely given up their drug of choice, but they are using less often. They see peers who have been in the program for several weeks not using and they are encouraged by the facilitator to comment on their peers' success. Many of them have failed other programs. Some are here by court order. It's their last chance. When asked by the facilitator at the end of the group session, "What's working in this group?" most of them comment that they feel respected, something that they have not felt before. Most say that the program is different and that they want to get better. They can't exactly verbalize what it is that makes it different. They just know that it is.

Same city, in a private practice, mid-morning, a professional counselor meets in an emergency session with a mother and her 11-year-old daughter who, the counselor learns, has been sexually abused by her stepfather. The mother, in tears, talks of her daughter as if she were ruined forever. The counselor listens carefully and notes how the daughter shared that her stepfather had abused her for months. She looks at the daughter, compliments her on her bravery, and mentions that she is glad to know someone who has so much courage. She compliments the mother too, on coming to visit with her that morning. She, too, must see the bravery in her daughter. The mother remarks that she is quite proud of her daughter and begins talking more about things other than the abuse. Soon the counselor learns that the girl is a stellar student, and in the choir at her church. She commends the daughter on such talents and her mother for rearing such a competent young girl. The girl relaxes, feeling that she can tell this counselor anything. She seems to listen to her and not tell her what to do or ask too many questions that she is not ready to answer. The session goes well. Another appointment is made. When the mother asks how long the girl needs to attend counseling, the counselor replies, "We'll leave that up to your daughter."

Early afternoon, in a community agency, a 22-year-old goes to therapy with her mother after a weight loss of 30 pounds in six months. The mother found her daughter purging in the bathroom last week and when she confronted her, the young woman broke down and told her mother how hard school had been for her recently. A dance major at a local university, she had been starving herself, eating only when necessary for energy to dance. The mother called her family doctor, who referred them to the therapist. When they meet, the young woman is terrified that the therapist will tell her to eat. This doesn't happen. Instead, the therapist is kind and understanding. She asks the young woman how purging helped her. Surprised at such questions, the young woman begins talking about her desire to be the best in her dance company and how she needed to keep the weight off to do so. The therapist really seems to understand, thinks the young woman. She begins to open up more. She does not feel threatened like she thought she would. She makes a second appointment.

In a high-rise medical facility near a hospital that same afternoon, an internal medicine specialist is scheduled to see Selma, a 72-year-old patient with chronic arthritis. She walks slowly into the office, sits down, and waits. She comes to the doctor often these days as she has lots of complaints. She lives alone and at least she can talk to the doctor and the nurses. The internal medicine specialist who will see Selma has revealed to his own therapist recently that his contact with chronically ill patients has become difficult for him. The therapist shared some solution focused ideas with the doctor. When he meets Selma and she begins talking about how hard it was to get out of bed and come to the appointment, the doctor says, "Then how did you do it? I know it was hard getting up, yet you did. I am quite impressed. Tell me your secret." Selma stops complaining momentarily and looks at her doctor and says, "I don't know, it was really hard. You just don't know." But the doctor doesn't give in to her complaint and says, "Yes, I do, and do you know what that says about you?" Selma seems a bit startled and asks, "What?" The doctor smiles and says, "That you refuse to let it keep you down." Selma smiles back.

In the late afternoon, a committee at the elementary school meets to discuss possible special education placement for Ron, age 11. Ron's grades have recently dropped and his father, a single parent, is concerned that it is because Ron's mother recently left the family for someone else, giving up her parental rights. After some preliminary data is gathered, the committee, consisting of Ron's teachers, the vice principal, and the school counselor, begin to notice that Ron's grades have been average to above average for most of his elementary school years. With this information, special education placement is set aside and instead, Ron is asked what he needs from his teachers. Ron, ready for placement or negative reactions, looks at the team and begins talking about how he wishes his father spent more time with him and was interested in his schoolwork. His mother was the primary parent prior to her leaving and while yes, Ron is quite angry at his mother leaving, he states that he needs somebody to help him with his schoolwork. It wouldn't hurt either, Ron says, if two of his teachers reminded him to turn in his class work before he left the classroom. He seems to be forgetting a lot lately, and says he's not sleeping well at night. The meeting shifts from placement to accommodating what Ron needs at the moment. Based on his prior successes, special education is not necessary.

Early that evening, across town at a local church, a therapist meets with a support group for parents who have lost their children. The room is filled with sad faces, yet the therapist begins with his usual question, "Tell me what has gone slightly better for each of you since we met last." Silence at first. There is always silence at first. Then one by one, people begin talking about getting back to work for the first time since their child's death and how hard it was. It was so hard coming home, they said. Heads nod and others begin talking about the holidays coming and buying ornaments for their lost children so that they are not forgotten during the holidays. The therapist says little. He lets them talk primarily, for they have told him before when he asked them, "What did we do that was helpful tonight?" that listening was the most important thing that he did. So he listens.

It's 11:00 on a school night and Jake, age 16, still isn't home. He is normally on time after football practice and hanging out with his friends. His parents trust him. So tonight after a few unanswered cell phone calls, they panic but try to stay calm. At 11:15 Jake comes in, looking frazzled and upset. He flops down on the couch before his parents have time to speak and says, "Mom, what is it with girls? You will never guess what Lauren did." They sit and talk and soon, the issue that Jake is an hour and 15 minutes late and didn't call is brought up. His parents would have previously grounded him for not calling and being late but tonight, they recognize that their son came home and talked to them for over an hour about where he was and what he was doing. They tell him that they were upset that he did not call and that it was not acceptable. But, they also tell him that normally he does call so they will not punish him this time. They recognize that this was a tough night. Jake looks at his parents and promises to call next time.

An employee shows up for work at the 24-hour restaurant late that same night and his boss meets him when he checks in his time card. "Rudy, you have been working here for six months. You are a great employee. Until last week you rarely came in late. What do you think you were doing all those months to get here on time? I want to see that Rudy again!" Rudy starts talking about going out too much with friends during the past week. The boss continues to say that he doesn't need to know why Rudy is late, just that he wants his "on-time employee back." He asks Rudy how he can begin doing that again. Rudy says he needs to get himself together. The boss smiles at him and leaves.

GET SMART AND CURIOUS

Some workshops begin with theory. I begin with cases such as these, sharing them with participants, asking them to think about what was done differently from traditional psychotherapy. I do this so that the participants begin thinking about what it means to become solution focused. Most of the participants tend to be engaged and anxious to learn more. The room is usually filled with therapists, social workers, school counselors, psychologists, and psychiatrists who come to learn about solution focused therapy, get some continuing education units, and perhaps explore a briefer model of therapy. Yet there are some who, clinging to their theories, are skeptical, and they ask questions:

> "What if you never get to the root of the problem behind the problem drinking? How can they possibly get past their denial?"
>
> "What about the bulimic patient? Don't you think she needs to be hospitalized to get better?"
>
> "The girl who was sexually abused obviously needs to deal with the abuse and talk about it or she will never be free."
>
> "I can't imagine a physician taking the time to talk to a patient like that. No one does that."
>
> "People who grieve must go through stages or they can't heal."

Each of these questions and statements leads to the next most often-asked question of: "Can solution focused therapy interventions be used on all clients?"

Let's answer that last question first. No, solution focused therapy cannot be *used* on all clients. It *can*, however, become a way of thinking for therapists to use with *all* clients. What's the difference? A real understanding of the solution focused model goes beyond the questions, the interventions (although there really aren't *any* of these), or complimenting. The real understanding occurs when a therapist sees clients and patients, employees and parents as people struggling to find a better way of living and they can't, yet. The therapist looks beyond the issues, the problems, the pathology, even the diagnoses and thinks, "How then, did they get to my office?" "How then, did this adolescent make it through the weekend without using drugs?" "How did the young girl gain courage to tell her mother, who loved her stepfather, that he had hurt her?"

These questions run through the mind of the solution focused therapists, almost rampantly, and create excitement and hope. There is an innate belief that no matter what their issue, situation, problem, or dilemma, most people simply want out of it. Yet, where do they go? They don't typically say to a therapist, "Take me back to when things were even more awful so I can dig in and understand why they were or are awful." Instead, they come to therapy, to groups, to family, to school to move forward. They just don't know how to do that.

The idea of a "solution focused therapist" means that a client who comes to see a solution focused therapist will be escorted through the session alongside the therapist in a respectful, understanding manner. The therapist will become a sort of field guide who will learn from the client about strengths, exceptions, and times when things weren't as awful, and then give feedback to the client. This new lens used by the therapist with the client results in the client feeling understood, relieved, less troubled, less sick, and more normal. The very experience of feeling that the issue at hand is solvable helps the client to relax and begin to explore how to make it so, again.

The next sections will discuss many different ways that the cases presented at the beginning of this chapter were dealt with by therapists. All are true stories. As you read them, notice that most of the clients or people were stuck in stories that did not work anymore. Once they knew where they were going, discovering how they made it before became simpler. There was hope. And this model is all about hope.

THE CHALLENGE OF CHEMICAL HABITS

In *Working With the Problem Drinker* Insoo Kim Berg and Scott Miller write about the importance of seeing past addictions toward healthy times. They write:

> If one accepts the premise that healthy patterns already exist but have simply gone unrecognized, then capitalizing on such patterns should lead to solutions without having to go through the traditional process of discovering the problem and then developing a solution. (Berg & Miller, 1992, p. 4)

This novel way of thinking reduces client resistance and produces much more collaboration between therapist and clients. Clients feel heard and understood. Therapists are not forced to provide an intervention. Instead, clients are encouraged to identify their own competencies, abilities, strengths, and healthy attributes, even if slight, as a means of solving the presenting problem. Thus, the conversations go differently.

I recall a young man, age 16, who was caught smoking marijuana inside his home. His mother, trying to save face, as she had smoked pot in her teens, told him he could not smoke in the house anymore. He therefore smoked in the yard. After a period of time, the mother became concerned about him and brought him to talk to me. He was quite proud of the fact that he still maintained a good grade average in school and held a job at a local shopping mall. "It's not a problem for me. I know how to beat the drug test at work, I have friends, and everything is cool. I just like it to relax." Seeing that he was not interested in therapy,

I acknowledged the fact that he was successful in school and at work and that it was simply admirable. I then mused to myself, how I certainly hoped that the problem with marijuana did not eventually grow bigger than he was able to control. He looked at me rather perplexed. I asked him: "How will you know, someday in the future, when the problem has gotten bigger than you?"

For a few minutes, he said nothing, and then he began: "I guess I would be spending more money on pot. I guess my grades would go down. Maybe I would skip school. But, Miss . . . that's not going to happen." I smiled and kept on writing. I then asked him for more clues that the problem was getting bigger. He continued with things such as possibly losing his job, giving pot to his little brother, still denying that such things would occur. I listed each of his predictions and made a copy for him. I told him that someday should the problem become bigger than he was, to call me.

I heard from his mother on a Sunday night about six months later. He still had the list in his wallet. He started therapy the next week.

Working with clients bothered by substance abuse issues involves working from the bottom up instead from the top down, which is where traditional substance abuse programs begin. Additionally, when working with a solution focused approach, clients are not labeled as "addicts" or "abusers," but as bothered by dangerous habits. This language, unique to the solution focused approach, creates for both client and therapist a context of possibilities, rather than disease or victimhood.

Beginning with the complicated symptoms, working top down means seeing that behind the alcohol or drug use are many complex issues that must be dealt with. This keeps clients in therapy for prolonged periods of time to gain insight. The attempt is to get to the bottom of things.

Working from the actual bottom up, the solution focused therapist may ask, "What does drinking do for you?" This rather controversial kind of question says many things to a client. First, it sends a message that the therapist understands that the usage has a purpose. This understanding lowers resistance. Second, it instigates information for both the therapist and client in the form of how the alcohol helps the person. Naturally, something that helps should not be scorned. Instead the therapist may inquire about other means that bring just a slight bit of similar satisfaction to the client. While not as satisfying as the drink, the client begins to explore with the therapist other times when he/she did something different that also felt good. That difference begins a new dialogue, which is collaborative.

In regard to collaboration, Berg and Miller write about how the traditional means of treating alcohol abuse often fail due to lack of such: "Very few in the alcohol treatment community have considered that the behaviors, which labels such as 'resistant' and 'in denial' are intended to describe, are at least as descriptive of the traditional alcohol treatment procedures as they are of the problem drinking population" (Berg & Miller, 1992, p. 21).

Berg and Miller write about visiting a shoe store in *The Miracle Method* (1995) and describe to the reader what it might be like to be told that there was only one brand, and one size, the perfect size, of shoe. They ask, "Would you stay in the store?" If you did, chances are that you would have your foot forced into the shoe by clerks, who had forced others' feet into their shoes as well. If you refused, you might be told that you were simply resistant. The same is true with drug abuse treatment. To say that there is only one way is disrespectful and dangerous.

People bothered by substance abuse problems were at one time free of the problem. Seeking out those times, situations, beliefs, and differences allows the client to regain dignity and see himself as competent. It also enables a better working relationship to develop. Additionally, therapists working with client goals, such as keeping their job, saving their marriage, getting healthier, or getting their boss off their back will find more cooperation than that of confrontation over a drinking or drug problem. These are the road signs to true recovery and they are the goals that the client will work toward, often giving up the substance in the process.

SURVIVORS OF SEXUAL ABUSE

Clients such as the young girl who reported sexual abuse by her stepfather are often focused completely on the issues of abuse. The issues, now out in the open, seem to suffocate the memory of any better times that the child has experienced, and place a label on her forehead of "victim." This keeps the client stuck and in a state of trauma, feeling as if there is no way out of the pain.

In the case presented earlier in this chapter, the therapist was open to listening to whatever the girl wanted to talk about, yet she was cautious to not ask the girl to go into details. Why not? Going back into the details seems to be a common technique in traditional psychotherapy, whose practitioners think that such a voyage helps people to deal with the abuse. According to Yvonne Dolan (a solution focused therapist; see chapter 5), a therapist such as the one who listened to the young girl was both respectful and helpful to steer clear of details. I heard Yvonne speak about her views on helping those clients bothered by sexual abuse in an early conference on solution focused therapy in New Orleans in the early 1990s. Her words suggested that "asking a client to go back through the details of abuse . . . is further abuse." Because of her statement, I have followed her suggestion and I never ask clients to disclose anything more than they want to disclose. The majority of clients don't disclose details and are often thankful that they aren't asked to do so. Those who do disclose, do so after several sessions. When they do, I acknowledge the details and then continue focusing them on life past the abuse.

"Solution focused questions (Lipchik, 1988; Lipchik & de Shazer, 1986) are carefully formulated queries asked by the therapist to help clients focus on what they are already doing that is working (even to some degree) on imagined solutions, and on ideas about how to make the solutions occur" (Dolan, 1991, p. 37). Such answers to questions give the therapist a sort of path to take that is within the client's scope of what is helpful.

I recall working with a young woman who had been date-raped at college. She was examined by a psychiatrist after the assault, who gave her medications and told her that probably the worst part for her was that her sexual encounter was against her religion. She was angry not only at the perpetrator, but the psychiatrist as well. It was he who encouraged her parents to make their daughter move on. It did not work. She kept vigilant over the event and continued to talk about it with her family, describing how it was destroying her mentally. She needed someone to believe that she wasn't ready to move on and to respect her wishes.

By the time I met Nan, she had stopped the medications on her own and simply wanted another viewpoint of how to deal with the assault. She began the session by saying that even though others felt she was becoming obsessed with the incident, she was not ready to put the "bomb that went off" (her description of the assault) in her life aside. She asked if I needed her to talk details and I replied that I only wanted to hear what she wanted me to know. So, she told me little about the assault. She did talk about who she was prior to the "event" and who she wanted to become again. Doing so, I learned a lot about Nan. Even though she was date-raped in December of her senior year at college, she was still able to complete her college degree with honors. She maintained her sorority officer status and continued applying for jobs in journalism. Once she graduated, she left the college town to get away from everything (the event occurred there) and moved 300 miles away. I saw all of these achievements as attempts to cope with the issues she had experienced, and verbalized her strength, passion, and survivorship. Yet, the issue remained a true thorn in her life.

Once, we discussed the miracle question and she immediately told me that in her miracle, she would get justice. From then on, we talked of justice, what it would look like, how it would impact her and the difference it would make. She began to pursue it legally, found a lawyer willing to take the case, and began to feel in control again. Her parents and psychiatrist had previously discouraged such "revenge," but Nan called it "justice" and it gave her some peace. She was on her way to moving past the event and into the rest of her life. When asked what we did in our work together, Nan replied that "you always let me decide where I was going and what I was going to do about it. People like me with situations like this have to have that kind of support. It put me in control at a time when I didn't feel I had any."

When speaking to clients who have experienced sexual abuse, talking about survivorship rather than victimhood is a language that attests to the client's strength and personal reputation. I often do an exercise with sexual abuse survivors that I refer to as Mirror, Mirror on the Wall. It is a group exercise (Metcalf, 1998, p. 94) designed to help clients begin to describe themselves differently. The facilitator asks the clients to imagine themselves as victims and to describe the actions, beliefs, and feelings that they would have as they went through their day believing that they were victims. After listing the answers on a whiteboard, the facilitator switches to a new description, a survivor. The clients then brainstorm the actions, beliefs, and feelings that they would have as they went through their day believing that they were survivors. Throughout the session, clients begin to understand that how they perceive themselves has much to do with how they react to their life. This is particularly helpful in a group setting, as fellow clients describe what they will begin doing differently and what beliefs they can develop to help them do so. The exercise ends with the facilitator asking the clients to choose either the victim or survivor role to play for the next week, as many days as possible.

Those who have been sexually abused respond well to the solution focused approach as it respects them, validates who they are as people, and places them in control. These clients, previously seen in traditional therapy offices as clients who will need years of therapy, often terminate within months.

UNHEALTHY EATING HABITS

Perhaps you have noticed that solution focused therapists look at what some may describe as "addictions" differently than traditional psychotherapists. This is not to say that solution focused therapists do not take their client's dangerous habits seriously; they do. What they do not do is see the person as diseased, as that very description leads to few possibilities for "cure." Instead, the solution focused therapist looks more at times when the habits are not as powerful over the individual and the individual uses more healthy ways to deal with life's challenges. "The therapist holds the belief that habits are not born with people but, rather, develop over time in response to some personal need" (Metcalf, 1998, p. 67).

In cases involving clients with unhealthy eating habits, I have discovered that by giving the client most of the control in therapy, a relationship that is both collaborative and open to new ideas develops. Traditional clinics for eating disorders involve nutritional training, meal monitoring, and developing weight gain/loss goals. After working in such a clinic early in my career, I recognized why the programs failed. Many of the clients found ways to get control over the programs by purging in their shoes and hiding them in the closet. Some would sit for hours, dividing their food into tiny pieces and moving it around their plates. They weren't about to give up control over something that they could control.

So, why not let them have control?

"Kim, age eighteen, weighed seventy-five pounds when I first met her. She was already beginning to experience chills, amenorrhea and hair loss. Her physician had become alarmed when her parents brought her in for a physical after she returned from her college freshman year in Paris" (Metcalf, 1998, p. 75). By eating only apples, Kim found some control over her out-of-control family. She had attended a prep school prior to college, and often found herself escaping into studying to drown out the yelling in her family over finances. Her brother disappointed her parents time after time and Kim desired to fix their sadness. Yet instead of doing it in a healthy manner, for herself as well, she dealt with stress by eating less. Her parents took her to see a nutritionist who scared Kim to death. "No way will I eat all that she prescribed for me."

I asked Kim in our initial session what she wanted to call what was occurring with her and she smiled and said, "I know what is going on but I would rather not talk about it like that." I then asked how she would like to talk about it and she said, "I need to get healthy." So, healthy it was. Over the next few sessions, we talked about how she could begin getting healthy. While it helped immensely to have a client who wanted to get healthy, Kim still showed the significant symptoms of anorexia, and was very cautious to choose foods that contained little to no fat. I insisted from the very beginning (as I do with all clients with eating disorders) that she see a physician every two weeks for checkups. She complied. Over the first few weeks, Kim designed her own meals and began putting aside her fear of becoming fat. One day, after hearing Kim's concerns about the pounds that she was slowly gaining, I looked at her and told her that she was, for sure, a weight loss expert who (I was certain) could lose the weight if she needed to in the future. She smiled at that description. It was an exception that made sense to her.

She gained sufficient weight over several months to please her doctor and we began family therapy at her request. Working with families who have a member struggling with an eating disorder can be tricky, as they feel their efforts to push their struggling member to eat is their responsibility. Instead, helping the family to monitor from a distance and become supportive to the client's need for control is a focus that is often developed between me and the client in front of the family members.

Nan did well, finished college, moved away from home, and called me several years later, married. While she said she still had to deal with being healthy, she was feeling in control.

HAVING PATIENT CONVERSATIONS

The internal medicine physician described in one of the introductory cases was as in need of some uplifting methods to see his job differently as his patients were to see themselves and their conditions differently. Hearing constant complaints and negative descriptions of the lives of his elderly patients, the physician had become burned out and was considering going back to his original position as a pharmacist. Instead, talking to him about what brought him through medical school into internal medicine made him reflect on several reasons why he chose his field. We also talked about the patients that he liked working with and the rewards he sometimes felt. Those thoughts had been taken over by his current burned-out status and while he could recognize the thoughts for what they were, he still needed tools to deal with the challenging patients.

I showed him the book *In Search of Solutions* by Bill O'Hanlon and Michelle Weiner-Davis (2003) and told him that it explained the kind of model that I used with him and other clients. He said he had wondered what I was doing when I asked him "different kinds of questions" and found them very thought-provoking. He bought the book and when he returned to the next session, he reported that he was feeling less burned out, had spent more time with his family (which we had sorted out in session as an exception to his feeling burned out) and was enjoying his time at home. As for his patients, such as Selma, he began listening to their complaints and then wondering out loud how they still made it to their appointments, remembered their medicine (sometimes), dealt with their chronic pain, still went to Bingo, visited their grandchildren, and so forth. He found that he got satisfaction when they stopped complaining to ponder his questions. They got satisfaction too, from a physician who seemed to see their lives as more promising.

In medical facilities, family therapy with a solution focused approach is quite helpful, particularly in acute cases where family involvement can make the difference in recovery. When the solution focused family therapist asks the patient what he/she needs to talk about, it is often different than what the therapist or even family wants to talk about. The patient knows what is helpful and what is not during a tough time, while well-meaning family members impose their solutions, sometimes meeting resistance. Instead, going one week at a time, with a miracle question to assist the goal setting, patients have a second chance to make some progress. I recall one elderly patient, wheelchair bound, who told one of my supervisees that in his miracle, his friends would be taking him to the bar to watch football again. When asked by the supervisee how that made a difference, he said he felt like he was one of the guys again. Since the "guys" came to visit the patient weekly, the supervisee decided to step in one day when they were visiting, and compliment them for visiting their friend so often. She asked her patient to tell her again what he liked about his friends and he went into old stories of doing a variety of activities. She left when they were still musing over old times. When Thanksgiving came, and his family was too far to visit, the guys took him to one of their houses and they watched football all day. He had so much fun, and told them so, that they made their outings more close together.

In the medical field of psychiatry and medicine, patients are not the only ones who benefit. Alasdair Macdonald writes in chapter 16 about his role as manager of a hospital unit:

> Violent confrontations within the secure unit and the length of stay in the unit decreased as we became more solution-oriented. Our unit became so successful that we were often the only unit in North England with beds available for emergencies. At times we had contracts with other counties because our turnover had become so rapid that the staff complained that the unit was too quiet to be interesting! (Connie & Metcalf, in press)

LABEL-FREE SOLUTION FOCUSED EDUCATION

After spending over 12 years in public schools as a teacher and school counselor and working with children and adolescents in private practice for over 20 years, I have come to appreciate firsthand the usefulness of pursuing a solution focused approach in education. Educators struggle to help children and adolescents achieve success yet only seem to know one way to do so. It is as if educators see students as depositories of knowledge, and they are the depositors. When the students can't accept knowledge packaged in traditional ways, they are seen as resistant, unmotivated, or even unteachable. However, those stellar educators who see outside the box are often more successful and their students respond accordingly. While their styles are unconventional and sometimes questioned, they get results. They hear a different drummer. They are often solution focused and don't realize it.

It was typical for me as a school counselor to get referrals from teachers and administrators to see a student who was misbehaving, disrespectful, or unmotivated. I write later in this book about Tyler, a 16-year-old who needed a miracle and once he got part of it, skyrocketed to success (see chapter 14). His case was not uncommon. He needed his teachers to notice him. Other students were often misunderstood, as I would describe to them, in need of changing their reputation with their teachers. Together, we brainstormed what that miracle would look like in detail:

> "What will your teacher begin seeing you do in that miracle that will tell her the kind of student you can be?"
>
> "What will your teacher be doing that will help you to achieve this?"

> "What difference will that make to you? How will it change things for you at school, at home, other places?"
>
> "What if your teacher forgets sometimes? How will you keep this up so that you still benefit from your behaviors?"

These are different kinds of questions from those that a traditional school counselor might ask, as they are affirming, empowering, and goal oriented. In addition to questions like these of students, I asked them of teachers who complained:

> "I understand that Jose can really be difficult. I'll bet you have had difficult students like him before. What did you do that made a difference?"
>
> "Tell me about a time when Jose did not act up as much. What went on that day? Would you keep watching for a couple of days to find other times?"

In addition to asking these questions separately, I always got consent from both student and teacher to relay their answers to each other. Ideally, I tried more often than not to meet with both student and teacher together, and only for 10 to 15 minutes. That meeting did not involve talking about what the problems were. Instead, I started the meeting with:

> "This is a different kind of meeting. I brought you both here because I think you both have some ideas on how to make things better. Let's start by imagining what it will look like when things begin to get better in the classroom for both of you."
>
> "Teacher, tell me what will be signs that things are getting better? "
>
> "Student, tell me what you will be doing and your teacher will be doing when things get better?"
>
> "Tell me about the last time that happened on a small scale? Teacher? Student?"
>
> "What difference did that make?"
>
> "From these answers, what do you each think you could do for a day, as an experiment, to get back on track?"

While the solution focused questions are helpful, what is more helpful is the relationship change between student and teacher. This new way of seeing each other, often in a more positive way, goes a long way toward behavioral change.

Students dealing with poor academics benefit from a solution focused team meeting, where all teachers are present and have the opportunity to look through their records for times, projects, contexts, and learning situations where the student does slightly better. In a 5-year consultation, Davenport Community Schools decreased their special education referrals by over 50% utilizing a solution focused conversation that had three levels. The first, a parent conference with student present, was conducted by the teacher, using a solution focused approach. If the initial parent conference, which identified exceptions, was successful, special education as an option was dismissed. If not, a second-level meeting was held with all of the student's teachers, staff, administration, student, and parent present. Discussions took the form of identifying exceptions to low grades or performance. A team effort was undertaken, utilizing exceptions. If successful, again, special education was not considered. If not, a third-level meeting was held, identifying more exceptions but also considering health and mental challenges and their exceptions.

In *The Field Guide to the Solution Focused School* (Metcalf, 2008) this study explained further and in detail how the district found that not only did students who were suspected of needing special education stay in the least restrictive environment, they thrived. When the administration took on the solution focused approach for their team meetings and faculty meetings, morale increased and productivity became common. While implementing such a novel approach was not appreciated at first by teachers who were asked to take on challenging students in addition to their regular classroom curriculum, they too, eventually saw themselves as more competent and came to appreciate their students' differences as just that . . . differences, not disabilities.

GRIEF AND LOSS: LETTING TIME LEAD

My coauthor, Elliott Connie, relayed the story of the group early in this chapter, which consisted of parents who had lost their children too early in their lives. Elliott told me that when he first facilitated the group, he was a bit uncomfortable, as he had never lost a child and worried if he would relate to the members. Even the lead facilitator asked if he had experienced loss before. When Elliott said he had not, she looked frustrated and concerned.

By thinking with a solution focused approach, Elliott joined the group and was mesmerized by the group members. Each had his or her own unique story and each had begun to survive the loss. They did not need his leadership, they needed to be heard. After the group was over, Elliott asked a unique question of the group: "What did we do in here tonight that you found helpful, if anything?" When the group resoundingly responded with remarks such as, "You listened to us," Elliott was relieved. Afterward, the lead facilitator was quite complimentary. Elliott was again relieved. He had learned something that reinforced his thinking: that clients indeed can lead us if we allow them to do so.

From several years ago I recall Eve, a woman in her 50s, who came to therapy three months after her husband had passed away. He was quite ill and his passing was a blessing, she said, to him and to her family. Yet, she was still "stuck" as she put it to me, and her children were urging her to move on and get on with her life. She, however, wasn't ready to do so. While I consider myself to be a solution focused therapist, I sometimes mesh narrative therapy, especially the work of Michael White (1989), who elegantly writes about the importance of honoring the influence of those who leave us behind. White reminds us that until we who have lost someone can incorporate the loved one's influence as part of ourselves, we see the lost one as gone forever. However, by including those influences in the healing process, the grief becomes less painful and a determination to carry on the lost one's influence becomes more dominant, leading to a more productive way of living.

With these ideas in mind, I asked Eve to tell me about her husband and she readily agreed to do so. We spent a couple of sessions discussing who he was, what he liked to do, his illness, the joyful times she had with him, the difficult times they had as a couple, and her sadness about his leaving her all too soon. She seemed more alive herself when she talked about him; yet at intervals in our conversation, she asked if it was good that she was talking about him so much. I asked her how it helped and she said, "It feels good . . . other people keep telling me to move on."

I recall that the sessions moved into the holiday season, which made Eve sad. Once when she was in session, she told me she had gotten sadder that week, because typically during the holidays, she and her husband would decorate the house and buy an annual ornament. She said her kids weren't so sure she should decorate this year. I asked her what her husband enjoyed about the holidays and she said he wasn't much on decorating but he loved watching her decorate. As for the ornament, she usually picked it out and he liked whatever she chose. I asked her a question derived from Michael White's work (1989):

> Just for a moment, put aside what others are saying to you. If we were looking through Ralph's eyes right now, wherever he is, what would he say he would love to see you do?

It was an easy answer. She said, "Decorate the house and buy that ornament." Brightly, she questioned: "So that's okay?" I answered, "Would it honor Ralph?" She replied, "Absolutely."

She came back the next week to tell me about her decorations and the ornament. Her kids were puzzled but she was much brighter. She then told me, "I have to tell you something else I do that troubles my kids. . . . I watch a video Ralph made before he died . . . several times a day." Again, she asked if I thought doing that was okay and again, I responded with, "How does it help?" She said, "I feel as if he's still partially here. . . . I feel close to him." I replied, "Then, I hope you will continue. How wonderful that you have discovered something that helps you feel close to him."

The sessions continued and I learned more about Eve's coping. She frequently smelled Ralph's aftershave and wondered if that was all right. I kept on responding with, "How is it helpful?" and she began smiling at me each time I did so. Soon, she appeared brighter, more animated, and ready for the holidays. When the holidays ended and she returned to therapy, she said, "You know, we talk about what Ralph liked watching me do. One thing we talked about before he died was my completing my G.E.D. [General Equivalency Diploma]. I looked into the library schedule last week and signed up for a course to help me prepare." I told her how impressed I was that she was keeping Ralph's influence alive! She then went on to tell me that she had called her employer and told her that she was ready to return to work part-time in two weeks. She said to me, "I think it's time."

Eve went back to work and began to study for her test. When she came to the last session, I asked her what we did during our time together that was helpful, if anything. She responded: "You never pushed me or judged me . . . you let me do it my way."

A NEW LENS FOR PARENTING

As a marriage and family therapist, I have the chance rather often to hear complaints about children and adolescents from their parents. Sometimes the complaints are about a specific incident, which, parents believe, if left unpunished or unaddressed will lead to more incidents. While this way of thinking is rational, it sometimes keeps parents from looking at their children with a wider lens.

Andrea, age 16, was brought to therapy by her parents. Her mother called for the appointment and asked if both she and her husband could bring Andrea. As a family therapist, I was delighted, as too often, parents call and make appointments for their children and plan on staying in the waiting room. Andrea's mother asked if I would consult with her and her husband after the appointment and I responded with an invitation to join Andrea in the session itself. The mother was quite relieved and told me that she and her husband were quite worried about Andrea's recent behavior. She did not go into too many details and I was thankful for that. As a solution focused therapist and family therapist, I prefer to wait until the session and be told by everyone present what the issue is that brought them to therapy. Then I can watch for reactions, listen for exceptions, and everyone knows what I know. I don't like secrets.

Andrea and her parents arrived and once seated, Andrea burst into tears and said to me, "They are the greatest parents ever . . ." The parents became tearful and described the reason for the session. Andrea had gone on a trip with her friends to a beach in South Texas, some 300 miles from home, one night at 3:00 A.M., after telling her mother that she was spending the night with a friend. The group came home the next night and dropped Andrea off at her house. Andrea went into her home, woke up her parents and told them: "I have to tell you the truth . . . I was not at Cindy's house . . . I went to Corpus Christi with my friends. I am so sorry that I lied to you." Andrea's parents listened, thanked her for telling them the truth, and grounded her for two weeks.

In the session, Andrea admitted to her wrongdoing and her parents looked at me and said, "This is the first time she has ever done such a thing . . . we just don't want it to continue." Upon which, looking at what I had just witnessed, I said, "So, for sixteen years and four months, your daughter has done what you asked her to do in a respectful manner? How have you done this . . . reared such a respectful young lady? And to hear that she went inside after she made a mistake and apologized to you . . . [turning to Andrea] how did you do that?" The family was quiet for a few moments and then Andrea looked at me and said: "I told you, they are great parents."

I saw Andrea one more time after that session and together we discussed how going to the beach was helpful to her. She described being quite stressed at school, as she was in all Advanced Placement classes and at work, where she was a hostess three nights a week at a restaurant. We brainstormed other places to go besides a beach 300 miles away and she came up with going to the local lake the next time she was stressed. She called a week later and said everything was great and she didn't need to come back. A phone call to her parents confirmed the same. Again, I commended them on rearing an incredible daughter.

When parents come to therapy, it is helpful to see past the issues at hand so that children and adolescents can have a chance to defend against their negative reputations and allow their parents to see them differently. It is also helpful to look for situations where negative behaviors do not occur. I am often asked to do attention deficit hyperactivity disorder assessments. I never use the traditional checklist. Instead, I have a conversation about "energy" and when the energy goes untamed and when it is tamed (Epston & White, 1990). When I hear that the energy is tame at school but wild at home, I don't recognize that ADHD is the culprit. Instead, we explore what is different at school. All too many children have told me that "I get sent to the office if I misbehave at school but nothing happens at home but getting yelled at." This soon offers new exceptions to parents, who recognize that perhaps they have a part in the situation.

With adolescents, the challenges are greater, yet a solution focused approach has often revealed needs that parents did not recognize. One high school student told me that she had no curfew and got into trouble way too often. When her parents came to the school for family therapy, they were shocked. They had thought that freedom created more responsibility. Not according to the daughter. She wanted structure. She even came up with a plan in my office where she could earn privileges.

The solution focused therapist will gain additional information that can lead to specific goals and helpful exceptions if incorporating family interactions and conversations into therapy. It may be useful to ask a few beginning questions such as:

"What will be different as things begin to change for the better at home?"

"Who will be doing things differently?"

"What will your mother/father/stepparent say you will be doing that will make things better for her/him?"

"When was the last time you did that on a small scale?"

"What were others doing that helped you do that?"

The key in working with families is to see each family member as your cotherapist. Allow each person in the room to express exceptions. If a person chooses to talk about what he or she does not want happening, say thanks and ask: "What will be happening instead?" The atmosphere you create will survive long outside the therapy room. The exceptions you discover will transform perceptions and change relationships.

HAND OVER THE EXCEPTIONS, NOT THE PINK SLIP

Our son, Roger, spent his first few years out of college as a manager at the Cheers restaurant in Boston. He had accompanied me on several trips to do workshops and often talked about how applicable SFT was for the workplace. He told me how it changed his managerial style from that of focusing on what employees did not do to what they did do, even when they were remiss in their responsibilities. On one occasion, he talked to a young woman who had been employed at Cheers for several years about her tardiness. The woman was apparently ready for some dismissal verbiage but instead, Roger told her: "You have been an employee here for three years, which is as long as I have been here. During those years, when I look at your personnel file, I see that you were on time and got good reviews. Lately, I notice that you are late occasionally. I wonder what you used to do to get here on time?" The young woman sat silent for a few minutes, unsure of what to say. After a while, she began talking about things that were different for her lately. Roger asked how he could help and she told him it was she who needed to alter some things. The conversation ended with Roger telling her that he would be looking out for the great employee she had been in the past. She improved.

Imagine a workplace where more of this happened. Recently, I watched a YouTube.com clip titled "Validation." In the clip, a parking attendant sits with the validation stamp ready, yet before he stamps each person's parking ticket, he validates them with compliments. Within a short while, the parking garage is filled with more and more customers and the parking attendant's line is out into the street.

While compliments are a small part of the SFT approach, they can turn around a negative conversation into one that is more future-focused and cooperative. Steve de Shazer writes:

> First we connect the present to the future (ignoring the past, except past successes) then we compliment the clients on what they are already doing that is useful and/or good for them, and then—once they know we are on their side—we can make a suggestion for something new that they might do which is, or at least might be, good for them. (de Shazer, 1985, p. 15)

Imagine the possibilities of helping challenging clients to become more cooperative and collaborative using this approach. The nagging parent becomes a passionate parent who took the time to come with her child to therapy and help the child become his best. The teacher who complains nonstop becomes a teacher with a mission to help a student improve because the teacher sees potential and that's why she pushes so hard. The adolescent who is unmotivated to do chores or schoolwork is a person who has the means to be someone different yet is uncertain when to unleash his potential. While these descriptions may seem to be reaching, in a sense they are . . . they are reaching out to clients who are not cooperative in a way that says, as de Shazer states above, "I am on your side. Tell me what it is that you want to accomplish." Many employees, students, parents, families, and individuals have not had opportunities to be listened to in this manner.

In many of the chapters in this book, you will read about dozens of clients who experienced therapy in a novel fashion and because of the new context, opened the door to change. It is rare to have a client come in and say to us, "Tell me what to do and I will do exactly as you say to become who you think I should be." Instead, clients come in wanting direction, but not recognizing that they can create their own direction. It is in that context that SFT shines the brightest.

SUMMARY

This chapter describes a variety of situations where SFT is a valuable tool for creating a context where change can occur. To name more situations where SFT is helpful would take many more pages! Instead, suffice it to say that the applications are endless because people have an endless list of concerns that they bring to therapy. What has been delightful to me, after practicing SFT for the last 18 years, is the assistance, the theory, and the ideas that SFT have given to me with even the most difficult of situations. From the tearful parent who was saddened that her child needed a heart transplant to live, to the young woman needing to make a decision to terminate a pregnancy or keep the baby, to the adolescent who slept in his car to avoid his abusive father, I have had the opportunity and honor to work with each of these scenarios and watched my clients succeed.

My wish is that you will see more in SFT than techniques or strategies and allow yourself to step down from the role of expert and experiment with this task: Choose one client in the near future, and simply be curious with how that client has coped, dealt with, and survived so far, the ordeals and situations that bring him to you. Then, just talk about your wonderings with the client. The answers you hear may turn out to be . . . exceptional.

REFERENCES

Berg, I. K., & Miller, S. (1992). *Working with the problem drinker.* New York: Norton.

Berg, I. K., & Miller, S. (1995). *The miracle method.* New York: Norton.

de Shazer, S. (1985). *Keys to solutions in brief therapy.* New York: Norton.

Dolan, Y. (1991). *Resolving sexual abuse.* New York: Norton.

Epston, D., & White, M. (1990). *Narrative means to therapeutic ends.* New York: Norton.

Lipchik, E. & de Shazer, S. (1986). *The purposeful interview.* Journal of Strategic and Systemic Therapies, 5(1&2), 88-99.

Lipchik, E. (1988). *Interviewing with a constructive ear.* Dulwich Center Newsletter. Australian Post Publications, 3-7.

Metcalf, L. (1998). *Solution focused group therapy.* New York: Free Press.

Metcalf, L. (2008). *A field guide to the solution focused school.* San Francisco: Wiley.

O'Hanlon, W., & Weiner-Davis, M. (2003). *In search of solutions.* New York: Norton.

White, M. (1989). *Saying hullo again: The incorporation of the lost relationship in the resolution of grief.* Selected papers, prepublication pamphlet of collected works. Adelaide, Australia: Dulwich Centre Publications.

3 A Solution Focused Journey

EVE LIPCHIK

Everything should be made as simple as possible but not simpler.

—Albert Einstein

THE DECISION TO BECOME A THERAPIST

Life is so unpredictable! I would never have believed my career path if someone had predicted it! I grew up in New York City and had an undergraduate degree in communications from New York University. I had my heart set on being a TV script writer or playwright. Marriage and the birth of three children put that on the back burner. My family and I were living in Rochester, New York, when my youngest child started kindergarten and I began to turn my mind toward a career again. However, in the interim I had decided that rather than writing, I wanted to do something that would help people in some other way.

One of my neighbors was a child aide in a research project called the Primary Mental Health Project (Cowen et al., 1997) that was run by the Clinical Psychology Department of the University of Rochester. She loved her job, which entailed working with elementary school children one-on-one, and often shared exciting stories about it with me. The goal of this project was to prevent emotional problems in adolescents by addressing the problems as soon as the children entered school. A 10-year pilot study that assessed children when they entered kindergarten found that 10% of them had developed emotional problems by the time they entered junior high. Even though the Rochester schools had enough funding for one full-time school social worker and psychologist at each school at the time, two people could not do individual therapy with so many children in addition to fulfilling their other obligations. That is why the psychology department came up with the idea of child aides, a paraprofessional position for women who, for purposes of the continuing research, would be devoid of any experience in teaching, psychology, or social work. These women were trained to do play therapy by clinical professors at the university and also by select consultants. I fit the requirements for the job, but I had some hesitation. After 10 years of being a stay-at-home mom, I thought I might like a non-child-related occupation. However, the fact that I had enjoyed volunteering in my children's classrooms gave me the incentive to give it a try.

The training was extensive and exciting. It was strictly psychodynamic; so much so, that we were warned never to talk to a parent of one of our patients because it could contaminate our relationship with the child. I fell in love with the work instantly and began to read everything I could about play therapy, specifically, and psychodynamic therapy, in general. It took less than a year for me to decide that I wanted to become a professional in this work, so I matriculated as a master's degree candidate in the human services program at the university. (The University of Rochester did not have a social work program. The highly competitive clinical psychology program was heavily research oriented and would not accept me because of my goals.)

I continued to work as a child aide at the same time that I studied for my degree. As I began to understand more about the process of change from the psychodynamic perspective, questions arose in my mind. Would my seeing the children twice a week at school for 45 minutes really produce changes that would make a difference in the long run? Wouldn't the parents have to understand what we were doing with the children and perhaps do something different, too? Since children are constantly developing and changing, would they need therapy until they became adults? When I raised these questions with one of my supervisors, she suggested I take some seminars in family therapy offered by the Department of Psychiatry at Strong Memorial Hospital. The chairman of that department was Dr. Lyman Wynne (Wynne, 1978), a founding father of the field of family therapy.

THE DISCOVERY OF FAMILY THERAPY

It was the early 1970s, and the family therapy seminars I attended focused on pioneers like Ackerman (1960), Bowen (1960), Boszormany-Nagy (Boszormany-Nagy & Spark, 1973), Skynner (1976), Minuchin (1974), and Whitaker (1976). I began to see that the questions that had arisen in my mind were not out of line. Looking at children's problems in the context of the family made sense.

In 1976, I moved to Milwaukee and attended the School of Social Welfare at the University of Wisconsin-Milwaukee for another year in order to earn a master's in social work instead of the master's degree in human services I had almost completed in Rochester. At UW-M I took all the family therapy courses that were offered. I was introduced to the work of Jay Haley and was fascinated by his very different way of thinking about change. Unfortunately, I was not able to get a field placement assignment with a family therapist.

I received my MSW in May of 1978, and was hired as a family therapist by a residential treatment center starting in September. I was quite excited to get a job so quickly but also anxious, because I had never treated a couple or a family with or without supervision.

Milwaukee had a Family Therapy Training Institute at Family Service of Milwaukee that led to certification by the American Association for Marriage and Family Therapy (AAMFT). It was a 40-hour-a-week program that lasted two years and consisted of seminars, as well as individual and group supervision, some of which was live. I inquired whether I could buy some family therapy supervision over the summer. Family Service had a long waiting list of clients in those days. Given my past clinical experience with children and adults, they offered me free supervision and the option to attend all seminars if I treated 10 cases per week. I accepted this offer, and was assigned Insoo Kim Berg as my supervisor. Within days of working there I recognized that I was totally unqualified to be a family therapist. The didactic studies of family therapy did not translate into clinical practice. I decided to sign up for the two-year program and asked to be released from my prospective job.

That was the beginning of the most valuable and exciting aspect of my career. My biggest challenge was to learn to think systemically. I remember an occasion about one year into the program when I had to excuse myself from finishing a case presentation because I became so confused between psychodynamic and systemic language and concepts. That was a turning point! I went home, opened the family therapy textbooks that

I had read before, and started to reread them. Now I was able to distinguish systemic thinking from psychodynamic thinking because of the practical experience and supervision I had obtained.

FROM BRIEF FAMILY THERAPY TO SOLUTION FOCUSED THERAPY

In the second year of the program, I began to participate with Insoo and her husband, Steve de Shazer, in some work they were doing outside the agency. Steve was intrigued with the developments at the Mental Research Institute (MRI). He had lived in Palo Alto a few years and taken some courses there. Eventually he befriended John Weakland and some of the staff. Steve had ideas about making the MRI model more systemic. The existing MRI Brief Therapy model like the Milan model saw therapist and team as distinct from the clients. The therapist hypothesized, diagnosed, and treated more like a physician than an integral part of a treatment system with clients. MRI and the Milan group also used a team approach which Steve and Insoo adopted. A "conductor," the name for the interviewing therapist, met with a family in the consultation room, while a team of therapists observed from behind a one-way mirror. The team could call the conductor out to make suggestions, or call into the room if there was a telephone hook-up. At the end of the session the conductor left the family and jointly with the team developed an "intervention message" that was read to the family when he returned to the consultation room. At MRI and Milan, this message was intended to create change by interrupting the dysfunctional interactional patterns that were believed to be maintaining or escalating the family's problems.

Steve had a different theoretical take on this process. His idea was to develop an ecosystemic model, called "brief family therapy" (de Shazer, 1982). Therapists and clients would form a treatment system, and the intervention would be isomorphically fitted to the clients' story. The changes that could occur would be open ended, and determined by how the clients reacted to the intervention. This was quite different from the MRI and Milan models, in which the intervention targeted a specific interactional pattern determined by the therapists.

Some of us at Family Service interested in exploring this idea with Steve met at his and Insoo's house once a week to observe cases. Our "clients" were anyone we knew, or friends of theirs who had a problem and were willing to be our guinea pigs. The team sat in the dining room or on the stairs while the interview was conducted in the living room. All sessions were videotaped so they could be discussed later.

Steve drew on a binocular theory of change (de Shazer, 1982, pp. 7–18) for this new model. This theory suggested that clients viewed their situation negatively because of a limited perspective, as though they were seeing with only one eye. The conductor collected information about this monocular problematic view and the team then composed an intervention message that was isomorphic with the clients' view but reframed just enough (positively) to offer a different dimension (like depth perception). This new way of viewing the problem was believed to have the potential for opening up new possibilities for change.

One of the important similarities between the MRI model and brief family therapy was Milton Erickson's influence with regard to circumventing resistance. At MRI, the concept was called "position" in relation to clients (Fisch, Weakland, & Segal, 1982, pp. 89–109) while Steve de Shazer called this concept "cooperating with how clients cooperate" (de Shazer, 1982, pp. 9–15). Basically, the difference is one of semantics. The point is to assess clients' worldviews and to utilize them to eliminate resistance. For example, if a client is reluctant to disclose certain information, the therapist compliments her on knowing how to protect herself and not to talk about things she is not ready to reveal. If a client is assessed as needing a lot of control, the therapist would not assign a task. Instead, she would mention a task as something that may be helpful but that the client may or may not want to try.

In those early days of experimentation our team members had varying backgrounds. One had a degree in communication theory; another in behavior theory; one was a physician; and several were social workers. I was the "psychodynamic" one. This variety of perspectives was greatly valued at the time. We believed that our differences enriched the intervention message. When we met as a team we would associate very freely about our reaction to the clients' stories and then blend them into one message. The conductor of the interview always had the final say because the person doing the direct interviewing had information about the family that the observers did not have access to: nonverbal language and dynamic cues in the emotional field between people in conversation. This fact was validated later when we worked with one-way mirrors. When unexpected circumstances required a switch of role from team member to conductor, we discovered that we had a totally different attitude toward the client. Behind the mirror we might have been opinionated and partisan. Face to face with the same client, we experienced more empathy and acceptance. Obviously, both views are valuable, precisely because they provide more information than either one does alone.

In 1979, Steve de Shazer and Jim Derks left Family Service and rented an office to start the Brief Family Therapy Center (BFTC). The large room was divided in half by a narrow viewing room about five feet in depth that had two one-way mirrors, each one facing one interviewing room. There was a sound system that allowed for two separate teams, facing opposite mirrors, to monitor a case at the same time using ear phones. I have to confess most of us were so excited about what we were doing, and so hungry to participate in all cases, that we often would try to listen to both cases at the same time by switching earphones with each other.

In 1980, we had a daily staff of five people at BFTC: Steve and Insoo, Jim Derks, Marilyn LaCourt, who had also been a student at the Family Therapy Training Institute, and me. Elam Nunnally, a professor of social work at UW-Milwaukee, was with us regularly a few times a week. We also had a stable of interested therapists who visited. It was the five core members, however, who would sit together to watch cases, make videotapes, and spend hours analyzing what we were doing and how to improve it. As we worked together our thinking blended more and more, and the variety of perspectives faded. To some degree that fading was a loss, but the benefit was that the sum total of our similar ideas was still greater than the individual insights.

I was never more stimulated and excited than at that time. The theoretical discussions broadened my thinking and allowed me to see things in an entirely new way. I became aware of context, and developed the ability to see the big picture in relation to details as I had never been able to do before. This happened at work as well as in my personal life. I was not alone. We infected each other with our enthusiasm and became a creative organism. We had the hubris to think that no one had the ability to help our clients as well as we did. In retrospect, this seems quite adolescent, but I think this confidence was necessary for the success of the creative process.

Lest it might sound as though this creative process was always smooth sailing for me, I need to confess that the role of conductor was a stumbling block when I first started to work with the group. I didn't get it. "Just go in there and ask all the questions we need behind the mirror for the intervention message," I was told. This confused me more. It felt stilted and distracting to conduct an interview during which I was to ask questions others might want answers to as well as those I wanted answered. I tried my best, but always felt a lack of connection with the clients. It was this very discomfort that led me to concentrate my thinking on the purpose of the interview and its interventive possibilities (Lipchik, 1988a; Lipchik & de Shazer, 1986). To some degree this foreshadowed the switch from considering the intervention message as the main change agent to understanding the interview to be the intervention, as it was in solution focused therapy.

In 1981, our group attended a meeting in Connecticut where the cutting-edge systemic thinkers in the world convened. There, Lyman Wynne of Rochester, New York, saw a tape of one of our cases and became very interested in our group. Lyman later came to visit us in Milwaukee to watch us work, and soon we were getting other notable visitors like Brad Keeney, Bill O'Hanlon, John Weakland, Carl Tomm, and others.

THE BIRTH OF SOLUTION FOCUSED THERAPY

The change from brief family therapy to solution focused brief therapy came about accidentally. Although brief family therapy had distinguished itself from the MRI model by being ecosystemic, it was still like that model in terms of its problem focus and strategic nature. As our creative process continued, Steve introduced new theoretical concepts, such as the concept of "fit" (de Shazer, 1985, pp. 59–64) based on the statement of the 14th-century philosopher William of Ockham that "what can be done with fewer means is done in vain with many"(de Shazer, 1985, p. 58). This guiding principle spurred us on to make brief family therapy interventions as simple and fitting as possible. Steve likened the fit (de Shazer, 1985, pp. 59–64) of an intervention to the construction of a master key that unlocks the client's ability to solve his problem.

The use of formula tasks at the end of the session was an idea we experimented with to that end. The first session formula task tended to be, "Make a list of what you want to change." Then one day someone behind the mirror said, "Let's ask them what they *don't* want to change." This flight of ideas behind the mirror was characteristic for the team. We all thought that was a good idea and the interviewing therapist agreed. To our amazement the clients came back with the homework done, and the report that they were much better. This gave us food for thought and we decided to do it again. The result was the same. Subsequently, we researched the response to this question and found that by asking clients to focus on exceptions rather than the problem, improvement tended to occur. We theorized that focusing on exceptions offered clients the recognition that things were not as stuck as they thought they were. When clients felt more hopeful they were more energized and motivated to do something different. Consequently, we began to ask a lot of questions about reported changes, no matter how small, especially if there were others, as well, and what needed to happen for changes to continue and increase. Frequently, this process helped people reach their goals in only a few sessions. Eventually, we developed a series of questions, and even decision trees, to deal with the cases in which goals were not met so quickly. This new way of thinking shifted the interview into the position of being as crucial as, if not more so than, the intervention message had been. That is how SFT was born (de Shazer, 1988)!

Shortly after we made our discovery, I reviewed one of my former brief family therapy tapes during which I had spent three sessions discussing the problem with the client in order to fully understand how to develop a fit. When I considered this case from the new perspective I realized that the first three sessions would now be unnecessary. I could start treatment by immediately focusing on when the problem did not occur. That is how dramatic the change was from the problem-focused brief family therapy to a solution focused model.

The years that followed were exciting and gratifying. Steve wrote about our work and he and Insoo started to travel near and far to teach it. Soon some of us followed in their footsteps. The timing was also right for a brief, effective model because of the changes in health and mental health reimbursements. Solution focused therapy was an ideal product for managed care.

SOLUTION FOCUSED THERAPY TRAINING

Soon we had a full-blown training program at BFTC. I was totally committed to the solution focused manner of working, and loved teaching it. I enjoyed empowering the trainees to empower their clients. It was such a contrast from how I was supervised. With the exception of Insoo Kim Berg, my previous supervisors had been psychodynamic. They analyzed my process notes from the position of experts and sometimes did not even hesitate to interpret my actions.

Our training protocol at BFTC was geared to therapists who had a master's degree and were in practice. The program lasted one year and took place once afternoon and evening per week. We originally started the trainees with weeks of theory seminars and observation of trainers before sending them into the room with clients. When the trainees finally faced clients, they were usually very unsure of themselves, which affected the therapeutic relationship. This was evidenced by the fact that many clients did not return after the first session.

To rectify this situation, we changed the protocol. The trainees were sent into the room with clients the second week after they started and the theoretical seminars were presented gradually on a weekly basis. Now the trainees were extremely anxious about being thrown into the water so suddenly, but we pacified them by allowing them to take a list of questions into the interviewing room with them. The problem with that solution was that it was difficult to help them ask the questions at the right time and in the right context without interrupting the sessions constantly with calls from behind the mirror. Even though the trainees were less anxious overall, it became necessary to take the crib sheets away from them after several weeks for the sake of the therapeutic relationship. My own way of dealing with this stage was to ask trainees to stop thinking of the questions for a few sessions, but just to listen and respond to clients unless we called them from behind the mirror. It turned out that when their attention was diverted from asking the "right" question, they actually asked the questions very appropriately. Therapeutic relationships improved markedly, and there were fewer dropouts. I also believe that this method benefited the overall learning process, because when questions were called in, the trainees experienced them in the context of their connection with the clients. Previously, it happened more than once that a solution focused question like, "When aren't you so devastated?" was asked in the first few minutes of a first session of a client who was experiencing an emotional crisis.

HOW COMPUTERIZING SOLUTION FOCUSED THERAPY CHANGED ME

In 1984, Steve and Wally Gingrich, a professor at the School of Social Work at the University of Wisconsin-Milwaukee who had become part of our group, became interested in developing a computer program to determine which formulized task to assign at the end of the first session.

A master's degree candidate in computer science working on artificial intelligence, Hannah Goodman, wrote the program, which was called "Briefer" (de Shazer, 1988, pp. 14–19). Although it worked fairly well, we never made use of it. Later an attempt was made with some engineers from Marquette University to expand the project to include subsequent sessions but this did not lead to any substantial results.

It was during our work on "Briefer" that my thinking about solution focused therapy began to change. The researcher interviewed each of us to chart how we decide what to ask, what to ignore, and how to respond to clients. This work with Hannah really brought home the complexity of the therapeutic process to me. I began to see clearly that the questions alone are not the answer to successful solution focused therapy because the process is not strictly verbal. It is about body language, facial expressions, tone of voice, and emotions. It has a lot to do with our stance in relation to clients ("cooperating with how clients cooperate"). We who had started solution focused therapy and were practicing it successfully were not emphasizing these nonverbal aspects in our writing and training. The literature coming out of our organization at the time, including mine, shows that clearly. In looking back, it seems we were working so hard to simplify and formulize the solution focused therapy process that we forgot to humanize it with the therapeutic relationship. Later research (Lambert, 1992; Lambert & Bergin, 1994) pointed out that 40% of therapeutic success is the therapeutic relationship and only 15% the type of therapy practiced.

ICF CONSULTANTS, INC.

In 1988, with Marilyn Bonjean, a former supervisee at BFTC who later had a private practice there, I started a small agency called ICF Consultants. Marilyn shared my interest in exploring what makes therapy work. We developed an informal research project for that purpose. At the start of the second session, and every session thereafter, clients were given a short questionnaire to fill out. They were asked whether there had been any change since the last session, and if so, what they remembered from the last session that might account for that change. We, in turn, filled out a questionnaire at the end of each session about what we remembered happening in the session that might lead to some report of change in the next session. To our amazement, the 80 or so clients we studied said approximately the same thing: what made a difference for them was the feeling that they were understood and respected. The statements we made on our questionnaires about specific techniques or interventions were never mentioned. Of course, the strength-based solution focused philosophy provided the underpinnings for the clients' reports of comfort and safety. However, this study corroborated the research mentioned above about the power of the therapeutic relationship compared to therapy models.

At ICF I changed my way of training once again. I started with six hours of didactic seminars and illustrative videotapes before the students saw clients in front of the mirror. This didactic training covered the basic philosophy and techniques of solution focused therapy, but above all, it focused on the theoretical assumptions. I had come to the conclusion that if a therapist internalizes the assumptions then he or she will not feel at a loss about what question to ask next. Assumptions provide a framework for therapy and shape the therapist's attitude. They are guideposts. Assumptions serve to remind therapists not to feel as stuck as the client. To be helpful to clients, therapists have to transmit a positive attitude and hope.

For example, if a client complains about lack of progress after a few sessions, a therapist might experience a feeling of failure and be uncertain about what to do next. A review of solution focused assumptions will produce a number of responses that suggest how to proceed. For the case of the dissatisfied client, "Nothing is all negative" or "A small change can lead to bigger changes" can provide direction. Both these assumptions prompt the therapist to search her mind for something the client has said or done in past sessions that is evidence of some progress. If she remembers a small change she will want to bring it to the client's attention in a subtle manner that does not contradict the client's complaint. She might say, "I'm sorry you feel that way, but it is good that you are assertive and have shared that with me. What were your expectations and hopes when you first came in?" The client may say she hoped for more rapid progress. In an empathic manner, the therapist can "seem to remember" that the client mentioned a small change previously. If the client acknowledges this, the therapist can explain that small, gradual changes are more lasting than a sudden leap that may not last. She can continue by asking, "Are there any other small changes that you have noticed lately?" The hope is that the realization of some change may prompt the client's memory about other changes as well. If there have been no other changes, the therapist's next question can be, "What small change would you like to tell me about next time we meet?" "How would you notice that change?" "Who else might notice it?" Frequently, clients have sudden recall of a small change as a result of questions like this.

"Nothing is all negative" similarly keeps the therapist from slipping into the client's hopelessness and provides impetus for continuing to search for small changes. Clients often need prompting, like, "Nothing is different, even a little bit?" "What were you hoping you could report to me today?" The expectations are usually unrealistic and therapists have to help clients lower them, at the same time that they normalize gradual improvement. The other importance of the assumptions is that they serve as a reminder to therapists to keep their ears finely tuned for the minutiae that clients report.

"Clients have resources to help themselves" is another one of the assumptions. However, it is the therapist's job to find those resources and highlight them for clients. Regardless how insignificant a positive quality or change may seem, it is important to jump on it with, "Is that different?" This question focuses the client's attention on a point she may otherwise have disregarded. Whether this point is different or not does not matter, because it is grist for the mill in either case. If it is different, the therapist can build on it with more questions about how more of it can happen, and what else may be different. If it is not different, this fact can be the starting point for a conversation about what is necessary for something different to happen.

Solution Focused Therapy as I Experience It Today

Since 1988, ICF has grown to include seven associates. However, the one-way mirrors and cameras we originally installed for teamwork and training are idle. The financial repercussions of managed care prevent therapists from performing unpaid team work. Most of our staff work part-time at several places to make ends meet and get needed benefits such as health insurance. Therapists are paid by the hour and cannot afford the time to sit behind the mirror. It would not be ethical to charge for an observing team unless it is an exceptional situation and the insurance company agrees to pay for this kind of a treatment process. The increasingly stringent privacy laws have also made videotaping less desirable.

My teaching opportunities have changed over the past years, as well. The financial restraints result in less demand for individual and group training. I am more likely to be hired by agencies that provide community-based services, to train their therapists to work more briefly.

For example, I am presently consulting and teaching at an agency that provides in-home treatment for foster and residential care. Their therapists are all salaried. They also have a group of master's degree therapists who do not have the hours required for licensure yet and who are accumulating these on the job. The trainees come in a group once a month for three hours. I give them a few basic lectures about solution focused therapy with an emphasis on the assumptions, but from the first session on, I spend only half the allotted time on theory and techniques, and the rest of the time discussing their cases. I weave solution focused thinking into the case discussion. This seems to engage the therapists quickly and intensely because it is very relevant for them from the start.

In the residential program I teach solution focused therapy to people who may only have a high school or bachelor's degree. I have learned that I have to use a different approach with these trainees. I have found that lecturing, providing handouts, and showing videotapes does not engage them. What works is the same approach I use for clients: meeting them where they are and listening to them empathically. I begin by letting them tell me about their work problems. I may spend some time on their units to show them that I really want to understand the difficulties of their jobs. Seeing them on the unit allows me to observe their interaction with clients. These trainees trust me much more when I talk with them about clients I have observed in action. They are also more receptive when I wonder about alternative ways of responding to clients. For example, I recently helped unit staff to reduce acting-out behaviors by suggesting they compliment a child immediately if he does not protest or act out in response to a command. Formerly, when the staff did not get a response to a command, or got an angry one, they repeated the command louder and firmer, which resulted in an escalation that led to major upheavals.

My Relationship With Clients

I start my sessions by asking clients what they want to know about me and our agency. They are usually surprised by that and ask questions like, "How long have you been doing this?" or "What kind of a degree do you have?" Of course, some people take this opportunity to ask a lot of detailed questions, including personal ones. My response to personal questions is that I am married and have children and grandchildren. I don't go into further detail.

I am frequently asked to explain how I work. My answer to that is that I do not see problems as pathology; that I consider each person, couple, or family as unique and as having strengths and resources even though they may now be feeling stuck. I explain that my focus will be on the present and the future, rather than on the past, and on helping them figure out a solution to their problem. I always ask whether they have had therapy before and what they found helpful about it and what they did not find helpful. Reports about what clients did not like about previous therapies tell me what not to do when I work with them. Many clients who have seen other therapists before have told me that they were disappointed because the therapist just listened and did not say much. They want to know whether I will be a more active participant in the process, and I tell them I certainly will be. Sometimes clients, usually controlling ones, have a chip on their shoulder when they come in. For example, they'll ask for my credentials and respond with, "Oh, you don't have a PhD?" "No, I don't have one," I reply. If they say that they expected to work with someone with top credentials, I say I understand, and ask if they would like me to refer them to someone who has a PhD. Interestingly, these clients usually drop the subject and stay. Many young therapists are asked how much experience they have, or whether they are married and have children. I do not have that problem any more, but the best policy is to be honest at all times and offer a referral. Clients have to be comfortable in the therapeutic relationship and trust their therapist. If they express discomfort and are not given a choice, therapy is less likely to be successful.

Most of the face-to-face feedback that I have had from clients over the years is that solution focused therapy is helpful. I ask what that means to them, in particular, and their answers corroborate the informal research we did at ICF Consultants, namely, that they feel understood and respected. The feeling of respect is the result of the collaborative nature of SFT. Periodic questions like, "Are we talking about what you want to talk about?" "Do you feel you are getting the help you hoped for?" "Do you feel progress?" convey that the therapist values the client's opinion. If a client ever gives a negative reply I ask, "Could you share with me what you were hoping for?" "What would you like me to ask you about that I am not asking?" Since we cannot read clients' minds it is important for them to have the opportunity to provide feedback about the therapy process. However, many clients will not feel comfortable giving feedback, particularly if it is not positive. This lack of communication between them and the therapist can prolong treatment.

It is understandable that clients want to leave feeling that the hour has been worthwhile. More often than not the feedback after a session is, "I feel so much better now," but at times heavy issues have to be faced and clients are upset when they leave. They may have had to face reality for the first time, which may not be easy. Like any other therapy, solution focused therapy is not about making people feel good, but about helping them make choices that will make them feel better about themselves and their relationships in the long run.

How Solution Focused Therapy Has Affected Me Personally

I enjoy solution focused work much more than I did psychodynamic work. I do not experience the burnout I used to feel, nor the frustration of dealing with clients' resistance. I like the fact that clients get helped much faster. Perhaps that has something to do with my need to see results faster and not have people dependent on me for years. I trust the solution focused way of thinking and all that goes with it, and that trust has given me confidence. I suspect clients sense that the trust, as well, and that it gives them hope and security in turn. Nevertheless, I feel the longer I do this work the more humble I become about what I have yet to learn. Over the years one is presented so many different situations that one can never handle them all with ease. "Every person is unique" is one of the solution focused assumptions. Every case is unique, as well, and I try to approach it with that in mind. If I were to think, "Oh, this situation is just like the one I treated four months ago," and try to duplicate what I did then, I would probably not be helpful. I would also be totally bored. Each case is a new challenge and an opportunity for learning.

At every opportunity I try to impress on therapists interested in this approach not to see it as a formula but as a very creative, exciting process. I have reached an age when people are beginning to ask me when I will retire. My answer is always, "What would I do that would be as exciting as looking forward to the next intake?"

While I am certain that this model has benefited my clients far more and much faster than any of my previous work, I cannot honestly say that it has changed attitudes and behaviors in my personal life to a great extent. Many of my solution focused colleagues report that they have developed a much more positive outlook on life. I do not think that has happened to me. My default reaction is to see the glass half empty instead of half full. What has changed, though, is that I have become more self-reflective. I can recognize my mind-set sooner and try to help myself. Sometimes I do some self-talk in my head or on the computer. I have a conversation in which I ask myself solution focused questions about my issue. Other times, I use some of the exercises I give clients to help myself. An example would be writing about what bothers me and then tearing it up and watching it disappear in the garbage can. Other times I ask myself, "What should I do, or how should I behave right now, so that I feel good about myself later when I look back at this situation?"

Early in my career I sometimes tried to think like a therapist when I was interacting with family and friends. That became particularly tempting when I was first enamored of solution focused questions. This phase is long past though. Now I know the boundary between my personal and professional life and have no desire to cross it.

CONCLUSION

It is hard to believe that my solution focused journey has lasted almost 30 years. It has been so exciting and rewarding that it seems much shorter. I have learned so much from my supervisors, clients, supervisees, trainees, and people who have attended my workshops. I am aware that I have become increasingly respectful of clients over the years. There were aspects of our work at BFTC while developing the model that I no longer agree with. I think we were theoretically client-centered, but not practically so. Our early practice and trainings reflected an authoritarian, if not arrogant, attitude. If clients did not agree to the team approach, or the one-way mirror, we told them we would not see them, and referred them out. The irreverence behind the mirror, which I hinted at previously, was not truly client-centered. Today, I believe the clients' comfort and feeling of safety are far more important than any methodology. Genuine respect for the humanity of the client is the essential part of being client-centered for me now.

The most significant change that has occurred in my thinking about solution focused therapy since the late 1980s is that I have come to value the theoretical underpinnings as much as, if not more than, the techniques. The more well-known solution focused therapy became, the more it seemed to be thought of, or presented, in a formulaic manner. The techniques like the exception question, the miracle question, and the scaling question (de Shazer, 1991, p. 148) took on a life of their own and were thought to solve all problems, regardless of how long-standing and severe they were. The therapeutic relationship was reduced to brief joining at the beginning of the first session. The concept of "cooperating with how clients cooperate" to circumvent resistance was no longer mentioned. This reductionism eventually led to my decision to write a book (Lipchik, 2002). Its purpose was to put some meat on these now skeletal questions by providing context and underpinnings for the questions, and to make solution focused therapy more respectable for many therapists who believe that it is superficial and ineffective in many situations.

An important aspect of this change was to make emotions explicit and acceptable as part of solution focused therapy (Kiser, Piercy, & Lipchik, 1993; Lipchik, 1999). The MRI Brief Therapy Model as well as brief family therapy did not see emotions as relevant to the therapeutic process. Emotions were considered ephemeral and very subjective, while behaviors were seen as concrete and easy to track by clients and therapists when changes occur. Steve de Shazer used to remove the facial tissues from the consultation room before his clients came because he felt that the facial tissues would focus them on their emotions and hamper change. Yet most clients describe their problems in emotional terms. The inclusion of emotions broadens possibilities for solutions. One can build solutions on exceptional feelings just as well as on exceptional behaviors. I am certain there are many excellent solution focused therapists who disagree with me. But then, each therapist is unique, just like every client we treat!

I feel privileged to have been part of the development of solution focused therapy. I hope that many therapists have enjoyed practicing it as much as I have and have had the satisfaction of helping people more quickly and effectively. Most of all I hope that solution focused therapy will be valued for its elegance and practicality for many years to come.

EDITOR'S COMMENT

I simply do not have the words to express how I felt when I was informed that Eve Lipchik had agreed to contribute her chapter to this book. I have been a fan of hers for some time and very much enjoyed the way she incorporated emotions and the therapeutic relationship into her work with solution focused therapy. This was mentioned several times in her chapter; she incorporates emotions in a way that no one else in the field does. As a founding member of the Brief Family Therapy Center in Milwaukee, Wisconsin, along with Steve de Shazer and Insoo Kim Berg, she can talk about this theory in a way that many others cannot because she played a role in the development of the approach from its inception. She does this with such honesty and passion that I felt as though I was there experiencing the early days of SFT.

—Elliott Connie

REFERENCES

Ackerman, N. (1960). *Treating the troubled family.* New York: Basic Books.

Boszormany-Nagy, I., & Spark, G. I. (1973). *Invisible loyalties. Reciprocity in intergenerational family therapy.* New York: Harper & Row.

Bowen, M. (1960). Family psychotherapy. *American Journal of Orthopsychiatry, 31,* 40–60.

Cowen, E. L., Hightown, A. D., Pedro-Carroll, J., Wock, W. C., & Wyman, P. A., & Haffey, W. G. (1997). *School-based prevention for children at risk: The primary mental health project.* Washington, DC: American Psychological Association.

de Shazer, S. (1982). *Patterns of brief family therapy: An ecosystemic approach.* New York: Guilford Press.

de Shazer, S. (1985). *Keys to solutions in brief therapy.* New York: Norton.

de Shazer, S. (1988). *Clues: Investigating solutions in brief therapy.* New York: Norton.

de Shazer, S. (1991). *Putting difference to work.* New York: Norton.

Fisch, R., Weakland, J. H., & Segal, L. (1982). *The tactics of change: Doing therapy briefly.* San Francisco, CA: Jossey-Bass.

Kiser, D., Piercy, F. P., & Lipchik, E. (1993). The integration of emotions in solution-focused therapy. *Journal of Marital and Family Therapy, 19*(3), 232–242.

Lambert, M. J. (1992). Implications of outcome research for psychotherapy integration. In J. Norcross & M. R. Goldfried (Eds.), *Handbook of psychotherapy integration* (pp. 94–129). New York: Free Press.

Lambert, M. J., & Bergin, A. E. (1994). The effectiveness of psychotherapy. In A. E. Bergin & S. L. Garfield (Eds.), *Handbook of psychotherapy and behavior change* (pp. 143–189). New York: Wiley.

Lipchik, E. (Ed.). (1988a). *Interviewing.* Rockville, MD: Aspen.

Lipchik, E. (1988b). Interviewing with a constructive ear. *Dulwich Centre Newsletter,* pp. 3–7.

Lipchik, E. (1999). *Theoretical and practical thoughts about expanding the solution-focused approach to include emotions.* In W.A. Ray & S. de Shazer (eds.). Evolving brief therapies: Essays in honor of John Weakland (pp. 157–172) , Galena, IL: Geist and Russell Companies, Ltd.

Lipchik, E. (2002). *Beyond technique in solution-focused therapy: Working with emotions and the therapeutic relationship.* New York: Guilford Press.

Lipchik, E., & de Shazer, S. (1986). The purposeful interview. *Journal of Strategic and Systemic Therapies, 5*(1&2), 88–99.
Minuchin, S. (1974). *Families and family therapy.* Cambridge, MA: Harvard University Press.
Skynner, R. (1976). *Systems of family and marital psychotherapy.* New York: Brunner/Mazel.
Whitaker, C. A. (1976). A family is a four-dimensional relationship. In P. J. Guerin (Ed.), *Family therapy: Theory and practice.* New York: Garden Press.
Wynne, L. C. (1978). Knotted relationships, communication deviances, and metabinding. In M. M. Berger (Ed.), *Beyond the double bind.* New York: Brunner/Mazel.

4 Respectful Optimism and Satisfying Subtlety

YVONNE DOLAN

It is better to light a candle than curse the darkness.

—Eleanor Roosevelt

Q. How did you first learn about solution focused therapy?

A. I was working at a shelter for runaway and homeless youth in New Orleans, Louisiana, in the early 1980s when I first learned about solution focused brief therapy. Funded primarily by church groups and charity contributions, the shelter had so little money that we were only able to house and counsel each child for three weeks. Many of the children I worked with had been sexually abused; most had been emotionally abused, neglected, and battered, and some had been sold or coerced into prostitution by parents or caregivers. In most cases, one or both parents were missing, in jail, or incapacitated by severe drug and alcohol abuse or chronic mental health problems. Having been trained in strategic therapy and in Ericksonian psychotherapy and hypnosis, I was naturally curious about new developments in brief therapy and so I began reading articles and issues of Steve de Shazer's newsletter, *The Underground Railroad.*

In 1983 I phoned the Milwaukee Brief Therapy Center (BFTC) to arrange a visit. Steve de Shazer answered the phone and, since I already was a bit in awe of him and Insoo, I was momentarily speechless. I then apologized for the lapse, explaining that I was a *very* shy person. Little did I know that I was at that very moment talking to one of the shyest people I would ever meet! It was the beginning of a deep and poignant friendship based at least in part on mutual disclosures about our personal struggles to overcome social awkwardness.

I traveled to BFTC that summer with Charlie Johnson (a long-time subscriber to *The Underground Railroad,* also my then partner) and we spent several days behind the mirror observing therapy sessions. We were staying in Insoo and Steve's guest room, and every evening we sat around and talked about the sessions we had observed and asked Insoo and Steve a lot of questions. I remember being struck by Steve's view that "how" questions about symptoms were a lot more useful question than "why" questions; also by the fact that he saw his background in philosophy (particularly logic) and the work of Derrida and Wittgenstein as particularly relevant to the practice of psychotherapy. Insoo was warm, welcoming, and enthusiastic. At the time, she and I both shared a sewing hobby and made a lot of jokes about the fact that there was always a box of fabric under one of our beds.

We thoroughly enjoyed observing the live sessions at BFTC from behind the mirror and I immediately felt that I had finally "come home" to a therapeutic approach and culture that embodied my core beliefs about the nature of therapeutic change, the significance of demonstrating respect as well as empathy to both clients and colleagues, and the necessity of making the approach fit the client's needs rather than vice versa.

Nevertheless, I was quite taken aback when on the second day of our visit, Insoo firmly told us that our observation period was over and we were now expected to be active team members. We both did our best, and apparently Steve and Insoo thought we did okay because afterward they invited us to come back to BFTC whenever we were able. They also kindly offered to come and sit behind the mirror on the brief therapy team we were planning to start in Denver.

We subsequently returned home and started a team largely based on what we had learned that week at the Milwaukee BFTC. Steve and Insoo came to visit often and we all became good friends, establishing a relationship that endured until their respective deaths. They came several times a year and always spent at least one afternoon or evening with our team behind the mirror; the team subsequently became the solutions group headed by Charlie and it continues to this day. Steve and Insoo did not charge us for their consultations. However, we willingly sponsored several workshops for them. These events, along with visits to BFTC, and assisting with training at BFTC over the years (since 1993), afforded me with a lot of invaluable hands-on training and ongoing experience in the evolution of solution focused brief therapy.

The atmosphere at BFTC at that time was fascinating to me. In addition to Steve and Insoo, I met other members of their team including Eve Lipchik, Kate Kowalski, Michele Weiner-Davis, Wally Gingerich, Gale Miller, Elam Nunnally, Jim Kral, and several others whose names now escape me. Every person I met at BFTC at that time struck me as very intelligent. There was a shared goal of discovering what questions or behaviors resulted in positive therapeutic changes and everyone appeared passionately invested in it. The relationships between team members impressed me at the time (1983) as egalitarian, friendly, and informal. The discussions I recall from those days seemed rather extraordinary, quite unlike what I would have expected to hear among the staff at other outpatient mental health clinics or social service agencies at the time.

For example, the topics could range from team members' straightforward observations of the live sessions they had seen that week; to arguments about the relevance of philosophy, linguistics, strategic therapy, or Batesonian theory to their ongoing work with clients; to the comparative virtues of various research designs to the cultural, social, and therapeutic relevance of contemporary music and art! The atmosphere between team members seemed extremely nonjudgmental and people managed to be playful at times despite the intellectual rigor of the discussions and the hard work involved in working with such a large and varied clientele. For example, I remember hearing that the male BFTC team members had a chili-making competition with blind tastings to determine the best chili, and that Steve de Shazer, Wally Gingerich, and Michele Weiner-Davis shared an affinity for imported licorice. Team members took walks together and shared an occasional pizza and beer.

Most significantly, everyone on the team expressed what appeared to be a very genuine interest in finding out what others thought—and this included the clients, whose views were treated with great respect. The clients were considered to possess genuine expertise and knowledge about their lives and what would be necessary to dissolve the problems that brought them in. I remember saying at the time that the atmosphere at BFTC seemed to be an "ego-free" zone.

BFTC was essentially an inner-city outpatient clinic, with a very wide range of clients, including homeless heroin addicts, severe alcoholics, chronically mentally ill people, multiproblem families who had previously exhausted all the local county social services, highly educated upper-income people struggling to make high-level career decisions, couples experiencing domestic abuse, children with school problems, parents of children exhibiting problematic behaviors like bed wetting and defiance, and so forth.

The staff of BFTC had a policy of working with whoever showed up rather than (for example) requesting that the entire family come in, or that members of a couple be seen alone. This was considered rather unusual, even radical at the time.

All clients were requested to sign release forms so that the tapes could be later studied for educational purposes. Most were willing to do so, and as a result, almost every session was videotaped. Afterwards, Insoo, Steve, and various other team members would spend hours observing the videotapes, keeping track of any question or behavior the therapist or client said or did that resulted in positive therapeutic change during and after the session. These behaviors were recorded, preserved, and subsequently utilized in other sessions. Questions and behaviors that were not demonstrated to be helpful (or in some cases appeared to even interfere with positive change) were discarded.

Q. What characteristics of the model drew you toward it?

A. I was immediately drawn to the practicality, effectiveness, respectfulness, and optimism of the approach, as well as its flexibility and satisfying subtlety. While some refer to the solution focused "model," I prefer "approach." When we[1] were working on *More Than Miracles: The State of the Art of Solution Focused Brief Therapy* (de Shazer et al., 2007), Steve de Shazer and Insoo Kim Berg advised against calling the solution focused approach a "model" because doing so implied a rigidity of technique and theory that contradicted its tenets and risked stultifying its further growth and development.

Q. How did you discover that solution focused therapy was the model that seemed to fit with your way of working with clients?

A. As I mentioned earlier, I first got interested in this approach while working with traumatized homeless adolescents in the early 1980s. Later I worked with many other clients who had suffered sexual, physical, and emotional abuse as well as other traumas. A common characteristic of traumatic experiences is that the client's experience is one of feeling out of control and at the mercy of another person or situation. SFT's collaborative stance and strong emphasis on the client's expertise—about the realities of his or her life situation and what needs to happen in order to solve or at least improve the problem—provides an opposite sort of experience that helps to counterbalance this.

I also found that the emphasis on solution building, rather than problem assessment, was liberating for both the therapist and client—especially for traumatized clients, who oftentimes have already been asked to repeatedly recount the details of horrific experiences to a long series of caregivers and intake workers before arriving at the first therapy session. SF sessions typically begin with a description of what the client wants to be different as a result of the session or how others will know that the session was helpful. This supplies a much-needed perspective of hope, which is then combined with the practicality provided by scaling questions that identify real-life actions the client can take to immediately began to improve or better cope with the situation or condition that caused him or her to seek therapy. I consider it both cruel and immoral for therapists to engage in long-term therapies that unnecessarily prolong clients' suffering when effective short-term therapies such as SFT are available.

Q. How has utilizing solution focused therapy impacted your work with clients? (Please mention if you utilized a previous model and the difference you noticed in clients and yourself after switching to SFT.)

A. I came to SFT with a background in Ericksonian Utilization.[2] The SF approach immediately made perfect sense to me because I had learned the importance of respecting the client's position and the value of utilizing rather than opposing their perspectives. I suppose the biggest change that occurred in my work as a result of learning the SF approach was that I began using Ericksonian hypnosis much less, instead simply utilizing the intensified responsiveness and focus that occurs naturally in my clients in response to detailed SF questions involving their heartfelt longings and aspirations—questions that gradually evolve during our shared solution development process.

Q. How would your clients describe your work with them?

A. When working with clients who have experienced other therapy approaches, I consistently hear how much they appreciate the fact that I do not tell them what to do but instead take the time to listen to their perspective and then ask practical questions that help them identify what they need to do in order to get the results they want. Many of my clients tell me that I ask "good questions" and report that they spent time thinking about a scaling question I asked or the miracle question in between sessions.

Q. What is it about SFT that makes it so effective?

A. When done well, the SFT approach utilizes language with such precision and deliberation that it becomes a highly personalized response specific to each client. The therapist's responses and questions are carefully calibrated to consistently and respectfully communicate to the client that the client is being listened to with great diligence, concentration, and care, and that his or her ideas are being considered thoughtfully. Like any other approach done well, SFT includes messages that congruently communicate respect, caring, and genuine good wishes toward the client.

Q. Describe one of your favorite cases and how it impacted your work as a therapist

A. I have had many "favorite" cases, but if I had to pick just one it would be the following: A young woman in her 20s came to me and described a history of severe sexual and physical abuse. She was very intelligent and had read all the literature about the correlation between abuse and various debilitating symptoms such as drug and alcohol abuse, self-harm, sexual dysfunction, and so forth. She explained that when she contemplated the future she feared she would live as a result of her extremely violent, abusive childhood, she thought of killing herself. On the other hand, whenever she allowed herself to build what she described as "air castles," in which she fantasized about dreams that seemed (to her) far out of reach like going to college, becoming a famous chef, or falling for a "decent man who would be faithful and love" her, she was momentarily better, but afterwards cried her eyes out.

I didn't do anything special with her, mostly just listened in a caring way. When there was an occasional pause, I asked gentle scaling questions about her "air castle" fantasies (in which achieving her fantasy was 10, and 0 was before she even imagined these dreams). We joked a lot about how she was from Missouri (she wasn't from there in reality) because it was called the "show me" state and she was definitely a show-me-first type of person: She repeatedly asserted that she was not capable of believing anything good could happen to her until after it actually happened—and even then, it would probably take a while for her to believe it.

Despite the fact that she initially responded to my scaling questions with a lot of sarcasm and "I don't know," I gently persevered in asking them. Gradually she was able to identify small concrete things she could choose to do that would allow her to begin to move in the direction of some of the things she wanted, like earning money for tuition at the local junior college and getting her teeth fixed so that she would feel more courageous about trying to find a boyfriend. It took a long time, but one by one she achieved the things she longed for, many of which she had trouble believing were possible even when they were on the brink of taking place, like for example her college graduation. She had trouble really believing she was going to graduate until *after* she received her diploma.

I saw her on and off for over 5 years, usually once or twice a month. When I confided this to Steve de Shazer and Insoo Kim Berg, my long-time mentors, they said, "Remember that Brief is a relative term. It should be no longer and not one bit shorter than necessary." Steve later included this advice in the forward he wrote for my book, *Resolving Sexual Abuse.*

Q. Has the use of solution focused therapy impacted you in your personal life? If so, please explain.

A. I have used the Miracle Question to help identify personal goals in my life, and have sometimes used my own Letter from the Future technique (in which I write a letter from a future perspective describing what my life is like after my personal miracle has happened). I am convinced that there are many things in my life that I might not have achieved without doing this. In some cases, such as teaching workshops, I might not have even realized what I wanted to do if it had not come up as part of my description of a personal miracle. For example, although I have always loved animals, I assumed that having a dog was out of the question until one came up in my personal miracle description. These days, post "miracle," my little furry four-footed sweetie, Tchotsky, and I are inseparable and I have become a much more joyous person.

Q. What are some key personality traits that you think are shared amongst solution focused practitioners?

A. Patience, humility, optimism, humor, and flexibility.

Q. What are some common mistakes that therapists trying on the model make most often? If you had a chance to guide them differently, how would you do so?

A. The most common mistakes are failing to devote sufficient time to finding out what the client wants to have happen as a result of therapy and using SF techniques rigidly rather than applying them intelligently and sensitively in the context of the sort of highly personalized, congruently respectful, and caring conversation that characterizes all good therapy. No approach, including SFT, will work well if it is practiced rigidly or insensitively with disregard for the client's feelings or unique life circumstances, or without congruently communicating caring and respect. Omitting these things can sometimes result in solution "forced" therapy, but never good solution focused therapy.

Q. What are some things you notice students doing while trying on this model that lets you know this model may fit them?

A. They congruently communicate respect for the client's point of view and life experiences, observe behavior rather than jumping to conclusions, and are good at asking specific detail-oriented questions.

Q. If you were training therapists in the solution focused therapy model, what strategies would you use to train them and how would you present the material?

A. Since I train therapists in the SF approach all over the world, this is a strategy I use in real life. Oftentimes my attendees are people who are new to SFT, or are using other approaches, feel skeptical about the SF approach, and are apparently only attending to satisfy their boss or supervisor. After giving them the bare basics of the SF approach, I invite each person to try the following exercise with three other colleagues: One person role-plays a current client with whom they are struggling or who they consider to be difficult or resistant to therapy. The other three people take turns role-playing therapists working with this "client." The person playing the client is asked to notice which of the three "therapists'" questions, behaviors, or comments are most useful or helpful.

The three therapists sit in a semicircle facing the client, and each takes equal turns talking with the client. Per turn, each therapist is allowed to ask one question or make one statement to the client. Once the client responds, it is the next therapist's turn. One therapist is asked to faithfully adhere to the SF approach described in the workshop, incorporating the SF techniques of scaling, compliments, and detail-oriented questions. The other two therapists are invited to use whatever problem-focused technique they wish.

After 30 minutes, the client is invited to leave the room for a 5-minute break. During this time the therapists compare impressions and try to predict what the client will say was most useful and essentially what they felt worked best. When the client finally discloses what was actually most helpful from his or her perspective, the result is typically quite surprising, revealing, and rather dramatically instructive. It is always the SF approach that the client describes as most helpful. Frequently, people are amazed by how much more respected, supported by, and cooperative toward the SF therapist the client feels, as opposed to the two who role-played a problem-focused approach. Afterwards I ask each group to describe what they learned from the exercise and people are typically very specific and enthusiastic about their observations of what they or others did that worked effectively.

Q. If you could pick a pioneer solution focused therapist who impacted your work, whom would you name and why?

A. It would be impossible to choose between Insoo and Steve, so I will credit them both. I cotaught with both Steve and Insoo on many occasions and spent a lot of time observing their work. From Insoo, I learned the value of beginning sessions by first joining with clients through focusing on their hopes, longings, strengths, preferences, and already existing competencies. This has a powerful hope-instilling effect on the rest of the session as well as the entire course of the therapeutic process.

From Steve, I learned the importance of taking emotions seriously by appreciating them as understandable responses to the specific contexts or situations in which they originate in the client's real life rather than conferring on them an unwarranted sense of solidity. Speaking of feelings of sadness or fearfulness apart from the real-life situations in which they typically originate (for example, the loss of a loved one, a job, or worries about a specific risk or danger) by labeling them as symptoms or entities such as "depression" or "anxiety" makes it much more difficult for therapists and clients to recognize that their emotional intensity is inherently transient. Therapists who speak of painful emotions as if they are stable, solid objects are arguably doing their clients a serious disservice. Because SFT focuses on observing the transiency of emotion rather than attempting to determine the "cause" of the "symptom," the comforting awareness that "this too shall pass" is rarely lost during the therapeutic process.

I also am grateful for what I learned from observing Eve Lipchik, whose gracious, empathic manner with clients I much admired, from Harry Korman, who often incorporates gentle humor into his solution focused sessions, from Luc Isebaert, who elegantly demonstrated how

SF can be effectively applied in medical and drug and alcohol treatment settings, and from Bill O'Hanlon and Brian Cade, who invented a technique of asking clients to describe a series of frames from a videotape of what their life after the SF miracle would look like.

Q. What developments would you like to see in the future of this model?

A. I would like to see numerous research projects in order to further demonstrate its effectiveness and legitimacy.

EDITOR'S COMMENT

When Elliott and I approached many of the kind practitioners in this book to write a chapter for us, Yvonne Dolan was one of the first to reply enthusiastically about the project. Throughout her account in this chapter, I picked up on her initial excitement in learning the model, practicing the model, and teaching it to trainees. No wonder replying to us was a given.

I appreciated Yvonne Dolan in the early 1990s when I attended one of the first solution focused therapy association meetings in New Orleans. Her words about being more respectful to survivors of sexual abuse resonated with me as she talked of how encouraging clients to talk about the abuse was, in fact, more abuse. I keep her words in my head when I work with clients and cite her constantly when I teach therapists. She has always been a model for me in this area and continues to impress me with her integration of hypnosis and solution focused therapy. How fortunate we are to read of her upbringing into solution focused therapy and to read of her admiration for those originators who clearly valued her as well. Her obvious tenacity for hearing emotions and knowing how to direct her elegant questions for clients demonstrates that solution focused therapy is more than questions and techniques. I gathered much from reading Yvonne's work and perhaps the most important message to me was that a solution focused therapist always evolves, and it is her clients that help to create that evolution.

—Linda Metcalf

NOTES

1. Terry Trepper, Harry Korman, Eric McCollum, and I coauthored *More Than Miracles* with the late Steve de Shazer and Insoo Kim Berg during the final years of their respective lives.

2. Although it wasn't published until 1985, I had just finished writing a book *(A Path With a Heart: Ericksonian Utilization with Resistant and Chronic Clients)* on therapeutic utilization of client's symptoms, perceptions, cognitions, and behaviors shortly before I visited BFTC for the first time.

REFERENCE

de Shazer, S., & Dolan, Y., with Korman, H., Trepper, T., Berg, I. K., & McCollum, E. (2007). *More Than Miracles: The State of the Art of Solution-Focused Brief Therapy.* Binghamton, NY: Haworth Press.

5 Working in the Dark

CHRIS IVESON

Words were originally magic.

—Freud and de Shazer

Q. How did you first learn about solution focused therapy (SFT)?

A. I met Harvey Ratner and Evan George in 1986 when I took a job in a family therapy clinic in London. That year, too, I met Bill O'Hanlon at a workshop. I was inspired, but had difficulty replicating Bill's ideas in my own practice. Evan, Harvey, and I all taught family therapy so we tried to keep up to date with new developments. They were talking of doing some work together on solution focused brief therapy and I muscled in on the plan. In the autumn of 1988 I joined them in a three-month project to teach ourselves solution focused therapy, with *Keys to Solutions in Brief Therapy* (de Shazer, 1985) and later, when it became available, *Clues: Investigating Solutions in Brief Therapy* (de Shazer, 1988). On Wednesday afternoons each of us saw a client, while being observed and supervised by the other two. We tried to see people in the most difficult circumstances and especially statutory (or mandated) clients. This was a very creative period and at the end of the three months we decided to continue, gradually dropping all our previous ideas and practices.

We wanted to meet de Shazer, but we couldn't afford to go to Milwaukee and neither could we persuade any of the family therapy institutions to invite him over. We decided to take a risk and invite him ourselves. His fee was modest; he said he would throw Insoo in for the same price and we arranged his trip a year in advance. Meanwhile, we presented our work at a conference and then wrote *Problem to Solution* (George et al., 2001). Steve was a little surprised that we had written a book before meeting him and for a while he was reluctant to read it! However, eventually he did read it and produced a very generous foreword. His first visit to us in May 1990 was a great success. We have videos of both him and Insoo working with us, and of the 250 participants at the workshop, many went on to become solution focused therapists. That workshop was BRIEF's first event, though it was another four years before we became a totally independent clinic and training center.

Q. How did you discover that SFT was the model that seemed to fit with your way of working with clients?

A. It was reading the literature with Evan and Harvey that brought the possibilities of solution focused ideas alive. Once I began to grasp it then I felt I had come home. I had been drawn to family therapy as a student social worker in 1971, seeing it as an alternative to the pathology-dominated ideas of the time. Though the phrase had not been coined, the early family therapy was very strengths-based, and this had immediate appeal to me. What family therapy lacked was a procedure for identifying and utilizing strengths except by focusing on problems and so gradually it drifted into its own brand of pathologizing clients. Solution focused brief therapy provided a means both to identify and utilize the client's resources. It was like discovering the Holy Grail and realizing it was staring us in the face all along.

Q. What characteristics of this model drew you toward it?

A. It was the notion of *exceptions* that really bowled me over. This totally simple idea that for every problem there were embryonic solutions already in place was such a revelation and yet so obvious. One of the seminal moments in my solution focused career was a very early case of agoraphobia. Following a traumatic event, the client had been self-incarcerated in a 15th-floor apartment alone for two years. An hour-long home visit produced no exceptions and not a little annoyance in the client. It also produced a large worm of doubt in my mind. Luckily, my colleagues Harvey and Evan persuaded me to give it another go, so two weeks later I returned.

Half an hour into this second session, I was quietly wishing ill to Harvey, Evan, and the still unmet Steve de Shazer when a very large dog walked into the room. As it bent down to lick my ear I commented on its fitness and asked my client who took it for walks. Looking at me as if I was mad she said, "I do of course! Who do you think! You know I live alone!" It took another half an hour to tease out and replant this daily *exception*. The client then canceled the next session but a month later sent a postcard from the holiday destination she had been planning to visit at the time of her trauma. Writing about it now, I am almost tempted to go back to that early way of working!

Exceptions and the simplicity of the model and the fact that it offered absolutely not a toehold on diagnosis, assessment, or pathology was a draw: there was no room, anywhere, to hypothesize about the client and the cause or reason for the problem. I remember running a two-day workshop on hypothesizing in family therapy just as I was moving into solution focused work. I said to myself, "This is the last time you'll do this one!" and was not without worry as my family therapy teaching paid for our holidays! Luckily solution focused teaching proved even more popular! Eventually.

Q. How has utilizing SFT impacted your work with clients? (Please mention if you utilized a previous model and the difference you noticed in clients and yourself after switching to SFT.)

A. It was a long time ago! I was never formally trained in family therapy and my work reflected this. The clinic I worked in was heavily influenced by Salvador Minuchin, who had spent a year there. I too had been drawn to him because of his work with slum families. I was also very taken by the MRI's work and by Jay Haley's (what was to become very dated) work on adolescents. Basically my work was a mishmash and though I was probably reasonably effective, I could not have very coherently described why I did what I did at any given moment. I remember that our early solution focused work *seemed* more effective than what I had been doing previously, but have no evidence to support that feeling. What I remember is enjoying work much more—not just the new approach but the increasingly close collaboration with Harvey and Evan.

I was talking to a group of social workers about the beginnings of solution focused therapy in the early 1980s when someone contradicted me and said, "It must have begun in the early 1970s because I was doing it then!" I hotly denied this allegation and demanded evidence. She was a social worker for Banardo's, a large UK-based child care organization, and part of her job was to supervise ex-clients wanting access to their records. In one case I had been the social worker and had been the only contributor to the file who wrote of the client's strengths and possibilities! That was in 1973. It was another 15 years before I discovered what I had been looking for!

It is too long ago to remember how existing clients responded to the change in my practice. I suspect not a lot, since it is the affirmative side of solution focus that most strikes people as different and that was already present in my work. What they might have noticed is a big increase in my confidence. I remember absolutely basking in the new sense of knowing what I was doing! I also remember therapy being less of a struggle both for me and my clients. It was still hard work but with a much clearer sense of purpose and technique. I imagine this could have enhanced my effectiveness if only because I appeared more confident to my clients.

At the time all this began I was running a series of workshops entitled "Vive la Resistance" (not realizing that resistance was already dead!) based heavily on the MRI model but with a very heavy stress on the idea that resistance was where the client's greatest strength lay so it should be honored, preserved, and utilized. Not really that different from early de Shazer.

Having now done nothing other than solution focused work for 20 years, I am surprised by how fascinating I still find the work. I think I owe the root of this satisfaction to Steve de Shazer's application of Occkam's Razor: what we can do with fewer means we should not do with many. The minimalism engendered by the constant application of Occkam's Razor has been a tremendously creative force in our work. Minimalism is often jokingly referred to as a reductionist process ending up with the therapeutic equivalent of the white on whites in the modernist art movement of the middle of the last century. The principle is to examine everything we do and as far as possible test its usefulness. If doing without it doesn't affect outcomes, then it can't be necessary.

The first to go was the "customer, complainant, visitor" categorization; then tasks; then problem descriptions; then the miracle as a metaphorical device; then the break; and then the end-of-session compliments. However, these omissions do not lead to shorter sessions. Instead they lead to new developments. Losing the client categories led directly to the assumption that all clients (including mandated clients) were motivated; giving up tasks meant greater attention could be paid to the client as the therapist would not need to shape the conversation toward a task; problem descriptions, necessary when working through exceptions, were rendered unnecessary by asking clients what their best hopes were from the therapy; descriptions of possible futures were elicited without the introduction of miracles, thus making the therapy far more prosaic and unmemorable and, therefore, less prone to leaving large footprints. Similarly, dispensing with the break and message leaves clients with their own voices. The upshot of this is that we have become far more skilled at drawing out detail, both of possible futures and those actual pasts that might lead to them.

Q. How would your clients describe your work with them? Have any of your clients who might have experienced another model of therapy commented on the difference (if any) that they perceived when working with you?

A. I'm not sure clients are always very interested in the process as long as it works. Some do notice a positivity, but not necessarily one that they like! Often clients describe the experience as having someone listen to their problems (even though we haven't actually talked about them). Probably those most likely to notice a difference are those with a poor experience of another form of counseling. But sometimes first timers can be pleasantly surprised. Yesterday I asked a first-time client (a woman wanting to get her children back from local authority care), "Would you like to come again?" She replied: "Ooo! Yes, please! It's my first time and I didn't expect it to be like this. I thought you'd just tell me what to do!"

And sometimes clients have noticed the difference and decided it's not a difference that suits their preferences.

Q. What is it about SFT that makes it so effective?

A. My most recent thoughts on this is that we only pick up what is already there: Whatever a client does tomorrow they could have done yesterday and if we trace the history of any success it will be as long and complex of a history traced back from a problem. All we perhaps do is raise the client's perception of what is possible—but the "what is possible" has to be there in the first place. From our point of view, we work in the dark. We cannot know what is possible so when we help a client describe a preferred future and there is no improvement, we cannot know whether the lack of improvement was because what was being sought after was actually impossible, or whether we just did a bad job in raising the client's perceptions, or we helped the client see more possibility and the client decided not to pursue it, or whatever else! Since we can't know what is going on, we are left with trusting the process and doing some sort of outcome research to verify that enough people we see make sufficient progress to justify continuing to offer this type of therapy.

Alongside this, I think our conversations are most helpful to clients when we do not interfere with their lives (with tasks, action plans, or even any hint that we think they should do anything different) but simply help them describe what might be and what already is. I can't say this hands-off approach is any more successful but early indications are that it is briefer. Our last follow-up (22 clients) had an average of well under three sessions (with 80% reporting some lasting change and 50% reporting significant lasting change). How far under three would be too embarrassing to confess!

Q. Describe one of your favorite cases and how it impacted your work as a therapist.

A. A very well and expensively dressed woman came to therapy after seeing a mention of BRIEF in *Vogue* magazine. She told me her history of mental illness, drug addiction, and poverty. She had been a psychiatric inpatient, a homeless heroin addict, and an alcoholic. She decided this wasn't good enough and went into detox. This worked and she put together a successful life until some psychiatric symptoms reappeared. Before she knew it she was back in the hospital and then a homeless beggar on the drink and drugs. Again she decided she was worth more than this but couldn't face hospitalization. This time she detoxed herself and began to put together a new life. When I met her, she was running a very successful and profitable property business but her symptoms of paranoia were returning: That morning she had punched a man on the London Underground for brushing against her in a grossly overcrowded carriage! She said that she couldn't face doing the whole round again and this was her last chance. She also said she knew her difficulties sprang from the sexual abuse she was subjected to as a baby and child but did not want to discuss this. In this case the miracle was that "the past no longer has the power to mess with my future."

The story of the moment of change in this woman's life is to me so moving I can no longer tell it. It makes me cry! So, as she was happily paying for her third and last session she jokingly said that her friends couldn't believe the transformation they had witnessed even compared to how she was before the latest crisis. They kept asking her what happened in the therapy and she laughed that she could never remember—it was a complete blank! She then suddenly went serious and steely and after a deep breath said, "Before I go I've got something to say that you probably don't want to hear!" I steeled myself for the criticism as she continued, "I know that I would be dead by now if I hadn't come to see you but I've got to be honest and tell you that despite that, you have not touched my life one bit!" She looked very relieved but also looked as if she was expecting an argument from me. No such thing! I answered: "I can honestly say that is the best compliment I have ever received as a therapist and I would like you to know that you haven't touched my life either. And I'll always remember you." "And I'll always remember you," were her parting words.

Q. Has the use of SFT impacted you in your personal life? If so, please explain.

A. I would like to say no: Work is work and life is life! Unfortunately, Harvey, Evan, and our wives all met at the clinic Christmas party two months after we had started our initial Brief Therapy Project in 1988. The wives had never met before and when they got talking they all reported a distinct improvement in their husbands' behavior over the past few weeks. This would suggest that happiness is a two-way street: happy at work, happy at home, and vice versa.

Otherwise I try to keep solution focused work out of my life. It is a way of constructing and managing a professional (purpose-specific) conversation, not a way of being spontaneous. I did ask my daughter a scaling question once. She was about 8 years old and looked at me with haughty disdain before walking away. My punishment was to be spoken to only in numbers for the next few days; "Hi, Charlotte, how are you this morning?" "4." On the other hand, her younger sister, Florence, at about the same age was instrumental in helping us set up BRIEF. We were in paid jobs in an NHS clinic and for some months had been talking about setting up on our own. It was a risky business venture that all three would have to agree on. On one occasion when Harvey was the most cautious about the move, he and his family were at my house. All the children were playing Monopoly, and Harvey and I, like dads everywhere, were being annoying. Florence suddenly piped up: "Harvey, if Old Kent Road meant you'd never set up your own clinic and Mayfair means that you definitely will, where on the board would you say you are today?"

Harvey laughed, looked impressed, and complimented Florence. Without a flicker in her penetrating eyes, she persisted: "So where *would* you say you are now, Harvey?"

"Oh, you really want an answer?" said Harvey who then looked carefully at the board before picking Trafalgar Square. He then looked at me with great surprise and said, "Did I just say Trafalgar Square? That's good enough for me! Let's do it!!" So we did.

Q. What are some key personality traits that you think are shared among solution focused practitioners?

A. I seriously hope there are none. I know there is lots of gushing and positivity (not to say piety) in conversations among solution focused people and that was there among the early family therapists, and I assume within any group of people at the heart of something new and potentially big. I think solution focused work is a way of doing rather than a way of being, and I think any being can learn to do it. I assume that solution focused people are much the same as any other group: The greater the number the greater the range of good, bad, and otherwise people.

Q. What are some common mistakes that therapists trying on the model make most often? If you had a chance to guide them differently, how would you do so?

A. Without doubt it is failing to get a working answer to the question, "What are your best hopes from our work together?" (or whatever contract-building question is used to kick off the process). Some people forget to ask it, some ask it but forget to wait for an answer, some people accept negative answers (getting rid of something rather than creating something), some people accept "means" rather than "ends" answers, all of which curtail or even derail the effectiveness of the work.

I saw an example in a case presented by a very well-known and respected solution focused therapist. He was arguing that solution focused therapy, as it is generally known, is not up to certain tasks and needs something else. He cited an example of the work as failing until the something else was introduced. It was good effective therapy but the solution focused part didn't work because it was very poor! The client's goal was to have another family member do as he was told. This to us is not a goal but rather a means to a goal or as we would think of it a means to a hoped-for outcome. We would seek this by asking what difference the obedience would make and similar questions until we had a hoped-for outcome having to do with living life well. That would have opened up a very different conversation rather than one bound to wreck itself on the rocks of oppression and conformity!

Second favorite is thinking solution focused work is a positive approach and so just be Polyanna-ishly positive. I ban the word *positive* from my workshops and anyone who uses it is sent home immediately in bare feet and carrying a sack of rocks (as millstones are now hard to come by).

Q. What are some things you notice students doing while trying on this model that lets you know this model may fit them?

A. I don't see it as a question of fit. Probably the majority of people we have taught over the past 20 years have been sent to the course. It has been arranged by their managers and they are expected to attend. This made us nervous to begin with, so we had some initial differences. We decided to treat all participants as equally motivated (just as we were doing with our mandated clients) and since then have rarely had anything but interested and hard-working course members. I think anyone can do it and if we are not assessing clients, why assess students? (Unless, of course, we are accrediting them.)

A recent example: I was presenting at a management conference and through the entire two hours there was one man at the back looking fiercely disapproving. I knew that he was definitely not the person to look at, so I tried to look for a smiling nodding person, of which there were many. But Mr. Disapproval kept drawing my eye like a candle draws a moth. I had to exert all my discipline and trust of the process to keep my energy levels up to the required standard to deliver what was hoped from me. I just about managed it and as soon as the break came I almost ran for the door to find a quiet corner to recover. Mr. Disapproval was heading for the same door and we'd reach it together if I wasn't careful. I speeded up as unobtrusively as possible and so did he! I had three micro-seconds to plan my face (a sort of "you don't bother me" look) before we collided. As I was trying to put the plan into action he said: "I'm glad I caught you. You know, I came to one of your courses ten years ago. It was the best thing I've ever done and it changed my life completely. I just wanted to thank you!"

So, who am I to make judgments about students?

Q. If you were training therapists in the SFT model, what strategies would you use to train them and how would you present the material?

A. This is how I make my money and how we fund our free clinic, so I eat, drink, and sleep this question. The answer changes year by year and even week by week in productive times. My framework for thinking about it is to see solution focused therapy like a craft—carpentry, for example. It can only be taught by doing. A carpenter could talk about his work, demonstrate his work, give lectures on the molecular construction of wood—and still the student would not be able to saw a simple piece of wood at a right angle. That could only come with practice, and lots of it. Once that skill has been achieved the new carpenter can build almost anything; not necessarily elegantly but certainly serviceably. Later mastery of more sophisticated techniques will enable great efficiency and elegance but won't add that much to usefulness.

BRIEF builds all its training around exercises aimed at skills development. In that sense the training is like the therapy: We set up conversations that help people do things they hadn't realized they could do.

Just as I'm writing this Evan has sauntered down from a course he's running upstairs and told me of a new exercise he's been trying out: simple, effective in creating difference, and the best way to teach interactional questioning I've ever come across. I'm going to try it out next week. What it is to have friends!

Q. If you could pick a pioneer solution focused therapist who impacted your work, who would you name and why?

A. Steve de Shazer. We learned how to do it from his books and year on year we continued to learn how to do it from his visits to us. Though we used to joke with him that he would never pass our diploma course (because we had become so different), he always supported us. In one slightly outraged response to something I had written, an SFT practitioner was horrified that I disagreed with Steve. In a rare response to such debates, Steve wrote to say his great mentor, John Weakland, had not believed anyone could be briefer or more minimalist than he was. I think Steve knew that as John was to him he was to us.

Q. What developments would you like to see in the future of this model?

A. I'm not sure how I would like to see the model develop but I do have ideas about some of the processes that might help development (in whatever direction it goes) occur. The most important of these is a greater rigor in the writings and discussions of solution focused therapy. Too often there is an "Anything goes," "If it works it's solution focused" view taken. Cognitive behavioral therapy (CBT) works, electroconvulsive therapy (ECT) works. Neither is solution focused. A more rigorous and disciplined approach to discussion would be more revealing and is likely to generate new ideas and developments. Steve had this approach as do some of the current contributors to the literature: Harry Korman, Mark Beyerbach, and Rayya Ghul. Each of these contributors are among those who effectively look at the underlying principles, try to maintain philosophical coherence, and engage in dialogues (through the SFT-L list serve) that add to understanding. I would like to see a lot more of this and a bit less of the "Oh, what jolly good people we are and because we are solution focused we can do anything as long as it works!" Oh well!

EDITOR'S COMMENT

Chris Iveson has given us permission to bask in the glory of what happens between client and therapist, which keeps most of us learning from our clients year after year. How kind of him to be so descriptive of the woman whose life was quite different than it was prior to meeting Chris. Yet Chris remains humble and relaxed, and perhaps this is where his charm is most easily seen. I appreciate his banishing "positive" from his workshops. Solution focused therapy, I tell my trainees, is not positive; rather, it is curious. Chris brings his curiosity to his sessions and to this chapter, hoping that the model will continue to evolve with rigor and discipline so that we can use the guides presented to us by de Shazer and evolve from there. Chris shares thoughts of how many of us felt in the early days of being a therapist, struggling to do a good job and wanting to know more about how to do it best. Then Chris acknowledges that perhaps not knowing is knowing so much more. I appreciate Chris's conviction to the model and his colleagues for eliminating even the slightest extra bit of weight from the model so more thinking can flow during sessions. May we all work in the dark a little more often.

—Linda Metcalf

REFERENCES

de Shazer, S. (1985). *Keys to solutions in brief therapy.* New York: Norton.
de Shazer, S. (1988). *Clues: Investigating solutions in brief therapy.* New York: Norton.

6 The Three-Hour "A-ha" Moment

ALISON JOHNSON

Education is the ability to listen to almost anything without losing your temper or your self-confidence.

—Robert Frost

INTRODUCTION TO THE SOLUTION FOCUSED THERAPY MODEL

I was in my second year of graduate school for my doctorate in clinical psychology when I first encountered solution focused therapy (SFT). As a student in my school's cross-cultural program, I was enrolled in a course entitled "Cross-Cultural Families," taught by the division head. He was absent for one lecture, and a substitute from the faculty had agreed to cover for him. She chose as her topic "Solution-Focused Brief Therapy for Cross-Cultural Families." My personal a-ha! moment lasted the entire three hours of that lecture.

During that course, she showed a videotape of Insoo Kim Berg working with an African American couple. She described basic principles of SFT and had us practice some of its techniques of listening and questioning. As I listened and participated, my excitement grew in the idealistic fashion, perhaps, of the student learner. I was hearing ideas and ways of helping the person that made sense to me, without requiring the positing of specific unseen—and unseeable—mechanisms of thought and emotion. It was my first introduction to postmodern philosophy (something that, interestingly, was omitted from the course on the history of psychology), and I was, frankly, hooked.

I don't claim to be an expert on postmodernism; however, there are certain tenets that I believe fit within that philosophy: first, that there is not a single absolute truth, but many truths; and following from that, that it is not possible to completely understand another's truth. Upon hearing this explained in that first three-hour encounter with SFT, I was able to make a connection with my understanding of working cross-culturally. Rather than impose my limited outside understanding into another person's world experience, I was suddenly freed to be not-knowing and open to others' ways of describing themselves. I was enchanted by the possibilities of exploring my curiosity about another's world and working toward minimal misunderstanding together. This process in SFT involves honoring the client's expertise in his (or her) own life, trusting his intimate knowledge of his circumstances, and questioning respectfully and with curiosity to discover the tools he already possesses that will help him build the solution that is right for him. This does not negate the therapist's expertise; however, the SFT therapist's expertise is not prescriptive. It consists not of directing the client to some right course of action through superior knowledge and understanding, but of having useful conversations, seeking to minimize the difference in power in the therapy relationship and assist the client to be the leader in moving toward an individualized solution.

As a part of developing minimal misunderstanding, I was also enchanted to find that choice of language was a focus in SFT. I have been a word-lover since I suppose the age of six months, when I began to label everything around me with a baby's lisp. I can't remember learning to read, but I know I was gifted with an original edition of Rudyard Kipling's *Just So Stories* on my fourth birthday, and was reading it to myself. Suffice it to say that I have been a wordsmith up to the present day. To forward my understanding of the roots of SFT, I eagerly obtained and read Steve de Shazer's *Words Were Originally Magic* at the recommendation of the professor. I carry inside me a two-word postmodern summary of that substantial volume: *Don't assume!* Even the apparently simple choice of words that a person uses to describe a problem can be explored to achieve less misunderstanding. A case in point is the word choice I made above, in describing the person I work with as a client rather than a patient. Many psychologists choose the word *patient* with greater or lesser degrees of consciousness. It denotes a person under medical treatment who is having things done to him or her, rather than an active participant in a two-way process. *Patient* comes from the Latin word that means "to suffer." I choose the word *client* to emphasize that I am rendering a professional service to another person who is my customer or patron. This person, while leaning on my skills for a while (*client* comes from the Latin for "to lean") is an active participant in the process of directing his life. Such a lot of meaning in such a small word choice!

Another characteristic of the model that intrigued me was the concept that the problem and the solution are not related. I struggled with this for a while. The idea that there is a direct link between problem and its resolution is a concept that is not only hallowed in psychotherapy, but has become ingrained in modern American culture as well. There is a notion that we need to talk about the problem, fully understand the problem, master the occurrence of the problem, and then suddenly the solution will become obvious—usually by engaging in the opposite of what was done to begin with. Tie a knot, untie the knot. The trouble is, we rarely notice that even the notion of *opposite* is something that must be learned, and that many real-world problems demand fundamentally different solutions. If you spill a glass of water, you don't un-spill it; you must mop it up. This is a fundamentally different act from tipping a cup over the floor (or from its opposite, which I suppose would be tipping the floor back over the cup). Another example lives in the carpenter's saying, "You can saw a long board short, but you can't saw a short board long." The solution, of course, involves moving away from the too-short board and getting a different board, one that will meet your building needs. Life problems are approached in a similar manner, by stepping back, looking away from the problem, and asking, "What do I want or need? What will make a difference in this situation?"

This focus on the solution naturally leads to a focus on the future rather than the past. Something that puzzled me about other forms of psychotherapy was that much time seemed spent at looking where you've been rather than where you want to go. The traditional invitation to conversation in therapy seems to be, "So, what brings you here today?" This frequently results in the dialogue heading off into the past, into problems, perhaps hypotheses about the problems' origins, and discussion of emotions usually thought of as negative, unpleasant, or undesirable. The invitation to conversation that I use—and this is by no means prescriptive—is, "So . . . what would you like to see different or better in your life as a result of our meeting?" Most people react with some sort of surprise to my question. They stop and think. The question draws them to consider where they are and where they want to be. The dialogue spends more time in the present and in imagining the future, although the past is often mined for successes and honored for being the foundation for the present moment.

SFT means moving from not-knowing into minimal misunderstanding, honoring the client's expertise in his or her own life, paying attention to choices of language, and focusing on solution-building into the future rather than problem-exploring into the past. The first three concepts are more undercover—in other words, I tend to keep them in my head and demonstrate by my actions in the therapy room the attitudes and practices that they entail. The fourth principle is often made explicit when clients ask how therapy is done (if they've never been to therapy before) or how my particular therapy might be similar to or different from other treatment modalities they have experienced.

THE PROFESSIONAL IMPACT OF SOLUTION FOCUSED THERAPY

Having had minimal experience working with clients at the time I encountered SFT, my discovery of the fitness of the model for me came about as I developed as a psychologist. The program that I attended was rather structured, requiring each student to take one foundational course each in psychodynamic psychotherapy and cognitive behavioral therapy. I discovered that neither of these ways of thinking were that good a fit for me, and yet I learned enough about them to be able to understand each modality's philosophy and perspective. As I later moved into the wider world and society of psychology and psychologists, I found it helpful to be able to have conversations with them using the language of their particular set of beliefs. My developing professional self dove into the absorption of solution focused brief therapy as much as possible. It being my treatment modality of choice from the start, I rarely used other models until I was in individual private practice.

Since my academic schedule was crammed full of requirements for both the clinical psychology program and my cross-cultural subspecialty, I found alternative ways to increase my learning of SFT. Aside from devouring book after book, I enrolled in a one-year SFT practicum with the same professor who had lectured on that fateful day. We had 15 hours per week of SFT: client contact hours, individual and group supervision from a solution focused perspective, and plenty of practice discussing and translating our solution focused understanding of a case into the more traditional style of writing intakes, chart notes, reports, and discharge summaries. Our outpatient mental health clinic, which was on the school's campus, had the advantage of being equipped with video cameras in each room, as well as a one-way mirror room, which our group appropriated as often as possible to engage in the team process that so enhances SFT. The most useful thing I did at this point was to join a solution focused listserv at the recommendation of my professor. This forum was (and is) a wonderful place to gather with like-minded people, ask questions, and try out new ideas, while feeling accepted and encouraged in my professional growth.

It seems that there are two components to the use of a model: the ideas and philosophies that inform the work that we do, and the skill sets and techniques that arise from those ideas. As a student, I learned carefully all of the techniques of SFT and applied them with increasing understanding of their purpose in the forgiving atmosphere of a graduate school program. True confession time, however: At this point in my life, I am not an SFT purist. The main technique I have left behind on my journey is the session break, in which the therapist steps out of the room just before the end of the session in order to reflect on what has happened during the session. Sometimes it seems that asking the miracle question is not appropriate, or that asking, "What's better?" may not be helpful to a particular client. At the present, my most common detour is into cognitive behavioral therapy techniques, using systematic desensitization with graduated exposure for people with simple phobias, and teaching relaxation skills of various sorts to people experiencing severe anxiety. The path I am constantly working to stay on, however, is the internal one, remaining solution focused in my ideas as much as possible. This is often a struggle, but I am heartened by the metaphor of a rocket heading toward the moon: It is off course more than 90% of the time, yet it still gets there! I begin each session with a future- and goal-focused question, I use the miracle question in almost every first session, I hunt for positives already occurring in the client's life, and I compliment as much as possible without laying it on too thick.

Clients have responded to this in several different ways. "This isn't how I expected therapy would be" seems to be the most common remark from clients who are new to seeking professional help in making life changes. They then follow it with something hopeful, commenting on its positive outlook or the interactive conversational style. Clients who have experienced therapy before have noted the difference as well. “This seems so much more hopeful and positive,” stated one client. She described how she had been afraid of having to dig into the past and revisit painful memories, which she had to do in previous therapy, and this time around she had delayed getting help because of this fear. After our first session together, she felt more optimistic about her abilities and strengths. She achieved her stated goal after about four sessions, and we agreed to end our work, with an invitation from me to return whenever she felt like she wanted more assistance. She returned after half a year as another major life change arose, and dove right into our work together. It seemed as though the second time around she was not afraid of me or of our process together, and was very brave in sharing her fears with me about her new challenges.

Another client and I spent much of one session discussing her need to go slowly. She related past therapy experiences in which she felt that therapists had become impatient with her need to discuss parts of her life history repeatedly. She expressed appreciation that I would listen to her tell the same story over and over. I replied something to the effect that it must be very important to her to revisit those memories, perhaps so that she can figure out the proper place to put them, and the proper importance to put on them, as she lives her life now. I attempted to express my respect for her way of doing things that might be different from how others do it or what others might expect. A few sessions after this conversation she began to take on new activities, assisted her adult child to move out of the family home, and was engaging in better self-care. One day, she was reflecting on her new changes, and said, “I sometimes wonder why I didn’t do these things a long time ago, when I was younger and could have done more—I’ve wasted so much time. And then I think, ‘So what?’ If I can’t do *this*” (she held her hands apart, one low, one high) “I can still do *this*” (she narrowed the gap considerably) “and then a little more, and then a little more.” I smiled and nodded, gently expressing how impressed I was at her being able to make the changes slowly and step by step, because those were most likely to become good habits. Inside, however, I was thinking, “*Woo-hoo!*” It’s always such a pleasure to me to see when a client begins to pick up solution focused thinking habits.

The catchphrases “Go slow” and “never work harder than your client” come to mind when I reflect on working with this woman. I have to remind myself of these fairly often in my practice! For this woman, I had the sense that my internal "woo-hoo" would have been too much, too startling or overdone. For others, it might be appropriate. I have been known to cheer, applaud, shake hands, or give the occasional high-five when circumstances seemed to warrant it. Other treatment modalities might refer to this type of behavior by the therapist as "boundary-crossing." I see it as an example of SFT encouraging the therapist to attend closely to and follow the client's lead in conversational style, which builds rapport and helps us move toward solutions. Ultimately, SFT allows me to be more myself in the therapy room, and I believe this is what makes SFT so effective. Treatment modality doesn't make a difference in outcome—it's the therapeutic relationship that is the most important therapy-related factor. When the treatment modality feels like a good fit to me as therapist, I do a better job at applying it and am able to use it more effectively. No two of us are alike, clients or therapists, so it only makes sense to have a variety of models to shape one's process of work. Each therapist will move toward the philosophy that makes the most sense to him or her and will evolve effective ways of applying the chosen model. The humbling thing in all this is that most of the change clients experience has to do with factors outside of therapy. Each client finds his individualized solution, and can be encouraged to use those extratherapeutic factors to his best advantage.

LIFE OUTSIDE THE THERAPY ROOM

Through and beyond graduate school, my life became more solution focused in activity and attitude. I continued to work with my mentor, who was not only my professor, but became my dissertation advisor as well. My research compared SFT with other treatment modalities on the dimension of client satisfaction. (Essentially, satisfaction was statistically equivalent across modalities, but SFT arrived at that level of satisfaction in fewer sessions than the other treatments.) After four years of graduate school, having steeped myself in SFT, I simply couldn't quit. During my internship at a community college in southern California, I met through the solution focused listserv Tomasz Switek, a Polish therapist who shared a common interest in the effects of SFT. After some online conversations, we thought it would be a good idea to look at how SFT had affected us as practitioners. We developed a survey that explored the effects of SFT practice across several life domains, which we advertised online through the listserv. Enough people responded for us to develop a paper to deliver at the European Brief Therapy Association's conference in 2001. Tomasz and I met face-to-face for the first time the day before we gave our talk. Attending and speaking at that conference was an exhilarating experience—to put faces to the names and online voices that I had conversed with for many of my grad school years was like meeting old friends for the first time, and I was sorry when the conference came to an end.

At the same time that this was happening, my life was becoming more complex. My husband and I were in the early years of running a business that occupied much time and energy, which we hoped to grow to the point that it would either take care of itself or we would be able to sell it. (As it turned out, we were able to achieve the latter.) One day I received an e-mail from John Briggs at the Brief Family Therapy Center (BFTC) in Milwaukee. He said they had noticed my posts to the listserv and were wondering if I might be interested in coming out to Milwaukee for an interview.

"Would I? Is the pope . . .? Does a bear . . .?" After screaming like I had won a game show prize, and calling my mentor and my husband and my internship supervisor, I arranged for a flight to Wisconsin. I have to admit I had more than my share of rock-star mentality about meeting the crew at BFTC. However, they were more than welcoming, and did everything possible to help me relax and get on with the business of interviewing. We talked individually and in a group, and I took on about two or three client appointments in their classic model, with the team behind the mirror and videotape rolling. I remember that Insoo was warm and kind and cheerful, and Steve was serious and quiet with a flash and spark that would appear briefly. John was friendly and open and made me feel comfortable from the moment he picked me up at the airport. Theresa Zakutansky was easy to talk to and had a wonderful therapeutic and interpersonal style. After the day at the clinic, John toured me around Milwaukee, and then we reconvened at Steve and Insoo's home, where we shared a takeout pizza and great conversation about nonclinical stuff. I left wishing for more time with these people and feeling that I could definitely work there if they decided that I was a good fit for the job.

However, it was not to be. I was finishing my predoctoral internship and still had another year of postdoctoral supervision to complete to be eligible for licensure either in Wisconsin or in my home state of California. At that time, there was no one with a doctorate in psychology at BFTC who could have provided the requisite supervision, and my husband's and my business was also a factor in the decision. Both parties agreed that the timing was perhaps not right, although we both wished for it to happen. I am so grateful that I had the experience of arriving at the soul of solution focused brief therapy, which for me was the after-dinner conversation clustered around the round table in Steve and Insoo's dining room.

All these experiences most definitely became absorbed into my day-to-day way of thinking and operating in the world. I know that I now spend much less time analyzing a problem or trying to figure out why (or even how) something happened. I've become much more oriented toward what's going right in my life, and accepting as normal and natural that plans will go awry. In times of struggle, whether on the telephone with a customer service agent or in a deep and meaningful discussion with my spouse, I've learned the transferable skills of explaining what I want, stopping complaining and offering a solution, taking a break when necessary, and giving compliments. Frankly, I'm more cheerful and more relaxed overall, more accepting of others and myself and forgiving of myself if I forget to be accepting, and quicker to recover my equilibrium after something happens to disturb it. Reflecting on this, I know that this was a long, slow, gradual process, with some detours and bumps along the way, and I can think of plenty of room for improvement! This is an exciting thing, knowing that learning never stops, and I am one of the few people I know that looks forward to getting older. Living in a solution focused way for me is a quiet undercurrent, a mentality, or a practice. Some people practice music, some practice yoga, meditation, or religion, and some of us practice solution focused living. Each involves doing certain things as well as thinking a certain way, which helps to frame and organize one's life.

One thing I do is to maintain contacts through the solution focused listserv. It is a great way to observe the evolution of solution focused practice and connect to a group of like-minded people. It seems to have a low hierarchy compared to my profession of psychology, and therefore much less jockeying for status and position. Newcomers to the list are given welcomes, there is rarely acrimony although there is plenty of conflict and arguing back and forth, and there is a great deal of humor and affection exchanged. Solution focused people also seem to exhibit much less professional insecurity than psychologists. Insecurity may be present, but since psychologists are trained to find and analyze problems, it seems to show much more on the psychology listserv to which I belong. Another factor that may contribute to this low level of overt professional insecurity is that being solution focused is a transprofessional practice. At the time I write, there are the following professions participating on the listserv: psychiatrist, psychologist, social worker, marriage and family therapist, professional counselor, physical therapist, occupational therapist, life coach, business consultant, professor, student . . . and, I'm sure, others that I can't think of. There is a general respect for others' areas of expertise that eliminates the need to establish a one-up position. In general, I would say that solution focused people seem to enjoy being different from the mainstream, are curious, and are able not to take themselves too seriously.

TRAINING AND REFLECTION

When I was first learning SFT in a supervision group, all of us came in with different levels of skill and understanding. It seemed that some people had difficulty letting go of talking about the problem and looking for explanations of why the problem occurred. Other people became "solution forced," that is, thinking of what they would do if they were presented with the situation at hand, rather than helping the client draw from within himself his own unique solutions. Sometimes there would be a mechanical application of techniques instead of listening to the client's conversation for clues as to which direction to proceed toward a solution. It is difficult for me to think back to what mistakes people made, perhaps because of my solution focused training—I look more to the future and what people have done right, even a little bit, rather than to the past and what went wrong. Reminders such as "the problem and the solution are not related," "not-knowing," "go slow," "don't assume," and "lead from behind" were very helpful when we were sitting in the room with the client. Supervision was a time to dissect the principles behind each of these reminders in detail, and there were often forays into philosophy and ethics as we discussed our reasons for doing what we did and our choices for future action in the therapy room. Those explorations of our own personal life philosophies helped us clarify whether SFBT was a good fit for us as therapists.

So, suppose (great solution focused word!) . . . suppose I become a solution focused trainer and supervisor, the best I could be? What would be the first sign that this is happening? Well, I answer myself, the first thing I will see myself doing is getting more training in supervision. I will take a standard continuing education course for psychologists, and then retake a series of courses in basic training of SFT, not only to refresh my memory but also to observe the instructor. My ideal supervisory process would include providing individual, group, and peer supervision, with attention to specific case matters and skills to apply to them, as well as the discussion of solution focused philosophy and its integration into the constraints of one's professional world. This doesn't sound so different from supervision in any modality; what is the difference that makes a difference, I ask myself? I think it comes down to being meta-solution focused: applying the solution focused principles and processes to supervision as well. I will include such principles as leading from behind, starting where the student is and helping her move one step forward, noticing what is going right and building on that, providing compliments and suggestions, and moving away from the problem and working with people and their preferred future.

If I scale my progress as a solution focused supervisor, with 0 being "I have no clue" and 10 being "I am as good as Insoo and Steve," I would put myself at about a 3 and my mentor at an 8.5. Steve and Insoo were the pioneers who most directly influenced my development as a therapist, through their writings and teaching at conferences, and especially in their belief in me personally as good enough to do this stuff. My mentor, although not one of the well-known lights of SFT, was an influential pioneer in disseminating knowledge of SFT to a community that otherwise might not have experienced it. She also helped the most to shape me as a psychologist, albeit an unconventional one. So, what needs to happen for me to move from a 3 to a 4, or maybe just a 3.5? Head off to a conference somewhere, I suppose. Tune in with me soon to find out where I am on this journey!

The journey into the future of solution focused brief therapy itself is a road that is being constructed. The team of builders is a rather democratic one, with each participant having a voice that is soft or loud, tentative or insistent. I don't have a prediction for the direction the road may take. My dream is that others in my field know of SFBT as another equally effective approach to working with people, and that within the solution focused community, we continue to engage in the democratic and collaborative process of finding what works and doing more of it. Our road is perhaps built more slowly this way, but it is being built well, and is an inviting trip to take, whether on a short detour or a lifelong journey. I hope you come along!

EDITOR'S COMMENT

Through the SFT listserv I have had the great pleasure of corresponding with many practitioners that use this approach in their work. One of them was Dr. Johnson. When Dr. Metcalf and I discussed this project, this is the type of chapter that we envisioned. Dr. Johnson was candid in her descriptions of her approach to learning SFT and how it impacted her personally and professionally. My favorite part of this chapter was reading about her "a-ha" moment. My favorite moments in session occur when someone becomes enthusiastic in a way that lasts far beyond the moment. To watch a person become hopeful and never lose that excitement is inspiring and motivating to me. I am so thankful for Dr. Johnson's contribution to this project.

—Elliott Connie

7 This Is *Me*

TRACY TODD

If you limit your choices only to what seems possible or reasonable, you disconnect yourself from what you truly want, and all that is left is a compromise.

—Robert Fritz

Q. How did you first learn about solution focused therapy (SFT)?

A. Perusing the Iowa State University library bookshelves I discovered, tucked away, a little red book called *Patterns of Brief Family Therapy* by Steve de Shazer. Before I left the library, I had read the entire book. I immediately proceeded to my major professor's office and asked if she knew this stuff. She responded with, "No, but let's learn together." I then wrote a grant proposal to the university for $1,000 asking to bring Steve de Shazer to the university. The university informed me they were not accustomed to giving money to graduate students but they felt it was a worthy risk. As the saying goes, "One thing leads to another," and Iowa State University decided to host a conference on brief therapy. Keep in mind, I believe this was in 1987 when brief therapy and Steve de Shazer were not yet popular topics.

I met with Steve the night before for dinner, ice cream, and a long walk around Lake Laverne (a pond on the Iowa State University campus) discussing brief therapy. Imagine, a doctoral student conversing one-on-one with Steve de Shazer for an entire evening. The education was invaluable. We chatted, or should I say I interrogated and Steve patiently listened, corrected, and challenged my novice questions. What I learned that evening was that the next day was not going to be like any training or educational experience I had ever had before. Since I was asking questions like, "What about SFT with incest?" and his answers were nowhere near traditional, I knew fireworks were in store. I was only a student, but I knew therapists had sacred beliefs about certain populations. Knowing he was going to challenge those beliefs was both exciting and scary. Remember, I was the one touting this fantastic new model and wanting to share it with the State of Iowa. I did have flashes of being booted from the university. The most appreciative moments of that evening really had little to do with his seminar and more to do with the little questions he posed to me as we walked and talked:

"Where is that assumption coming from?"

"That comment really presupposes clients lack the ability to solve problems."

"Where did such disrespect for clients come from?"

Steve did not ask these questions maliciously, rather playfully. They were asked in a manner that simply made me think and become aware of the junk I was taking into the therapy room.

During the conference a conference participant predictably commented and asked Steve, "Sexual abuse issues are so serious, do you really feel this would work with that population?" Keep in mind, this question was not asked in an inquiring manner, rather with a defensive/combative tone. Steve very politely commented back that therapists need to be cautious about what problem they are treating. Are they treating the problem presented by the client, or the problem the therapist thinks the client should have because of a stated history? Although this particular participant became defiant, others in the audience had the epiphany look (I'm not sure such a look is well understood, only experienced). Immediately following the conference, participants were thanking Steve for the paradigm shift and there were many comments such as, "I'm not sure I can do this but I definitely need to consider how my beliefs are worsening the problem." From that point forward I never looked back. I attended trainings with Steve and Insoo over the next few years and that was my introduction to brief therapy.

Q. How did you discover that SFT was the model that seemed to fit with your way of working with clients?

A. After reading about five pages in the library I vividly remember saying to myself, "This is *me*," and there was no doubt in my mind. My only previous experience with clients was during internships and practicum, which I found very disturbing. Every week there was a meeting with classmates to "process" the therapy contacts. "Process" was code for "pathologize." Following a bit of critique about how each clinician conducted his or her presented session, there was exhaustive discussion about the ills of the clients. Such concepts as "adult child of ____," or "Your client appears to be ____." The disrespectful phrases were endless. To this day, I cringe when I hear such statements, even when useful. I knew the model fit with me when I presented cases starting by listing strengths, exceptions to problems, and specific nonproblem goals. I would give my solution focused presentation and then receive looks from classmates as though I had five eyes and four noses. They were perplexed and I was excited. Yep, that fit!

Q. What characteristics of the model drew you toward it?

A. In contrast to these clinical discussions, SFT begged discussion about strengths, exceptions to problems, and healthy envisioning of nonproblem time. Simply put, the ideas and conversations were significantly more in line with how I saw the world. I had always felt very uncomfortable and disgusted with the pathological interpretive qualities inherent in treatment models. I felt, and continue to feel to this day, that therapists who wield pathological interpretive powers abuse those powers. The SFT model is refreshing because it assumes there are nonproblem times and the therapist's job is to find, expand, and accentuate these times. This health orientation was the major draw.

Relatedly, I felt it was extremely disrespectful for me as a therapist to draw conclusions about someone I barely knew. This model did not require such actions and you could immediately start being helpful. Another attractive quality was the ability to immediately start helping clients. Although sometimes an exhaustive (and I do mean exhausting) history-taking session is needed, starting a session with, "Tell me when the problem doesn't occur" can quickly lead to momentum-building solution talk. Spending time discussing solutions rather than something that happened 13 years ago seems more respectful of my clients' time and situation.

Q. How has utilizing SFT impacted your work with clients? (Please mention if you utilized a previous model and the difference you noticed in clients and yourself after switching to SFT.)

A. Probably the most important quality of SFT in my work is the immediate hopefulness that is achieved by searching for exceptions. Getting to this information during the first contact (sometimes by phone, other times during the first session), creates an extremely positive momentum to build upon. My work with clients, which most therapists in the office comment on, results in laughter and fun during the first session. Solution focused therapy impacts my work by quickly changing the tone and emotional state of clients. Whether searching for exceptions, conversing about miracle questions, or scaling for a better time versus a not-so-good time, the unit of analysis is certainly different than clients expect; thereby creating a more positive therapy environment.

A little story fits nicely here. A few years ago a colleague of mine (who practiced very similarly to me) and I were seeing clients one afternoon. Since we were always in the office together on Tuesdays, we became familiar with one another's clients from seeing them in the waiting room. We would introduce one another to the clients for those situations where we needed to cover for one another (emergencies, vacations, etc.). One day I walked through the waiting room and chatted with my colleague's waiting clients. When I heard my colleague come out of her office, in a voice loud enough for her to hear, I said to her clients, "Watch out, she's crabby today." They laughed and I proceeded to get the mail. Upon my return, the clients locked me out of the office. Through the door they stated, "Say something nice about our therapist or we won't let you back in." Everyone was laughing and I of course did some groveling. They let me in and we all had a good laugh. During the session, they told my colleague that attending therapy in our office was extremely different than anywhere else they had had therapy. They noted that although discussing very serious issues, they always felt hopeful, confident, even playful. When my colleague asked about these qualities, they stated that even when sessions are tear-jerkers, they felt confident that solutions would get generated. Because of this hopefulness and recognition of similar therapy styles between my colleague and me, they did not feel this heavy burden when attending. Rather, they allowed themselves to have a sense of community within the agency. This community tone is what I truly appreciate about using this model.

Q. How would your clients describe your work with them? Have any of them who experienced another model of therapy commented on the difference (if any) that they perceived when working with you?

A. See above. Across the board, clients comment how different SFT is compared to other therapy (and therapists). I have heard comments such as, "This doesn't feel like therapy but I feel better," "Why don't all therapists do this type of therapy?" and "I haven't cried—are we doing therapy?" The difference is striking. Clients who saw other therapists and felt stuck (which, toward the end of my clinical career, constituted about 15% of my referrals) felt openly appreciative of the difference and immediate progress they were making based on their own experiences rather than therapist psychobabble.

I do feel it is important to note that some clients do have a sense of disbelief with SFT. Many times while making great progress in therapy a client would stop and ask, "When will we get to the real therapy?" Despite making gains, they felt they were being short-changed. I would simply visit their stated goals and ask what else they were trying to get accomplished. Amazing is the only word I can use by the responses. Clients having experienced other therapy styles would expect everything from (a) when will I begin to scream, to (b) why am I not crying, to (c) I feel great leaving therapy, how come? The popular belief that therapy is all about processing negative emotions rather than solving problems is quite evident when clients compare SFT with other models.

Q. What is it about SFT that makes it so effective?

A. Although there are some very powerful techniques that can help move therapy along, my personal opinion is that the potent qualities include (a) client self-awareness of strengths, resources, and resiliencies, and (b) the emotional tone a therapist can create by focusing on exceptions, miracle questions, and keeping conversations focused on solutions.

When asking about exceptions, miracles, or scaling, the cognitive shift made by clients in response to these questions is what I believe makes SFT so effective. This shift is aptly demonstrated when clients return to therapy a few months/years later. They will state, "We tried such and such," or "I looked for exceptions but that didn't work." These clients clearly indicate having made the shift, making attempts, and feeling more hopeful because they know we will search for solutions and they will not be "stuck in therapy" for a long period of time.

These same questions also create a much different tone during the session. This tone leads, in my opinion, more quickly to positive therapy momentum. Such positive momentum then builds upon itself and the therapy session quality is strikingly different.

Q. Describe one of your favorite cases and how it impacted your work as a therapist.

A. Over the course of nearly 10 years I saw a female client for a total of less than 10 sessions. She originally presented depression following the completion of genetic counseling resulting in her and her husband choosing not to have children. The odds were quite high they would have a child that would die within two years of birth. Saddened, and quickly becoming angry with family and friends because they now pointed out all the advantages of life without kids (a variation on the miracle question), she presented with moderate to severe symptoms of depression. During our first session I asked her to describe other "shitty situations in her history." She did so, believing this is how therapy should look (history talk of bad stuff). After collecting a few examples, I then asked if she considered herself a generally happy or sad person. She emphatically stated she was the family optimist (among all the extended family members) and known for her upbeat personality. I then inquired how she was able to remain so optimistic despite all the crappy things she described. At that point, she got it. She started identifying her cognitive abilities as well as resources that helped her through the situation. Throughout the 10 years, therapy was two sessions here, two sessions there. She would use the first session to give me her solution attempts and beliefs about why she was stuck. We would use the second session to discuss new solutions. Despite not seeing her for a few years, when I posted on our Web site the announcement I was leaving the practice, she was the first to call and congratulate me.

Q. Has the use of SFT impacted you in your personal life? If so, please explain.

A. SFT has impacted my own self-awareness and problem-solving abilities. When I'm down, in a rut, whatever, I engage in asking myself two questions, "When is my problem less than?" and "What would my life be like if a miracle happened?" From there I begin to examine unhelpful versus helpful patterns and habits.

SFT has also impacted my conversations with others. Although I'm like anyone else and can participate in pity parties, integrating solution talk with nontherapist friends and family members changes the dynamics in such a way that relationships are more genuine. I demonstrate empathy but also optimism, rather than buying into a reality or trying to talk them out of their reality.

Q. What are some key personality traits that you think are shared among solution focused practitioners?

A. I have had this conversation with many solution focused therapists. SFTs seem to have a "get things done" attitude combined with an adamant belief in client abilities. When I listen to therapists practicing other models, my perception (which could be in error) is that they relish being the expert, interpreting clinical problems, and being relied upon by clients. SFTs are quite different, almost opposite. The personality traits are focused more on health and wellness than treatment and pathology. The belief system is more focused on getting the clients started down a path of solutions and gain momentum—then *get out of their way.* This belief differs in that so many other models attract needy therapists who want to "be with their clients" through the hard times. Most SFTs believe that if they truly did their jobs, they should not need to be with their clients through those hard times.

Q. What are some common mistakes that therapists trying on the model make most often? If you had a chance to guide them differently, how would you do so?

A. Trying to move too fast. Jumping into miracles questions, searching for exceptions, scaling before the client feels heard and understood can be harmful to the relationship. Training becomes so focused on technique that the conversation is forgotten. All of psychotherapy tends to have a belief/training perspective that there needs to be therapy talk that is different than normative conversation. I tend to believe that normal conversations can exist while talking about serious issues. Herein lies the challenge: how to train normative conversation. I watch therapists, learning any model, try real hard to develop therapy talk. To me, that is not only disrespectful but also plays to the therapist's strengths rather than the clients. It is disrespectful because it lacks cultural sensitivity. Every client and client family is its own culture. We are taught to work from a client's cultural base. Introducing a new language (psychobabble) is not respectful of their language base. Also, therapy talk is what a therapist is good at and certainly not what most clients excel at.

Q. What are some things you notice students doing while trying on this model that lets you know this model may fit them?

A. Ease of discussion about information gathered. Some students, particularly those with therapy experience, tend to start using pathology talk and need to address the identified pathology before discussing the solution focused information. Other students do not feel this need or tendency. Students less interested in the "real" issues/explanations and more focused on describing the situation certainly demonstrate the ability to engage in successful solution focused therapy. The distinction between pathologically based interpretations and solution focused descriptions is cavernous. Those students who easily resist the temptation to stroll down the path of pathologically based interpretations have a higher likelihood of adapting to, or fitting, the model.

Q. If you were training therapists in the SFT model, what strategies would you use and how would you present the material?

A. I found that sending students out to simply converse with family or friends was the best training tool. I would ask them to ask, "How's it going?" and let the other ramble, usually about the ills of the day, for a period of time, then start to shift the conversation to SFT-type questions. I would ask the students to notice two things. First, how did the tone of the conversation change? Second, did the other notice the shift?

As students became better at the task, they would notice the conversational tone change. Importantly, if the other noticed the change in questioning, I told them to keep practicing. Getting responses such as, "What type of stupid question are you asking when you ask me 'if a miracle happens . . .?'" indicates a rough transition. If the transition goes unnoticed, it would indicate they are mastering the ability of working SFT questions into a conversation . . . exactly what is needed in therapy.

Q. If you could pick a pioneer solution focused therapist who impacted your work, who would you name and why?

A. Steve de Shazer. Few know that once upon a time Steve worked at the MRI. When he left, he left pondering the question, "What if we put the same energy and time into asking questions about nonproblem time?" This simple, but extremely profound idea was radically needed in psychotherapy. With many models and theories oriented toward problems, the field was ripe for such an idea. At that time, Steve was the *only* person talking about SFT. There were no other choices and SFT was represented very well through his diligence and perseverance.

Q. What developments would you like to see in the future of this model?

A. I'm willing to bet that you could interview 100 therapists identifying themselves as solution focused and most would not be able to give you the fundamental assumptions of SFT. I have grown a bit frustrated with the deconstruction of SFT into a heap of techniques. I hear therapists stating they do SFT because they use a few specific techniques. Yet, their conversation or case description reflects a belief system that I do not feel our pioneers would identify with SFT. I would like to see the model evolve beyond techniques toward a belief or paradigm. Currently, virtually every book on SFT is about either techniques or populations. What about treatment strategizing, or how a therapist belief system can enhance SFT, or what are accountability strategies when therapists begin thinking pathologically?

In so doing, I feel more techniques and applications would develop because the foundation is steeped in an SFT mind-set. New applications, from paper/pencil instruments, to interviewing questions, to experiential techniques, could be explored.

EDITOR'S COMMENT

As we began collaborating on this book, Dr. Metcalf predicted that we would find that people that subscribe to this theory seem to behave as if nothing were impossible. Dr. Todd fits this mode. From simply discovering this theory in the library, he somehow acquired funding to bring the developer of the theory to his school. This led to him spending what must have been a remarkable evening conversing with Steve de Shazer one-on-one. This was quite a feat—and yet notice that never once did he mention entertaining the thought of not succeeding. This optimism and expectation of success is certainly a theme among many practitioners in this volume—but perhaps no one expressed it better than the story told by Dr. Todd.

—Elliott Connie

8 Monty Python–Focused Therapy

BRIAN CADE

> Imagination is the beginning of creation. You imagine what you desire, you will what you imagine and at last you create what you will.
>
> —George Bernard Shaw

Q. How did you first learn about solution focused therapy (SFT)?

A. I am not really a solution focused therapist. I am not even sure I like the name; I prefer the term *future-focused.* Actually, as I look back through the years, I've never really been an anything in particular sort of therapist. If I had to nail my flag to one mast I would call myself a *brief therapist.* However, that sobriquet really doesn't mean very much anymore in that the outcome research shows that nearly all therapy is brief, whatever the optimum length the therapist thinks it ought to be. I started to call myself a *brief, interactional therapist,* but that was somewhat clumsy. On my business card, I call myself a *brief and family therapist.*

For a while, many years ago, the Milwaukee Brief Family Therapy Center produced a newsletter titled "The Underground Railroad." The idea originated in a hotel lobby conversation between Steve de Shazer, Paul Dell, and Lynn Hoffman during an American Association of Marriage and Family Therapy conference in Denver in 1980. It was given that title (Paul Dell's idea) because it was very difficult to describe what approach it reflected other than that it was for people who worked "this way." It appeared that practitioners who worked "this way" tended to recognize others who also worked "this way." An ever-expanding group of these practitioners began to communicate with each other through "The Underground Railroad," or by visiting each other's "shops" and watching each other through one-way mirrors, or by exchanging ideas in hotel bars during family therapy conferences over a beer or three (and sometimes more). Standing squarely behind those who worked "this way" stood the influence of Milton Erickson. As I have written elsewhere:

> Milton Erickson assumed people already had within their own personal experiences and histories all the necessary resources and competence from which to draw in order to surmount their difficulties. He did not operate from and, in fact, sought to avoid developing a clearly articulated theory of personality or of dysfunction although, in his lectures and writings, he often used the terminology of psychoanalytic thinking. He appeared to operate from an implicit theory of therapy, of how to interact with people to maximise the facilitation of change. Nor did he operate from a deficit-focused model. His main concern was with people's strengths and resources and it was with these that he engaged. He believed that all of us make the best choices we see as being available for ourselves at any given moment. The therapist's job is to listen carefully to, respect all communications from, and to meet the client in his or her own world rather than work from or impose elements of the therapist's world. (Cade, 2007, p. 27)

Q. What characteristics of this model drew you toward it?

A. I came across the work of Erickson through Jay Haley's early and seminal work, *Strategies of Psychotherapy* (1963), a book that dramatically changed the way I approached my practice. I then encountered the work of the Brief Therapy Center in Palo Alto (Watzlawick, Weakland, & Fisch, 1974; Weakland, Fisch, Watzlawick, & Bodin, 1974). I eventually met up with John Weakland, who was to become a friend and mentor at around the same time this was happening for Steve de Shazer and Insoo Kim Berg. It was Lynn Hoffman, over a quarter of a century ago, who suggested I make contact with Steve. She felt we had much in common. We began to correspond regularly by airmail until we met in the early 1980s. Over the ensuing years I made regular trips both to Milwaukee (where they would sometimes get me to see clients) and to Palo Alto. Steve, Insoo, and John also made trips to The Family Institute in Cardiff, Wales, where I initially worked; and later to Australia where I emigrated in 1985.

AN EARLY CASE STORY

A woman, after 20 years of psychiatric treatment, was struggling to stop taking the anti-anxiety medication she had been on for years, and to start making something of her life. She suffered from frequent panic attacks and was unable to swallow food without first drinking several glasses of whisky to relax her throat muscles. Only then could she eat anything. The food also had to be well mashed and she had recently bought a blender to make mushy soups for herself.

She was determined to finish with the drugs and, in her second session, she produced a diary in which she was marking with a tick those days she had survived without the help of the medication. I asked her how she was going to reward herself when she had successfully achieved 24 ticks in the diary. This thought intrigued her and she began to muse about how nice it would be to go to a restaurant and enjoy a full three-course meal without having to drown herself in alcohol.

"But, of course," she said sadly, "there'll be no chance of that. I'd end up gagging and choking and making a complete fool of myself."

I asked her what she would like to order if she were able to go ahead and give herself a treat. She first of all considered a range of hors d'œuvres and eventually decided on a prawn cocktail. For the main course she thought she would have a medium-rare steak with boiled potatoes and broccoli. She would prefer French fries but thought they might be too risky. To complete the meal, she decided on a coffee with a range of cheeses and cracker biscuits.

I asked whether she had a particular restaurant in mind. She told me of a quiet little place near where she lived. It had a number of single tables where a woman on her own would not be too conspicuous. I asked if she knew whether or not it had helpful staff. She confirmed that she thought they were.

"So you will be able to ask, without too much embarrassment, for a table against the wall close to a power point."

She looked puzzled for a few moments and then burst out laughing. "You mean to plug the food blender in?"

"Yes. The prawn cocktail would liquidize easily. And I'm sure the staff wouldn't mind if you popped briefly into the kitchen to rinse the blender out before the next course. You'd have to chop the steak up into small pieces, but the potatoes and broccoli should present you with no difficulties. I am unsure, however, about the cracker biscuits and the cheese. They might turn into a bit of a mess."

The woman was amused and continued to giggle for some time at the absurdity of the idea.

A week or so later, after achieving the 24 ticks in her diary, she drove to a small, picturesque country town. She booked herself into a hotel for the night and treated herself to a three-course meal. For her main course she ordered a medium-rare steak with French fries. The following year she wrote to me saying, "Absolutely no one else has *ever* helped me, but I feel you did; and I certainly hope *you* [here she includes the team behind the screen] all feel you did. If you would like to see me at any time, as (hopefully) one of your success stories, I will be happy to oblige."

This took place in the early 1980s. It was an example of working "this way." It bears a close family resemblance to what the gang at the Brief Family Therapy Center were up to at around that time. The woman was invited to project herself in the future to a time she had achieved a significant goal of her own and to visualize and describe how she would reward herself. Back then, I had read everything I could find either of or about Erickson including his 1954 paper, *Pseudo-Orientation in Time as a Hypnotherapeutic Procedure,* in which he wrote,

> These ideas are utilized to create a therapy situation in which the patient could respond effectively psychologically to desired therapeutic goals as actualities already achieved. This was done by employing hypnosis and using, conversely to age regression, a technique of orientation into the future. Thus, the patient was enabled to achieve a detached, dissociated, objective and yet subjective view of what he believed at the moment he had already accomplished. (Erickson, 1954, p. 261)

It would be about three more decades after that paper was written that one of Insoo's clients was to invent "The Miracle Question." It is interesting that current research that has nothing to do with therapy is now demonstrating how encouraging people to visualize themselves in the third person "engaging in a desirable future behaviour affected their self-perceptions and their likelihood of following through with that behaviour" (Libby, Shaeffer, Eibach, & Slemmer, 2007, p. 199).

OBSERVING RATHER THAN THEORIZING ABOUT THERAPY

What drew me to brief therapy back in the early 1970s was that it was the first therapy I had encountered that had essentially been developed from watching and analyzing therapy. In all other approaches I had encountered, the approach to therapy had been based on the tenets of a theory of pathology. In contrast, John Weakland described the origins of the brief therapy project as follows:

> To my mind we only had two or three basic ideas, which led to everything else. One, of course, was that we would work as a group. One person would be the therapist; the others would observe, and then everything would be recorded and discussed.
>
> But the two main principles that I think were responsible for the directions we took within that framework were, one, that we would focus on the client's main presenting complaint and STICK TO IT; not try to look around it or behind it or beneath it but stick to what's the main presenting complaint. And the other thing was that, by that time, we realised that it was not so easy to get people to change. So . . . we would try anything that we could think of that was legal or ethical regardless of whether it was conventional, or a long, long way from conventional thinking. I think things just grew out of that. (S. Chaney, personal communication, 1995)

Therapy was essentially focused on the future. I have a videotape of John Weakland in which he first asked the client what would be the acid test that would tell her she had achieved her therapy goal. He then proceeded to ask about the smallest but nevertheless significant step that would tell her she was on track. Over seven sessions the woman made more and more steps forward as John continued to advise her to slow down. John has described how the brief therapy project quickly rejected the usefulness of pathology and started working from the assumption that "people know how to be well" (Bavelas, McGee, Phillips, & Routledge, 2000). Again, recent research has shown how

> successful therapists . . . focused right at the beginning of the session markedly on what worked well for the patient. . . . These therapists were doing more than just supporting the patient's ego. They created an environment in which the patient felt he was perceived as a well functioning person. As soon as this was established, productive work on the patient's problems was more likely. Successful therapists also turned the focus of intervention away from the patient's problems in time. They did not let patients leave the session with aroused emotions but rather with even higher activated resources than patients experienced when they entered the session. (Gassmann & Grawe, 2006, pp. 9–10)

Continually reviewing the effects of their ways of intervening, the group would use more and more of those ways of talking with people that seemed to enhance change, and less and less of those that seemed either to inhibit change or turned out to be unnecessary.

Over the years I have been influenced by a number of people but I think John Weakland's influence remains at the core. My long friendship with Steve de Shazer was also extremely important at both a professional and a personal level. As far as I am concerned, the approach he and Insoo and their colleagues (and clients) developed, ultimately called solution focused therapy, evolved within the tradition of the careful watching of what worked, and doing more of it, and what didn't work (or was unnecessary) and doing less of it.

One important aspect of the solution focused approach which is perhaps the most helpful, particularly for beginners, is that the discipline of following it leads the therapist naturally to focus on those ways of communicating that are predictive of positive outcome, according to the outcome research. The following is a handout I use in training to summarize these.

SOME IMPORTANT RULES OF THUMB

- People tend only to hear when they themselves feel heard, validated, and respected.
- For a person to feel heard, a therapist/counselor must say something that indicates clearly to the client that they have *been* heard.
- People will *only* change (as opposed to just cooperate) in ways for which *they themselves* are a customer.
- It is important never to be more enthusiastic about the need for any particular change than is the client.

- "Resistance" is a sign that the therapist/counselor is using *more of the same* approach that is not going to work, and/or has become the customer for how the client ought to be, and/or colonized all of the arguments in favor of that change.
- Clients usually know what is right for them.

Q. What developments would you like to see in the future of this model?

A. One of my concerns about the approach, as in all approaches, is that practitioners measure themselves (or are measured by others) by the extent to which they adhere to the model rather than by the extent to which they continue to explore ways of being effective in helping people. In many discussions I had over the years with Steve, he seemed determined that the approach not be seen as a model for that very reason. In his and Gale Miller's paper, "Have You Heard the Latest About . . . ? Solution-focused Therapy as a Rumor," they state:

> We believe that it is useful to think about solution-focused therapy as a rumor. It is a set of stories that circulate within and through therapist communities. The stories are versions of the solution-focused therapy rumor. Whilst the names of the major characters usually remain stable, the plots and contexts that organize the action may vary from one story telling episode to the next. (Miller & de Shazer, 1998, p. 364)

Steve de Shazer and Gale Miller believed that solution focused therapy is what solution focused therapists *do,* not that solution focused therapists do what is formally laid down as solution focused therapy. Like many brief therapists, Steve was a maverick and an iconoclast: Would he be any less so with this approach, even though he was significantly involved with developing many of its ideas?

Typical of brief therapists over the years has been optimism about people; a focus on what Alan Wade describes as *the assumption of preexisting ability* rather than *the assumption of personal deficiency* (2000). They have tended to be experimenters, driven by a level of curiosity toward pushing the envelope. They have been interested in efficacy rather than conformity. Many of them have tended to view the world through the lens of humor, and some to have a taste for mischievousness.

Newcomers to the approach can find themselves becoming too enthusiastic, too formulaic. They can have a tendency to become either "solution forced" (see Nyland & Corsiglia, 1994), pursuing their clients relentlessly, hunting for exceptions and descriptions of miracles, impervious to client feedback; or, alternatively, they can be too easily deterred when a client at first finds it difficult to come up with anything. I give the example from one of my cases in which it was three sessions after the miracle question was asked that the client was finally able to come up with something.

Client: I really went crazy with the kids yesterday.

Cade: Remember that miracle I mentioned the first time we met? Suppose that had happened. What would you have done differently yesterday?

Client: I don't know. Maybe I would have walked out of the room and calmed myself down; maybe have made a cup of tea.

Q. If you were training therapists in the SFT model, what strategies would you use to train them and how would you present the material?

A. When training, I highlight the primary importance of the first rule of thumb (mentioned earlier in the chapter). I tell them that if they do nothing else other than give their clients the feeling of really being heard—perhaps for the first time—they will probably get good outcomes. When asked what a therapist has to learn, John Weakland replied, "It's going to sound dreadfully simple, but it is also very difficult to do consistently; and that is REALLY listen to what the client says and how they say it; really listen" (S. Chaney, personal communication, 1995).

Therefore, my second rule of thumb is of equal importance. For the client to feel heard, the therapist has to say something that maps sufficiently onto what the client is trying to communicate. This is where the discipline of the approach helps; in order to summarize and to compliment the client, the therapist must have focused carefully on what the client has said.

A COUPLE OF STORIES

The following story is about a man from whom I learned a great deal about never underestimating a client's resources or their potential motivation.

A family was referred to me by the Department of Community Services. It was described as one of their most difficult, long-term cases. The workers were at their wits' end and had heard that I had experience at engaging with chaotic families and wondered whether family therapy might help in this situation. The husband was verbally aggressive, evasive, and totally uncooperative. They had tried to get him to see a variety of psychiatrists, psychologists, and other professionals, but to no avail. There were six children. The older three were wards of the state and apparently wild and out of control. The wife was essentially struggling on her own to bring them up. The family had, at one point, been admitted to a residential assessment unit. The older children had climbed up onto the roof. Asked by the staff to help to get them down, the man had said, "You f— brought us here, you f— get them down!" He had then gone back to reading his newspaper.

I agreed to see the family if the referrer could find some neutral territory where we could meet. (I work from my own home and am not keen to see chaotic families there!) A place was found and, at the time agreed upon, I was making a cup of tea whilst waiting for somebody to arrive. I heard a noise behind me, turned, and there was the father. He was on his own. Somehow the referrer had managed to get him there and then had obviously driven off. The man was covered in tattoos. He was dressed in shorts and a T-shirt with a pair of sand shoes on his feet. He looked blankly past me with no sign of hostility, just that resigned, disengaged look that is often a feature of long-term welfare clients (like the war veteran's thousand-yard stare).

I looked up at him and asked, "What the f— are you doing here?"

He gave me a surprised look. "The welfare told me I've got to come and see you."

"I know, but what the f— are you doing here?"

He looked puzzled. "The welfare told me I've got to come and see you."

"I know but, from what I have heard, you must be sick to death of seeing people like me who tell you what to do, how to run your life, how to bring up your kids. So, what are you doing here?"

He readily agreed that he was fed up with all the intrusion into his life.

"So what are you doing here?"

"I told you. The welfare told me I've got to come and see you."

"You must be mad. If I'd had been you, I wouldn't have come. From what I hear, it sounds as if nobody has ever listened to you or asked you what you think or what you want for your family. So I'm still wondering why you're here."

He agreed that nobody had ever seemed interested in his point of view. They were all endlessly trying to foist their point of view onto him; to make him conform to their ideas.

"Look, now that you're here, would you like a cup of tea or coffee? It doesn't taste up to much, but at least it's hot."

"A coffee please, mate; milk and three sugars."

Over the rest of the session, this man told me about his love for his family and his wishes for them. He admitted he had not been a good father, but he didn't want his kids to go through what he had been through as a child. He had been moved from one foster home or residential facility to another. He had been physically, emotionally, and sexually abused in many of these places. He told me he ought to be of more help to his wife, and that he should do more to help out in the home. He told me he ought to spend more time with the children; maybe take them out to the park or take the eldest to football.

All I did throughout the rest of the session was continually acknowledge his obvious concern for his family, and suggest he didn't try to solve things too quickly, adding, "If you do decide to try some of these things, whatever you do, don't let the department know about it. Keep it as your secret."

The man came voluntarily to see me on quite a number of occasions over the next few months and started spending much more time at home and with the kids. For one of the appointments, he invited me home to meet his family. I sat and drank the cup of tea he made for me, from an obviously newly bought cup and saucer, while he sat proudly next to his wife on the sofa. I felt deeply privileged by the invitation. I had never greeted a client that way before and have never done so again. But I learned a lot from this man.

I use the various techniques associated with the solution focused approach with many (in fact most) of my cases. I find they sit easily alongside those aspects of my approach that I draw from my past contact with John Weakland, as well as alongside an aspect of my approach that I call "Monty Python focused therapy" (Cade, 1999).

Several years ago, I saw a 16-year-old young woman who, in addition to difficulties in her relationship with her father (her parents were divorced), was also preoccupied about her appearance. In spite of her mother's and other people's reassurances, and the fact that she claimed to have an endless queue of young men keen to take her out, she continued to obsess about the way she looked. When she told me about the interest being shown in her by this endless queue, I responded, "I assume they all have white canes, dark glasses, and guide-dogs, or are extremely hard-up and desperate."

She laughed and agreed with me that they must be. This kind of insulting banter remained an important thread running through our sessions together and at no time did I make a comment on how attractive she actually was. At the end of a session, when her mother had joined us to book the next appointment, the young woman suddenly said to me, "Come on now, Brian, admit it, I know that you really think I'm gorgeous."

My reply produced a howl of laughter: "You must be joking. You're the ugliest thing on two legs I have ever seen."

She later went on to disclose having endured a seriously abusive relationship when she was 14; the abuser had been about 3 years older. She had told nobody about this. I remain full of admiration at the way she addressed and confronted the painful aftermath of a horrifying and sustained period of physical and sexual abuse, and his demoralizing "brainwashing." I saw her again just recently. She is now at university. She told me she still has no shortage of men showing interest in her. She grinned and agreed with me when I responded, "Oh well! There's no accounting for taste."

Has the use of SFT impacted you in your personal life? If so, please explain.

"How come you always seem to see the other person's point of view?" complained my younger son, one time when he was expressing disapproval about somebody or other. The most significant impact that brief therapy has had on my life (apart from providing me with a living, that is) has been its introduction to me of the interactional view, the notion that nothing can be understood outside of its context. The more you are aware of the warp and weave of what goes to make up the tapestry of a person's life experiences, the easier it is to find an understanding and the less easy it is to judge. Positive reframing is always more than just a strategy; it reflects a way of viewing the world.

If there is one idea that perhaps has had a more profound pragmatic influence on me than any other, it is the notion that the attempted solution can so easily become the problem. *More of the same* leads to *more of the same,* creating a vicious circle ending in an exacerbation of difficulties or in remaining chronically stuck. Throughout my life—and particularly through the sometimes trying years of our children's adolescence—learning to do *less of the same* helped my wife and me avoid many a fruitless battle. Each of our children, since growing up, has in one way or another expressed appreciation of that. As my daughter said to me one day when we were out walking (she was then in her mid-20s), "Do you remember that time when I was a teenager, staying out late, night-clubbing, wearing short skirts, fish-net stockings, leather boots, and following those heavy-metal bands?"

"How can I forget?" I asked.

"Well, you and Mum did the right thing. If you had tried to stop me, I would just have rebelled more. But I always knew you were there for me."

Q. What do you see as the future of this approach?

A. As for what developments I would like for the future of the solution focused approach, I find that a difficult question to answer. As with developments in art, the logical way in which one approach seems to follow another only looks logical, perhaps even inevitable, with the benefit of hindsight. I just hope that the approach doesn't too quickly become accepted into academia and annualized. Although, having said that, I suppose it won't really matter. By then, the next generation of John Weaklands and Steve de Shazers will be off on some other iconoclastic tangent.

A FINAL STORY

In an interview given shortly before he died, asked what his favorite intervention was, John Weakland replied that if there was one thing he did regularly because it seemed to have very wide applicability it was, "[I]n some way or another to advise the client to go slow" (S. Chaney, personal communication, 1995). At the end of a therapy interview carried out during the day before he died, Steve de Shazer ended by advising the client who was planning to cut back on her drinking to revise her plan, to start in a less ambitious way. He said, "Take it easy; go slow."

EDITOR'S COMMENT

Only Brian Cade can take a relatively serious assignment such as the one we gave him for this book and, using humor, musings, and stories, turn it into such a masterpiece for us to think about. What has been so incredible throughout the process of compiling this book is the manner in which each practitioner has described what he or she does. Thus, Monty Python–Focused Therapy fits Brian well, since he is a character with many faces and mischievous antics with clients. Yet, obviously, his clients love him. They respond to his incredible ability to speak their language and be invited into their world. Brian makes sense to me when he says it doesn't really matter what we call this model, whether solution focused, brief therapy, or Monty Python Focused Therapy. It is what happens between two people when one of them, the therapist, really listens to what the other person has to say. But listening and hearing are difficult, as Brian suggests. Perhaps this may mean that in our training of future therapists, we engage more in exercises on relationship building and joining, as other practitioners have suggested.

Maybe this model is all about relationships. It's obviously not simply about questions. Perhaps we, too, should go slow. Not just to slow down the process or get our clients to slow down; that's a given. Let's go slow and enjoy what has evolved for us. And, as Brian says, get ready to see more, because there's lots more to see.

—Linda Metcalf

REFERENCES

Bavelas, J. B., McGee, D., Phillips, B., & Routledge, R. (2000). Microanalysis of communication in psychotherapy. *Human Systems: The Journal of Systemic Consultation and Management, 11,* 47–66.

Cade, B. W. (1999). Taking humour seriously: Monty Python-focused therapy. In W. Ray & S. de Shazer (Eds.), *Evolving brief therapies; In honor of John H. Weakland.* Iowa City, IA: Geist & Russell.

Cade, B. W. (2007). Springs, streams and tributaries: A history of the brief, solution-focused approach. In F. N. Thomas & T. Nelson (Eds.), *Handbook of solution-focused brief therapy: Clinical applications* (pp. 25–63). New York: Haworth Press.

Erickson, M. H. (1954). Pseudo-orientation in time as a hypnotherapeutic procedure. *Journal of Clinical and Experimental Hypnosis, 2,* 261–283.

Gassmann, D., & Grawe, K. (2006). General change mechanisms: The relation between problem activation and resource activation in successful and unsuccessful therapeutic interactions. *Clinical Psychology and Psychotherapy, 13,* 1–11.

Haley, J. (1963). *Strategies of psychotherapy.* New York: Grune and Stratton.

Libby, L. K., Shaeffer, E. M., Eibach, R. P., & Slemmer, J. A. (2007). Picture yourself at the polls: Visual perspective in mental imagery affects self-perception and behaviour. *Psychological Science, 18,* 199–203.

Miller, G., & de Shazer, S. (1998). Have you heard the latest about . . . ? Solution-focused therapy as a rumor. *Family Process, 37,* 363–377.

Nyland, D., & Corsiglia, V. (1994). Becoming solution-focused forced in brief therapy: Remembering something important we already knew. *Journal of Systemic Therapies, 13,* 5–12.

Wade, A. (2000). *Resistance to interpersonal violence: Implications for the practice of therapy.* Unpublished doctoral dissertation. Victoria, Canada: University of Victoria.

Watzlawick, P., Weakland, J. H., & Fisch, R. (1974). *Change: Principles of problem formation and problem resolution.* New York: Norton.

Weakland, J. H., Fisch, R., Watzlawick, P., & Bodin, A. (1974). Brief therapy: Focused problem resolution. *Family Process, 13,* 141–168.

9 Acceptance, Transparency, Research: Because the Others Want to Know

CYNTHIA FRANKLIN

A teacher affects eternity; he can never tell where his influence stops.

—Henry B. Adams

This chapter summarizes solution focused therapy (SFT) and my personal experience with the approach. I chronicle my journey as a researcher and teacher of SFT, including some of my personal experiences with Steve de Shazer and Insoo Kim Berg, who developed the SFT model. In particular, I describe how I learned SFT and provide details about my experiences applying it with children and adolescents in public school settings. Examples of cases and how clients respond to SFT, as well as some results from my research on SFT, are also presented. Finally, I discuss who my main mentors were and describe my views about what are the best ways for students and trainees to learn SFT.

THE BEGINNINGS OF SFT

The Brief Family Therapy Center (BFTC) in Milwaukee opened in 1978 and discovered the first solution focused techniques, "exceptions to problems," in 1982. Anyone that is familiar with the center will recognize the slogan "Solutions since 1982" that appeared on the center's Web site, videos, and memorabilia such as coffee cups. It was from that center that solution focused therapy was birthed and nurtured by two social workers and family therapists, Steve de Shazer and Insoo Kim Berg. It was chronicled in early and later writings such as de Shazer (1985, 1988), Insoo Kim Berg (1994), Berg and Miller (1992), and De Jong and Berg (2008).

The Brief Family Therapy Center was sometimes called the "Mental Research Institute (MRI) of the Midwest" and served as an experimental lab and think tank for new therapy ideas. This resulted in several therapists visiting and training at the center and contributing to the development of SFT (Berg & De Jong, 1996; Berg & Miller, 1992; Cade & O'Hanlon, 1993; de Shazer, Dolan, Korman, & Trepper, 2007; Lipchik, 2002). Therapists working in Milwaukee were interested in studying and improving effective and brief therapeutic techniques for helping clients change.

My professional social work training also started in 1978 and my career spanned more than a decade of schooling and work experience as a therapist before I entered a job in academia and discovered solution focused therapy. Concomitantly, during my career as a clinical social worker and family therapist, I was always interested in how people change and hastened to learn methods that could facilitate brief and effective change in clients. Originally, I received most of my training in behavioral therapies, behavioral couples therapy, cognitive behavioral therapy (CBT), and systems therapies. During my training I gained a great respect for therapists such as John Weakland, Jay Haley, Virginia Satir, and others that had worked at the Mental Research Institute (MRI) in Palo Alto, California. I focused on learning their perspectives on the formulations of problems and on the change process. My therapy training post-MSSW focused significantly on systems therapy training and I became a clinical member of the American Association of Marital and Family Therapy (AAMFT) while practicing as a full-time therapist. But for some reason I never encountered Steve and Insoo's work, other than a brief overview in the literature, until the early 1990s.

HOW I DISCOVERED SFT

In 1989 I received my PhD and became a faculty member at the University of Texas at Austin, a major research university in the southwest. As an assistant professor I was first trained in SFT while working on continuing education credits at an AAMFT summer institute. At that time, Tracy Todd was the SFT trainer at the institute in Santa Fe, New Mexico. Later I went on to receive additional training with Insoo Kim Berg and Steve de Shazer and I also had my entire research team trained in Milwaukee.

When I signed up for that very first workshop on SFT in New Mexico, I had no idea that it would shape my career, that I would build a relationship with Insoo Kim Berg that would last more than a decade, and that I would carry out research on SFT. In fact, I have to admit that I was more interested in vacationing in Santa Fe than the training! Once I got into Tracy Todd's workshop, however, I became very engaged in learning more about SFT. I remember thinking to myself that this would be a good approach with children and adolescents in school settings. School-based practice was where the focus of most of research and practice had been heading for about six years. So, the training that day sparked an interest in me to both learn SFT and possibly do research on it to see if my viewpoints were correct about its potential for schools.

MY FIT WITH SFT

What drew me to SFT is hard to pinpoint, but I seemed to have an intuitive appreciation for how it worked and how to practice it. Even though I had never seen a demonstration before the workshop in Santa Fe, I found myself volunteering to be the therapist in a live role-play in the workshop and discovered that I felt very comfortable trying out the therapy. It seemed to fit like a hand to a glove. Fortunately, being a good solution focused therapist and trainer, Tracy Todd also complimented me and told me that I was doing a great job demonstrating the SFT. Being an academic, I was used to thinking about therapy theoretically and empirically. What I immediately observed about SFT is that the approach used carefully posed questions from communication science to change client perceptions and to construct new responses. These change processes and SFT have been studied using experimental and process research in more recent times (Bavelas, Coates, & Johnson, 2000, 2002; Bavelas, McGee, Phillips, & Routledge, 2000; McGee, Del Vento, & Bavelas, 2005).

In Santa Fe, I was especially drawn to the behavioral and task-oriented aspects of SFT. I liked the way it used co-constructive language to move people toward collaborative goal setting and thought it was ingenious how SFT worked with the clients on envisioning new behaviors that could create change. I also liked how SFT focused on solutions instead of problems. I had always thought that focusing on behavioral change in a person's life and future was the best way to help. Perhaps because my mother drilled into me that "actions speak louder than words," I already believed that behavioral actions that lead to different responses are key to change. I also really resonated with the pragmatic focus of SFT. Insoo Kim Berg often said that change happened in the "details of everyday life" and I agree wholeheartedly with that statement, having repeated it on many occasions.

HUMANIST VALUES OF SFT

Upon reflection, I believe that my immediate acceptance of SFT seemed rooted in my values and SFT's strengths-based orientation. I quickly accepted the humanistic assumptions of the therapy, for example. What I mean by humanistic is the belief that it is important to build on the resources and motivation of clients because they know their problems best and are capable of generating their own solutions (Miller & de Shazer, 2000). I remember that many of the participants in the workshop in Santa Fe struggled with those assumptions and it was a dialogue in the workshop. In particular, some had a hard time accepting the belief that all people can make their own change and that this is an effective way to work with clients. Instead, they referred back to pathological frameworks and notions about how a client may have limited capacities for change. While limited capacities for change may exist, I observed that these objections missed the mark on understanding what SFT is all about because SFT was about working *with* a client's capacity, no matter what it was or what their circumstances might be. It was about "beginning where the client is" and working with them toward the best solutions for them. I had learned these assumptions during my social work training, so they seem to fit for me.

ACCEPTING THE STRENGTHS PERSPECTIVE

During my SFT training I observed that therapists usually either accepted the strengths perspective or not. A difference in opinion about the strengths perspective appears to be more than just prior therapeutic training, however. At the core of this struggle are a therapist's values and view about human beings. In 2002, Peter De Jong and I invited Insoo Kim Berg to do a workshop at the Council of Social Work Education (CSWE) and I saw the interactions that I first observed in Santa Fe play out again before a different audience. Insoo was involved in a spirited discussion about whether certain clients can change. This experience especially impressed on me how difficult it was for some professionals, regardless of their professional training, to accept the strengths orientation of SFT and the importance of doing so if you were to become a practitioner of this approach.

As I learned more about SFT I came to appreciate even more how its core components supported its strengths orientation and facilitated client change. For example, articles by de Shazer and Berg (1997) and Gingerich and Eisengart's (2000) systematic review of outcome studies on SFT categorized the therapy by the following techniques and core components:

1. Use of the Miracle Question
2. Use of scaling questions
3. A consulting break and giving the client a set of compliments
4. Assigning homework tasks
5. Looking for strengths or solutions
6. Goal setting
7. Looking for exceptions to the problem

Currently, these core components are important change techniques for SFT and each in its own unique way helps therapists focus on the strengths and resources of clients.

WORKING WITH CLIENTS: THE PROFESSIONAL IMPACT OF SFT

Because I was already in academia when I discovered SFT, most of my work with the approach has happened in research, teaching, and training settings. I also experimented with SFT in part-time private practice for a few years in the early 1990s, but that experience was very short-lived as I moved on to devote all my time to research and teaching. From 1993 to 1996, I conducted research in an agency in Austin, Texas, known as Youth Options, which worked with youth who were in crisis (especially those who were homeless or had run away from home). In that agency

I was able to team with a social worker, Jack Nowicki, who was trained in SFT, and together we offered a class for students on SFT and conducted some single case studies on the approach. When studied, we found that clients participating in the solution focused therapy changed on individual rating scales and standardized measures (Franklin, Corcoran, Nowicki, & Streeter, 1997).

I recall during the research at Youth Options that one family in particular seemed most impressed with the results they saw through SFT as compared to what they had seen when consulting with therapists that employed traditional therapy methods. Jack Nowicki conducted the first SFT session with an adolescent who had run away from home and her mother and partner. Since he worked in a youth agency, Jack was dressed very informally in a t-shirt and shorts. Both parents were high-level professionals and dressed the part in business suits. Unsolicited, the parents volunteered a comment about the results of SFT in a humorous way when asked at the end of the first session if they wanted to return for additional sessions. One partner said to the other, "This seems to be working much better than the other therapy." The second partner responded, "Yes, he is much better than the guy with the suit." Both parents agreed that they wanted to continue with the solution focused therapy. Jack and I both chuckled about the comment, but I also appreciated the transparency of the situation and how it was really a comment about the confidence these clients were gaining in the effectiveness of SFT.

Does SFT Work With Clients?

Many anecdotal stories like the one above can be offered to support the effectiveness of SFT, but I was eager to see the therapy examined with research studies. My goal was to see SFT become an empirically based intervention. The need for all kinds of research on SFT was definitely present but I was particularly interested in outcome studies with experimental designs. I spoke to Insoo Kim Berg about my desire to see more outcome research on SFT and I was grateful that she supported my efforts to see relevant studies completed. Both Insoo and Steve showed a genuine interest in improving research (de Shazer & Berg, 1997). Insoo also wanted the research on SFT to be examined and widely disseminated. Immediately prior to her death she envisioned an international book that would publish reviews of research studies in different countries. Fortunately, this book has gone forward and I am pleased to be a leader on that project.

In the early days of my research effort, not every SFT practitioner, however, was as enthusiastic. That is why Insoo and Steve's support was so vital to research moving forward. Steve de Shazer and I spoke on a panel at the European Brief Therapy Association (EBTA) in Salamanca, Spain, in 1998 and I recall a dialogue about whether research was really needed or not. Members of the audience challenged the need for research studies, suggesting that more attention should be given to marketing SFT instead. Someone asked why we should do this research. I will never forget Steve's clever reply: "Because the others want to know." In the coming years, and with the emergence of the evidence-based practice movement, it became very clear that the others did want to know and we needed to be more serious about our research studies on SFT.

MY JOURNEY AS AN SFT RESEARCHER

On my early journey as a researcher of SFT I was grateful to discover like-minded colleagues who were interested in research studies. Notable among these were Alasdair Macdonald in Great Britain and other members of the European Brief Therapy Association (EBTA) and Wally Gingerich (Gingerich & Eisengart, 2000) and Peter De Jong (De Jong & Hopwood, 1996), both social work colleagues in the United States. Later, I met many other research colleagues through the Solution-Focused Brief Therapy Association (SFBTA) research group meeting. That meeting continues to offer excellent networking for those interested in doing research on SFT.

Efforts at systematic research on SFT started during the 1990s. Alasdair Macdonald developed an SFT manual for research and conducted research in psychiatric clinics (Macdonald, 2005). Outcome studies started to accumulate and Wally Gingerich conducted the first-ever systematic review of SFT studies (Gingerich & Eisengart, 2000). Recently, two meta-analyses have been completed (Kim, 2008; Stams, Dekovic, Buist, & de Vries, 2006). The Research Committee of the Solution-Focused Brief Therapy Association developed a treatment manual in order to help standardize the implementation of SFT by practitioners and increase treatment fidelity of the model (Trepper et al., 2008). Three general ingredients of SFT are identified in the treatment manual: (a) use of conversations centered on clients' concerns; (b) conversations focused on co-constructing new meanings around client concerns; and (c) use of specific techniques to help clients co-construct a vision of a preferred future and drawing upon past success and strengths to help resolve issues (SFBTA Research Committee, 2008).

MY WORK IN SCHOOLS

While I did everything I could to facilitate interest in my students and colleagues toward outcome research on SFT, my own personal work focused on studies in schools. As I have previously summarized (Franklin, Kim, & Kelly, 2009) therapists began to use the SFT techniques in schools during the 1990s with the first publications and small research studies appearing in print around the mid-1990s (e.g., Kral, 1995; Metcalf, 1995; Murphy, 1996; Sklare, 1997). Since those early days, applications of SFT in schools has grown (e.g., Berg & Shilts, 2004; Franklin & Gerlach, 2007; Kelly, Kim, & Franklin, 2008; Metcalf, 2008; Murphy, 1996; Murphy & Duncan, 2007; Webb, 1999) with increasing reports of SFT interventions and programs being implemented in schools in both the United States and Europe (Kelly et al., 2008). The first two studies on SFT in schools that I completed were in 1995–1997 and conducted with 5th and 6th graders in a school district near San Antonio, Texas. These studies were later published in refereed journals (Franklin, Biever, Moore, Clemons & Scamardo, 2001; Franklin, Moore, & Hopson, 2008).

In those early studies, we used many of the training materials for schools that had been developed by Linda Metcalf (Metcalf, 1995). Metcalf was one of the first therapists to apply SFT in a school setting and her training materials for counselors and teachers are most useful. In addition, my research team were all trained by Steve de Shazer and Insoo Kim Berg and attended workshops in Milwaukee. I was very interested in maintaining the fidelity of the SFT approach and credit the training by Insoo and other progenitors of SFT as the reason why we were able to achieve good results in our studies in schools.

INTERESTING CASES

Many interesting cases emerged during my research studies on SFT in schools. One that I find most memorable involved a 6th-grade boy named Chris with classroom behavior and social skills problems. Chris was diagnosed with oppositional defiant disorder and liked to argue with peers and teachers. His teachers were most concerned that he did not have good social skills and was socially isolated within the school. Chris also set a goal to have more friends. This case is very memorable for me because it illustrates how important it is to collaborate with and follow clients in your work with them. Insoo often said to "lead from one step behind." Forcing SFT techniques goes against the collaborative conversations that are necessary to successfully apply the approach.

In the study we videotaped all the sessions with Chris and Kelly Moore, one of my doctoral students, who was the therapist on the case. Kelly was an excellent SFT therapist, but was working too hard to get an exception from Chris instead of adapting to his combative style and developing a collaborative conversation with him. During the initial session, she tried to get an exception for a time when he had a friend, but Chris kept insisting that he did not have any friends ever. The harder she tried to get Chris to identify someone that could be regarded as a friend, the more he insisted that he had no friends. So, most of the session was spent on this topic with little progress. The videotape of the session revealed the parallel process between Kelly and Chris and how the intensity between her trying to discover some positive friendships and his defiance had coalesced.

In the next session, I suggested that Kelly go in and tell Chris that she had been thinking about their conversation and she realized he was right. Some people just do not have friends. Kelly did not want to say this to the child, but she understood the reasoning. She went back into the session and told Chris that he was right; some people just did not have friends. She went on to say that in fact, some people are just meant not to have friends ever and have to adjust to being alone in life.

Spontaneously, Chris said he did have a friend! Kelly said, "No way!" The session then moved to details about the exception, and Kelly continued to show disbelief when Chris said he played with children and even spent the night at their house in the past. Kelly then bet Chris a Coke that he could not get a friend now and he said he could. She again said, "No way," and proceeded to ask him how he planned to do so. Chris told her he knew a boy in his class that he could invite to lunch and play with him. She continued to express disbelief that this could happen and bet him the Coke if he could do it by the next session. Kelly also stated that she would be checking with his teachers to see if it really happened. Chris took the bet that before next week's session, he would make a friend and invite him to lunch.

When Kelly checked with Chris's teacher, the teacher said he started having lunch with someone in his class and playing nicely with him. She said Chris usually sat alone in the lunchroom and she was pleasantly surprised at this change. Chris retuned to the session bragging about his success and expecting the Coke.

RESEARCH ON SFT IN SCHOOLS PROGRESSES

Research in schools on SFT has grown since 2000. Johnny Kim and I recently reviewed the outcome literature on SFT in schools (Kim & Franklin, 2008). This systematic review only included the most rigorous studies that used experimental designs, with standardized measures, and that met criteria for a solution focused intervention. In our review we found one experimental design study, six quasi-experimental design studies, and one single-case design study on SFT in schools. Most of these studies had arrived within the past two years of the review and this was a very encouraging sign that more research in schools was beginning to occur.

We were also encouraged by the amount of positive findings that emerged in the research. Some of the positive findings from the systematic review are as follows:

- Helps students reach goals
- Helps students alleviate their concerns
- Improves academic achievement (e.g., credits earned)
- Helps students reduce the intensity of their negative feelings
- Helps students reduce drug use
- Helps students manage their conduct problems (Franklin et al., 2001; Franklin et al., 2007; Froeschle, Smith, & Ricard, 2007; Kelly, Kim, & Franklin, 2008; Newsome, 2004)

Of course, there were some mixed results found in our systematic review on SFT outcomes in schools, but enough positive differences were found favoring SFT to view it as a promising intervention for school settings. The effect sizes we calculated and reported in the individual studies also showed SFT to be promising; most studies had medium and some large effect sizes. The results of this study made me think back to the solution focused workshop with Tracy Todd in Santa Fe, when I had said to myself that SFT could work in schools. It takes time to create an intervention and research it, but the research is starting to emerge.

My work has ventured into different ways to help schools apply SFT. School-based interventions may be implemented at different levels of the schools programs and with different groups within the school environment (Franklin, Kim, & Kelly, 2009), for example:

- Coach teachers in using solution-building talk (see the Working on What Works [WOWW] program, Kelly et al., 2008)
- Help at-risk students in individual, group, and family interventions (Murphy, 1996)
- Change interactions between parents, teachers, and students, such as parent/teacher meetings (Metcalf, 1995, 2008)
- Change the school culture, for example, when an entire school adopts the solution focused change philosophy and trains all staff (including teachers and principals) in SFT techniques (Franklin & Streeter, 2003, cited in Kelly, Kim, & Franklin, 2008, all cited in Franklin, Kim, & Kelly, 2009)

Mary Beth Harris and I developed a multicomponent intervention using SFT as a framework and integrating other methods such as cognitive behavioral and task groups to help pregnant and parenting teens (e.g., Harris & Franklin, 2007). In my work I also wanted to see SFT applied in a complete school context where everyone in the school was trained, from the top administrators to the lowest-ranking employee like the janitor. Like Metcalf (2008) I especially wanted to train teachers and principals and influence the school organization toward a solution focused culture. I got an opportunity to do so in 2001 when I was invited to Garza High School in Austin, Texas, to help their alternative school for dropout prevention. For the next seven years I worked with principal Vicki Baldwin and her staff to help them learn and apply SFT to help youths at risk of dropping out. I also conducted research on SFT at Garza (Franklin, Streeter, Kim, & Trippodi, 2007). Insoo Kim Berg became a trainer and consultant at Garza High School. The principal and Garza staff often affectionately said that Insoo and Steve had adopted the high school and Insoo jokingly would say, "Yes, I am a parent to a high school."

LIFE OUTSIDE THE THERAPY ROOM: PERSONAL EFFECTS OF SFT

On occasion, solution focused therapy has entered into personal discussions with my husband Jim. Jim is a stockbroker and trainer of other stockbrokers and he once observed a training tape I was going to show in my family therapy class. He watched as Insoo Kim Berg asked the miracle question and worked with the clients on the video. Jim turned and said to me, "Man, she is good. Can you teach me that miracle question?" So, I wrote it down for him. It led into a very stimulating conversation. His work had always seemed really different than mine; but I discovered the similarities from this discussion. Jim told me that SFT reminded him of consultative selling techniques, where he guided his financial clients who are stockbrokers to make sure they find out what the client wants and what the client goal is before providing them with financial options. He said it is always best to do what is best for the client. I was pretty impressed with his consideration for what the client wanted. We were building a mutual language and that opened up lots of interesting conversations about selling techniques and the values used in different types of selling.

What Are SFT Therapists Like?

Solution focused therapists are people who respect client self-determination and believe it is best when people can solve their own problems. They see that human beings want to change and do better for themselves. I believe they value offering clients choices and helping clients see the choices they have presented in themselves and in their situation. Therapists that use SFT want clients to recognize choices that they may not have thought about, as well as their own inherent strengths and capacities. Clients change best when choosing their own change, so the SFT therapist does not take too much control over the client's decisions but is patient and willing to stand back and let clients choose their own way and learn from the consequences of their experiences. Therapists practicing SFT are client-focused and value the viewpoints of those whom others might see as having less power and significance. Solution focused therapy is also a pragmatic approach; most therapists working in this tradition value pragmatism and optimism. I personally felt drawn to the futuristic, possibility thinking of the approach and the way SFT empowers people. I also believe that other solution focused therapists prefer the strengths orientation, as well.

TRAINING AND REFLECTION

There are five issues that I have repeatedly observed when trainees try to learn the SFT model. These issues often emerge as either questions or mistakes that early trainees make.

1. Students do not grasp the bigger picture of the change process involved in the SFT approach. They think it is all about the techniques and apply those in a forced or artificial manner. To correct this mistake, I think students need to be trained to understand that SFT is a purposeful conversation in which we need to know how to use ourselves to help people change. In order to effectively apply SFT, beginning therapists need to learn how to join with clients and how to use their communication skills and relationship skills to build rapport and to help people cooperate in a therapeutic relationship that is aimed at facilitating a process of change.
2. Trainees of SFT do not have the basic therapy skills to master the SFT approach. In order to apply SFT, students first need to learn the strengths orientation and be well trained in basic counseling approaches such as empathy, reflective listening, and reframing. When these skills are not well developed, I have observed that students misapply the SFT techniques and have difficulty learning how to build collaborative relationships. My observations suggest that it is a plus if therapy trainees have ample training in systems theory and that they benefit from training in understanding process approaches to therapy. I have found that some understanding of the MRI brief therapy and CBT is also a plus to learning and complements a student's speed of comprehension during SFT training. From my experience, those trained in psychodynamic and insight oriented approaches are harder to train and do not respond as favorably to SFT while those from learning and systems theories training grasp SFT better.
3. Students trying to learn SFT may assume the approach is simple and that it does not work with complex cases. To correct this assumption, I talk to students about how the therapy was developed on families with multiple problems and point to the many applications of the approach. I also tell them stories about Insoo's work and how she had a passion to help those in the child protective services—and those cases are not easy. I share my work with kids with externalizing behavior problems and the good results we got from that work. Finally, I tell them it is still an empirical question as to which client population SFT is best at helping; but we do know that it has been applied with complex cases and with clients that are mandated and perceived as being difficult to engage and help.

4. Students and practitioners often challenge me saying there is no research on SFT, or that it is not an evidence-based approach. To correct this viewpoint, I discuss the research evidence that exists for SFT and show how the model is moving toward an evidence-based approach. I point naysayers to the recent meta-analysis completed by one of my doctoral students, Johnny Kim (2008), and other reviews of the outcome literature (Gingerich & Eisengart, 2000; Stams et al., 2006). Furthermore, SFT was recognized by the Office of Juvenile Justice (OJJ) as a promising approach (Kim, Smock, Trepper, McCollum, & Franklin, 2008).
5. SFT is a lot like motivational interviewing (MI) and MI has a tremendous amount of research to back it up; so, some students ask, what is the advantage to learning SFT? First of all, I tell them that if SFT is just like MI, and MI works, then maybe that means SFT might work too. Second, I ask them, how do we really know that the two approaches are the same? Jan Bavelas and her research colleagues are empirically studying the differences using basic experimental research methods of microanalysis. When these researchers finish their study, we will have some evidence to discuss. In the meantime, I offer my opinion for discussion.

MI and SFT are not the same—even though when it comes to therapy, they are more similar than, say, SFT and emotion-focused therapy. From my observations there are, however, many important differences. MI is an approach to engage clients in a change process; SFT is an approach to engage clients in a solution-building process. MI focuses on engagement and the stages of change; SFT focuses on solutions to problems that a person wants to resolve, regardless of which stage of change they are in.

SFT and MI both honor client resistance and roll with the resistance but their approach to client motivation and change differs. MI therapists act to help clients move to the next stage of change; SFT starts with the belief that all clients want to change and it is the therapist's job to start where the client is in their process of change. Solution focused therapists help clients form a goal (something they want) which is a beginning to their solution-building process. Once the goal is clearly formed, clients can envision behaviors and tasks to create their own solutions. It is the solution focused therapist's job to create a conversation and context where the solutions can emerge from the clients instead of guiding clients with interventions that help clients move through the stages of change.

What Is the Best Way to Learn SFT?

The person that I have received the most training in SFT from was Insoo Kim Berg. I consider her to be my mentor in the approach. My observations of her suggest that SFT training is best accomplished when students can learn the philosophy and change process behind the SFT approach and master ways to use the language of change and SFT questioning techniques. Effective learning involves observations of master therapists doing the SFT approach and role-play experience practicing the techniques of SFT. Practice makes perfect so being supervised in practice with clients or learning in a supervised internship or in a training clinic is the best way to master the approach. However, to be true to SFT philosophy a practitioner of SFT may never become a brilliant strategist that knows all the techniques of change. A more humble idea about change is required because change comes from the client and the client's resources.

CORE KNOWLEDGE

I believe certain core knowledge also facilitates implementation of the SFT approach. Students that are being trained in SFT need knowledge in human development and change, as well as learning experience in effective use of relationship and communications skills, for example. When observing Insoo Kim Berg practicing SFT therapy I noticed that she continuously used effective communication skills and relationship-based counseling methods along with the techniques of SFT. I recall once asking her about her use of mirroring techniques and matching client language in a session. She smiled and said, "Oh, you mean the head to toe." Insoo definitely knew how to do the "head to toe" and watching her do it was fascinating to me. I also observed that Insoo practiced SFT as a relationship-based therapy and the importance of developing a cooperative relationship with clients was very central in her mind.

Insoo also took into consideration the developmental issues of clients when working with them. For example, we had Insoo in Austin on a numerous occasions and she would do live demonstrations or show her videos. In one workshop I remember she showed two videos of herself with a family with multiple problem called "Over the Hump I & II." This family was involved in many outside systems such as corrections and child protective services and had many issues to resolve, including substance abuse and parenting issues. The family was also very hostile toward helping professionals. In the first interview, Insoo demonstrated her amazing communication and relationship skills to help the family change their conversation from one of resistance toward helpers to saying they were cooperating and had made it "over the hump."

In the second video, the couple had made many dramatic changes (e.g., they stopped abusing substances, the husband had a job, their kids were returned to them, and they had their own home). Insoo focused on improving the couple's relationship in the interview. One of the workshop participants wanted to know why she did not focus more on the children's problems or the past pathological issues with the couple. Insoo responded that the clients had made many changes since their last interview. They had been a family on the verge of breakup and had many extreme problems outside the norm and would be considered dysfunctional. In the first interview (Over the Hump I), for example, the parents were complaining about things like prison release for substance abuse, and having their children removed from the home. Insoo went on to explain that the family was now developmentally different than in the first interview. In the second interview (Over the Hump II) they were more like a middle-class family complaining of issues with chores, school problems of their children, and relationship issues between them (i.e., the wife feeling ignored by her husband).

What I took from Insoo's response that day was that she honored the developmental changes in the family and complimented those changes, and proceeded to address their immediate concerns to improve the couple's relationship further. By following this course of action, Insoo recognized and supported the developmental changes and reinforced the stability and progress the family had made toward becoming a functional family system.

CONCLUSION

My journey as an SFT researcher and teacher has now spanned over 15 years and I am privileged to have been mentored and taught by both Insoo Kim Berg and Steve de Shazer while they were alive. SFT has continued to grow and advance since that fateful day in Santa Fe when I first discovered it. I witnessed the worldwide expansion of SFT in the 1990s and watched it become a very influential model of therapy. Insoo once told me that she believed that the increased popularity of SFT was hastened by the advent of managed behavioral care and the search for briefer therapeutic approaches. Since 2000, the research on SFT has also been growing and more experimental design studies have been completed that show the promising effects of SFT. The development of a treatment manual has also been a plus for researchers and practitioners that want to keep fidelity to SFT and study it further. Since Steve and Insoo's deaths in 2006 and 2007, respectively, all the training functions of the Brief Family Therapy Center have been transferred to the Solution-Focused Brief Therapy Association (sfbta.org), which continues to carry on the training tasks and dissemination of SFT books, videos, and other training materials. One of my main roles with SFT has been to work on conducting research that will help it become an empirically based treatment. As far as the establishment of SFT as an evidence-based approach goes, SFT has made considerable progress and I am confident that the best is yet to come.

EDITOR'S COMMENT

I appreciate Dr. Cynthia Franklin's honest, heartfelt description of how she found herself immersed in a workshop that changed her professional life. Her kind demeanor is also present throughout this chapter as she describes teaching students who are new to SFT and her patience to help them see that SFT is so much more than questions or techniques.

Cynthia's loyalty and affection toward Insoo is certainly a tribute to the impact that Insoo had on her life. I have become acquainted with Garza High School over the past few years and have met Vicki Baldwin, the former principal. I know the impact that Cynthia and Insoo have had on Garza and the passion that Cynthia has put forward to help the school succeed. It is successful—so successful that no other high school in its area has such academic success with students at risk, nor as minimal a dropout rate. Cynthia is a true pioneer in seeing what SFT can introduce to a school system.

Research is important to many in SFT now, although it wasn't always, as Cynthia has alluded. I am thankful to have Cynthia as one of the main researchers of the model, particularly since she has seen its applicability in so many settings. Yes, we need research findings, as they give credibility, yet as Cynthia relays, waiting for such findings does not cause solution focused therapists and new trainees in the approach to sit back and wait and see. The proof is already in the pudding. But when the proof ends up on paper, we will all be smiling.

—Linda Metcalf

REFERENCES

Bavelas, J. B., Coates, L., & Johnson, T. (2000). Listeners as co-narrators. *Journal of Personality and Social Psychology, 79,* 941–952.

Bavelas, J. B., Coates, L., & Johnson, T. (2002). Listener responses as a collaborative process: The role of gaze. *Journal of Communication, 52,* 566–580.

Bavelas, J. B., McGee, D., Phillips, B., & Routledge, R. (2000). Microanalysis of communication in psychotherapy. *Human Systems, 11,* 3–22.

Berg, I. K. (1994). *Family based services: A solution-focused approach.* New York: Norton.

Berg, I. K., & De Jong, P. (1996). Solution-building conversation: Co-constructing a sense of competence with clients. *Families in Society, 77,* 376–391.

Berg, I. K., & Miller, S. D. (1992). *Working with the problem drinker: A solution-focused approach.* New York: Norton.

Berg, I. K., & Shilts, L. (2004). *Classroom solutions: WOWW approach.* Milwaukee: Brief Family Therapy Center Press.

Cade, B., & O'Hanlon, W. (1993). *A brief guide to brief therapy.* New York: Norton.

De Jong, P., & Berg, I. K. (2008). *Interviewing for solutions.* Belmont, CA: Thompson.

de Shazer, S. (1985). *Keys to solutions in brief therapy.* New York: Norton.

de Shazer, S. (1988). *Clues: Investigating solutions in brief therapy.* New York: Norton.

de Shazer, S., & Berg, I. K. (1997). What works? Remarks on research aspects of solution-focused brief therapy. *Journal of Family Therapy, 19,* 121–124.

de Shazer, S., Dolan, Y., Korman, H., & Trepper, T. (2007). *More than miracles: The state of the art of solution-focused brief therapy.* Binghamton, NY: Haworth Press.

Franklin, C., Biever, J. L., Moore, K. C., Clemons, D., & Scamardo, M. (2001). Effectiveness of solution-focused therapy with children in a school setting. *Research on Social Work Practice, 11,* 411–434.

Franklin, C., Corcoran, J., Nowicki, J., & Streeter, C. (1997). Using client self-anchored scales to measure outcomes in solution-focused therapy. *Journal of Systemic Therapies, 16*(3), 246–265.

Franklin, C., & Gerlach, B. (2007). Clinical applications of solution-focused brief therapy in public schools. In T. S. Nelson & F. N. Thomas (Eds.), *Handbook of solution-focused brief therapy: Clinical applications* (pp. 168–169). Philadelphia, PA: Haworth Press.

Franklin, C., Kim, J. S., & Kelly, M. (2009). Solution-focused brief therapy in schools. In A. Roberts (Ed.), *Social workers desk reference* (2nd ed.). New York: Oxford University Press.

Franklin, C., Moore, K., & Hopson, L. (2008). Effectiveness of solution-focused brief therapy in a school setting. *Children & Schools, 30,* 15–26.

Franklin, C., Streeter, C. L., Kim, J. S., & Trippodi, S. J. (2007). The effectiveness of a solution-focused, public alternative school for dropout prevention and retrieval. *Children & Schools, 29,* 133–144.

Froeschle, J. G., Smith, R. L., & Ricard, R. (2007). The efficacy of a systematic substance abuse program for adolescent females. *Professional School Counseling, 10,* 498–505.

Gingerich, W., & Eisengart, S. (2000). Solution-focused brief therapy: A review of outcome research. *Family Process, 39,* 477–496.

Harris, M. B., & Franklin, C. (2007). *Taking charge: A school-based, life skills group program for adolescent mothers.* New York: Oxford University Press.

Kelly, M. S., Kim, J. S., & Franklin, C. (2008). *Solution-focused brief therapy in schools: A 360-degree view of the research and practice principles.* New York: Oxford University Press.

Kim, J. S. (2008). Examining the effectiveness of solution-focused brief therapy: A meta-analysis. *Research on Social Work Practice, 18,* 107–116.

Kim, J. S., & Franklin, C. (2008). Solution-focused brief therapy in schools: A review of the outcome literature. *Children and Youth Services Review.*

Kim, J. S., Smock, S., Trepper, T., McCollum, E., & Franklin, C. (2008). Is solution-focused brief therapy evidence-based? Manuscript under review.

Kral, R. (1995). *Solutions for schools.* Milwaukee: Brief Family Therapy Center Press.

Lipchik, E. (2002). *Beyond technique in solution focused therapy.* New York: Guilford Press.

Macdonald, A. (2005). Brief therapy in adult psychiatry: Fifteen years of practice. *Journal of Family Therapy, 67,* 65–75.

McGee, D., Del Vento, A., & Bavelas, J. B. (2005). An interactional model of questions as therapeutic interventions. *Journal of Marital and Family Therapy, 31,* 371–384.

Metcalf, L. (1995). *Counseling toward solutions: A practical solution-focused program for working with students, teachers, and parents.* San Francisco: Jossey-Bass.

Metcalf, L. (2008). *A field guide to counseling toward solutions.* San Francisco: Jossey-Bass.

Miller, G., & de Shazer, S. (2000). *Emotions in solution-focused therapy: A re-examination.* Family Process, 39, 5-23.

Murphy, J. J. (1996). Solution-focused brief therapy in the school. In S. D. Miller, M. A. Hubble, & B. S. Duncan (Eds.), *Handbook of solution-focused brief therapy* (pp. 184–204). San Francisco: Jossey-Bass.

Murphy, J. J., & Duncan, B. S. (2007). *Brief interventions for school problems* (2nd ed.). New York: Guilford Press.

Newsome, S. (2004). Solution-focused brief therapy (SFT) groupwork with at-risk junior high school students: Enhancing the bottom-line. *Research on Social Work Practice, 14,* 336–343.

Sklare, G. B. (1997). *Brief counseling that works: A solution-focused approach for school counselors.* Thousand Oaks, CA: Sage.

Springer, D. W., Lynch, C., & Rubin, A. (2000). Effects of a solution-focused mutual aid group for Hispanic children of incarcerated parents. *Child & Adolescent Social Work Journal, 17,* 431–432.

Stams, G. J., Dekovic, M., Buist, K., & de Vries, L. (2006). Effectiviteit van oplossingsgerichte korte therapie; een meta-analyse [Efficacy of solution-focused brief therapy: A meta-analysis]. *Gedragstherapie* [*Behavior Therapy*], 39, 81–94.

Trepper, T. S., McCollum, E. E., De Jong, P., Korman, H., Gingerich, W., & Franklin, C. (2008). Solution focused therapy treatment manual for working with individuals. Solution Focused Brief Therapy Association Research Committee. Retrieved May 20, 2008, from http://www.sfbta.org/Research.pdf

Webb, W. H. (1999). *Solutioning: Solution-focused interventions for counselors.* Philadelphia, PA: Accelerated Press.

10 The Evidence Base of SFT

SARA SMOCK

Everything absolute belongs to pathology. Joyous distrust is a sign of health.

—Friedrich Nietzsche

Q. How did you first learn about solution focused therapy (SFT)?

A. My first introduction to solution focused brief therapy was during my master's program in marriage and family therapy (MFT) at Purdue Calumet. During my second semester in the program I took a course on contemporary theories taught by Dr. Joseph Wetchler. In that class we learned about narrative therapy, collaborative language, and of course SFT. I can remember intently reading each word of the SFT readings and thinking, "I completely agree with everything." Although I was new to the field, I found myself being drawn into Steve de Shazer's writings. So, I looked for everything I could find on SFT to read. As I read more and more I grew fonder of the model.

During that semester, I also began seeing clients in the MFT clinic. I noticed myself drawing from SFT in the therapy room from the beginning. The interesting thing is that I wasn't consciously trying to use SFT, it just came naturally. When I sat in front of my clients the first thoughts that came to my mind were ones focused on the client's preferred future. I immediately knew that SFT was the best fit for me. As my master's training in MeFT continued, so grew my affection for the model.

Q. What characteristics of this model drew you toward it?

A. For me, the main attraction is the philosophical underpinnings of SFT. I believe that reality is individually co-constructed. One of my favorite SFT books is *Words Were Originally Magic* by Steve de Shazer. I echo the thought of language from a poststructuralism view. I truly believe that language is reality. The philosophical underpinnings of SFT and the fact that it is not a theory to explain behavior is so appealing.

I also agree with the core values of SFT. Everyone has all of the resources they need. So many approaches view the client as incapable of creating his or her desired path. I believe in the vast resources of every person. I also believe that it is more helpful to focus on one's desired future than problem solving. I could list each and every core value of SFT. They all resonate with my core being.

I was also attracted to the practical aspects of doing SFT. For example, I really liked how SFT can be used with mandated clients. As a new therapist, I was concerned about what to do for individuals, couples, and families that did not want to be in therapy. I quickly learned that a lot of clients, even those not mandated, didn't want to be in therapy. I found that using an SFT approach gave me the tools I needed to be respectful and help all of my clients.

Q. How has utilizing SFT impacted your work with clients? (Please mention if you utilized a previous model and the difference you noticed in clients and yourself after switching to SFT.)

A. As I mentioned earlier, I began learning and using SFT at the beginning of my training as a therapist. Thus, I can't comment about my professional life before SFT. I can talk about how SFT has impacted my work with clients over the years.

I believe that SFT has impacted my work the most in the area of respectfulness for my clients. I believe that the SF model gives room for me and my clients to work together in a respectful environment. The outcome of using a respectful therapy approach has been the results in my client's lives. My clients are able to work on their desired future and achieve the results *they* want.

The other way SFT has impacted my work as a therapist is learning to go slow. I have to admit that I am a product of our busy society that is always moving full steam ahead. SFT allows me and my clients to slow down and focus on the desired exceptions in life. It has taught me as a therapist to be a better listener, and thus a better therapist. I believe SFT has taught me and my clients so much.

Q. How would your clients describe your work with them? Have any of your clients who might have experienced another model of therapy commented on the difference (if any) that they perceived when working with you?

A. While I have never specifically asked my clients to describe their work with me, I have had clients make comments about their experience in working with me. My clients have stated that they feel comfortable in therapy with me. I believe this reflects the respectful environment SFT creates. Clients also comment on the hopeful environment of our sessions. I know that clients experience therapy differently but I hope that they all perceive the respectful nature of SFT.

Q. What is it about SFT that makes it so effective?

A. I think there are several things that make SFT effective but I believe it really boils down to one thing . . . allowing the client to be the expert of their desired future. From my experience, I have found that SFT is the only approach that truly listens to the client and bases therapy on the client's preferred future, not the therapist's. I am currently working on a research team that is examining the differences between SFT and cognitive behavioral therapy (CBT). We have learned several things to date about the differences between the two models. The one point that stands out the most is how SFT truly helps clients focus on their desired future. Other models, like CBT, may use goal setting and other future-oriented techniques, but fail to allow the client to direct the course of therapy. The therapist in SFT is trained to carefully listen (this is often challenging) to the client and ask questions that move clients toward identifying what they want their life to look like. To me, this is effective therapy.

I am sure you are wondering, how is focusing on the client's preferred future effective or what evidence do we have that this approach is effective? These questions are just a few that flood my thoughts constantly. Because I am a researcher at heart, my mission is to help provide evidence for the model that I believe in. During the SFBTA 2006 conference in Denver, I and several others began talking about what needed to occur for SFT to be nationally recognized as an evidence-based practice. We continued our discussion over the next few months and decided to submit published SFT studies to evidence-based practice (EBP) lists. To date there are numerous studies, several reviews of the research, and a few meta-analyses completed that showcase SFT's effectiveness (see Corcoran & Pillai, 2007; Kim, 2008; Stams, Dekovic, Buist, & de Vries, 2006). So we chose topic areas where several well-controlled studies existed (like education and substance abuse) and found the appropriate EBP lists to submit the articles. The greatest victory we have to date is that the Office of Juvenile Justice and Delinquency Prevention now recognizes SFT as a "promising" treatment (see for further information: http://www.dsgonline.com/mpg2.5/TitleV_MPG_Table_Ind_Rec.asp?ID = 712). The day we received the news of this recognition I was ecstatic. While some might think this was a small victory, I always believe that small change leads to big change. This is only the beginning. While I believe that SFT is effective from my experience as a therapist, it is important to continue the work of having SFT nationally and internationally recognized as an effective treatment. I have committed to dedicate my career to this endeavor.

Q. Describe one of your favorite cases and how it impacted your work as a therapist.

A. During my doctoral training I worked with children who had experienced physical and/or sexual abuse. I saw children as young as 3, as well as teenagers. Although I enjoyed working with all of the clients at this placement, one was especially memorable. I received a referral from the local police department for a young girl who had experienced a very traumatic incident. I'll call her Sue. Before meeting Sue or her family I had a conversation with the investigating officer. He described to me in detail the nature of the traumatic event. I can remember thinking that this girl had been through more than most people experience in their entire lives. After talking with the officer I met with Sue's parents. Sue's biological parents were divorced. The biological mother and stepmother had a good relationship and all three parents attended the first session. My first impression was wow! Here was a highly invested blended family where each parent took time off work to meet with their daughter's therapist. After meeting with the parents, I finally had the opportunity to meet with Sue. Sue came to session very aware of the traumatic event. I remember her being very tearful during that first meeting. Something told me that this family would be one of my favorites.

I began meeting regularly with Sue and her family. From the very beginning, I talked to Sue about what would be helpful for her during this time. Unsurprisingly, Sue came up with specifics about what she needed from her parents. She was able to identify what needed to occur surrounding the traumatic event. I asked Sue the miracle question and her response was that she would be brave if a miracle happened. We talked in detail about what she would notice if her miracle occurred. Sue said she would notice herself being brave at school, even in difficult situations. I then asked Sue what would need to happen for her to be brave at school. Sue came up with an idea to find a special stuffed animal to take to school and hold when she needed to be brave. I shared Sue's solution with her parents and they decided to take Sue to the store and let her pick out this special bear.

Sue's parents purchased the bear and talked to Sue's teacher about allowing her to hold the bear during the school day when she was feeling sad. The next week Sue brought her new bear to session and reported that she had taken the bear to school every day. She stated that when she would get scared or sad and wanted to be brave she would hold her bear. I asked Sue to scale her braveness and she was much higher than the previous week. I continued to meet with Sue and her family for several more weeks. Each session Sue reported feeling more and more brave. I asked the family when they would know that Sue no longer needed to come to therapy. Sue responded by stating that when she was able to be brave at school without holding her bear she would no longer need to come. Sue did just that. After a few more sessions Sue stated that she no longer needed to hold her bear to be brave. We had a final session the next week.

I believe the main reason why Sue and her family were so memorable to me as a therapist was their wholehearted belief in Sue's resources to overcome her trauma. They truly believed that Sue possessed the strength to be brave in difficult situations. Sue and her family were solution builders. I have had many other memorable cases but this one I'll never forget.

Q. Has the use of SFT impacted you in your personal life? If so, please explain.

A. As I have previously mentioned, I personally identify with the core values and beliefs of SFT. The model is not part of me but all of me; my worldview is reflected in SFT's tenets. I have learned about myself, others, and the power of language through SFT. The model is a constant reminder that hope exists!

Q. What are some key personality traits that you think are shared among solution focused practitioners?

A. Fortunately I have had the experience of being around SF therapists for some time. I have found that SF therapists not only view their clients differently but have a different outlook on life. One misconception about SFT is that SF therapists are always positive and wear rose-colored glasses. While it is true that SF therapists tend to have a more optimistic outlook on life, what really sets them apart from other therapists and people is their utmost respect for people. Possessing a nonjudgmental attitude toward other people and life seems to be the key characteristic of SF practitioners. I have never been around a group of more respectful people than SF therapists. It is so refreshing to work and interact with these individuals.

Q. What are some common mistakes that therapists trying on the model make most often? If you had a chance to guide them differently, how would you do so?

A. I think the most common mistake that new SF therapists make is trying to do SFT solely by using the interventions. This model is so much more than interventions. From my perspective, SF interventions are helpful suggestions of how to do SFT. In order to truly be an SF therapist, from my perspective, one must do the following: (a) truly believe in the philosophical underpinnings, (b) listen intently to your clients, (c) ask questions based on the client's conversation that moves the client closer to his or her desired future, (d) go slow with clients, and (e) do more of what works. Other details may exist but these five components, from my perspective, are essential to being an SF therapist. As you can tell, I didn't include the classic interventions in my list. It is not that I don't believe they are part of the model; it is that they are not the focus of the model from my perspective.

Q. What are some things you notice students doing while trying on this model that lets you know this model may fit them?

A. The main thing that lets me know that SFT is a good fit for my students/trainees lies in their core being. It all goes back to my response about the key traits of SF therapists. I think SFT is one of those models that either fits or it doesn't. If as a therapist you believe any of the following, SFT is *not* a good fit: (a) the therapist is the expert on what the client needs do, (b) it is important to understand the details of the presenting problem in order to reach a solution, and/or (c) therapy is about altering the personality/characteristic of a person. While there are other conflicting beliefs, these seem to be the more prominent.

Q. If you were training therapists in the SFT model, what strategies would you use to train them and how would you present the material?

A. My philosophy about training is the same as therapy; the trainee is the expert of how he or she learns best. I have had trainees share with me what works best for them and I have adapted my training to their needs. My trainees have expressed that they find role-plays to be extremely useful. When I am training therapists to do SFT in a group setting I give them an outline of the group format and ask volunteers to role-play. Those trainees not involved in the role-play watch the process from behind a one-way mirror. At the end of the training session, all of the trainees talk about what they noticed that worked, what was helpful, and what type of training experience would be helpful for the subsequent training sessions.

Another helpful tool in training, I have been told, is watching expert SF therapists on video. As a student I can remember watching full-length therapy sessions in my classes. I can remember feeling overwhelmed with all of the details. So, I have adjusted using videos in training a bit. One of the research teams I'm on uses a method called microanalysis to analyze small segments of video (Bavelas, McGee, Phillips, & Routledge, 2000). I have learned from this project that there is so much information contained in a small piece of tape that I only show short clips when I train SF therapists. I commonly will show them a few minutes of video and ask them to talk about what worked. In addition, I ask my trainees to discuss what they notice about the interaction between the client and the therapist. I believe that using video *clips* for training is not only helpful but essential.

Q. If you could pick a pioneer solution focused therapist who impacted your work, who would you name and why?

A. I would have to say several pioneers have impacted my work as an SF therapist. I will start at the beginning of my training. As a master's student, one of my professors, Terry Trepper, asked if any students were interested in doing an outcome study comparing SFT with a traditional model for substance abusers. Dr. Trepper, along with his colleague Dr. Eric McCollum, was working on a grant submission at the time and they were interested in having some pilot data. So, as a young and eager student *very* interested in SFT, I gladly volunteered. This project opened the door to meet other pioneers. Drs. Trepper and McCollum introduced me to Steve de Shazer, Insoo Kim Berg, Yvonne Dolan, and the list goes on and on. Honestly, there are too many pioneers to list that have positively influenced my work! I have been very fortunate to learn from them all of them.

Q. What developments would you like to see in the future of this model?

A. I am very interested in SFT research and having our model internationally recognized as an evidence-based approach. As previously mentioned, several individuals have begun making strides toward this goal. I am very passionate about this effort. It is so important for SFT to become recognized as an EBP for one main reason. Some insurance companies are already requiring that services be evidence-based. This means that if SFT is not listed on an EBP registry, therapists will not be allowed to use the model in their practice. While this trend is just beginning, my prediction is that within several years most insurance providers will require some type of documentation stating that the treatment being used is evidence-based. This reality should inspire all SF clinicians and researchers to do their part in getting SFT widely recognized as an EBP. It would be tragic to lose the ability to do what we know works for our clients.

You might be thinking, "What can I do to help?" One need is to have more outcome and process research published. If you have collected data but have not published it, I would encourage you to do so. If you have wanted to collect data on SFT, now is the time! Most EBP lists require published studies. If you aren't interested in doing research but have the freedom within your practice or agency to collect data, I would encourage you to partner with a researcher. By partnering with an SFT researcher, you can offer an invaluable resource to the field.

The Solution-Focused Brief Therapy Association (SFBTA) is making efforts to help clinicians and researchers connect to further the EBP effort. Their Web site (www.sfbta.org) provides links to clinicians and researchers in order to encourage collaboration. As new studies are completed, the Web site will offer updates on the results. Another way to help in our effort is to search for more EBP lists where SFT studies can be submitted. There are lots of lists giving their "EBP stamp" for specific populations. Identifying and sharing these lists with one another is important in our efforts. Additionally, everyone can help the SFT EBP movement at their local and state levels. Each state, and sometimes each county, determines the criteria for evidence-based practices. You can contact your local and state respective organizations (e.g., social work, marriage and family therapy, etc.) and ask them if they have criteria for evidence-based practices. Some states will consider treatments evidence-based if a model is listed on *any* EBP registry. Other states don't have specific criteria. While exploring who determines which models are evidence-based, you will find that it can be nebulous. Thus, understanding how your local and/or state system determines EBP is important. The more counties and states that recognize SFT as an EBP, and the more federal registries that give their stamp of approval, the better.

Again, I strongly encourage you to help in this effort. If you would like more information on how you can make a difference, please contact me. I know you are thinking that this sounds like an infomercial; it is. There is no way I can talk about the future of SFT without discussing the SFT evidence-based movement and my plea to everyone to do their part.

EDITOR'S COMMENT

I have had the pleasure of having several conversations with Dr. Smock and each time I was moved by her passion to build the evidence base of this approach. Each time, she strongly encouraged students and professionals to conduct research on the approach. She has also been generous with her research and resources. Building a research base and accomplishing the goal of having this approach accepted as evidence-based is a daunting task; it is heartening to know that Dr. Smock is one of many working toward this goal.

—Elliott Connie

REFERENCES

Bavelas, J. B., McGee, D., Phillips, B., & Routledge, R. (2000). Microanalysis of communication in psychotherapy. *Human Systems: The Journal of Systemic Consultation & Management, 11,* 47–66.

Corcoran, J., & Pillai, V. (2007). A review of the research on solution-focused therapy. *British Journal of Social Work, 10,* 1–9.

Kim, J. S. (2008). Examining the effectiveness of solution-focused brief therapy: A meta-analysis. *Research on Social Work Practice, 18,* 107–116.

Stams, G. J., Dekovic, M., Buist, K., & de Vries, L. (2006). Effectiviteit van oplossingsgerichte korte therapie; een meta-analyse [Efficacy of solution-focused brief therapy: A meta-analysis]. *Gedragstherapie* [*Behavior Therapy*], *39,* 81–94.

11 Learning With Enthusiasm

RAYYA GHUL

When you touch people with compassion, their good characteristics emerge.

—Madhav Ghimire

MY INTRODUCTION TO THE SOLUTION FOCUSED THERAPY MODEL

In 1995 I returned to work as an occupational therapist after a three-year maternity break. I was working part-time in a community mental health team and feeling rather lost. Although I had worked in mental health services off and on for the previous 15 years, I had never worked in the community and I was also feeling very rusty after having been at home. My manager told me that I could go on a training course to regain my confidence. I had no idea what to choose or what was on offer. A couple of days later, a flyer was put on my desk advertising courses in solution focused therapy. I had never heard of it but I thought it sounded interesting and my manager agreed to fund the training.

I didn't realize it at the time, but I was lucky enough to have picked up a flyer from the Brief Therapy Practice in London (now known simply as BRIEF), the organization which had pioneered the use of solution focused therapy in Britain and had strong links with Milwaukee where SFT had been developed by Steve de Shazer and Insoo Kim Berg. I signed up for a 4-day course and was very excited to be journeying up to London and back each day and doing something quite different from looking after small children.

My trainer was Evan George, one of the cofounders of the Brief Therapy Practice and coauthor of *Problem Into Solution* (George, Iveson, & Ratner, 1998). Evan is a quiet-spoken man who exudes an aura of compassion and I instantly warmed to his thoughtful and open style of training.

I am by nature an enthusiastic learner and I eagerly participated in the paired exercises. We were invited to look for the underlying assumptions to the questions we were trying out. I quickly saw that they assumed the client had preexisting strengths, qualities, and resources. I was pleased; this fitted in well with my philosophy as an occupational therapist. We focus on a person's ability rather than their disability and look for solutions to their barriers to daily living. I was looking forward to the point in the training when we were taught what to do with the clients to help them get better.

At the end of the third day, Evan showed a video of himself working with a woman. As I recall, she was a grandmother who was supporting her daughter and grandchildren and possibly undertook other support roles in her community. I think she had presented with depression. At one point Evan asked something like, "I'm curious, when does a busy person like you have time for yourself?" There was a visible shift in the woman's manner and she began to engage much more with building solutions. I was fascinated by how Evan had achieved this and went up to speak to him at the end of the day.

I asked him how he had known that this question was the right one to ask. Evan replied, "I didn't, I was just curious." I said, "Yes, but how did you work out what her problem was and know that was the right question?" He replied, "I didn't, I was just curious." I then asked the same question in two or three different ways and he still just responded by telling me he was "just curious."

I became more irritated and then angry with him each time, to the extent that my frustration led to me becoming tearful. Evan, who must have been quite perplexed, said, "What do you want, Rayya?" I replied, "I just want you to tell me how you did it, how did you know what to ask? You must have worked out what her problem was, and chosen the right question based on some sort of knowledge or reasoning and I want to know how you did that and I can't understand why you won't tell me!"

Evan was looking at me kindly and slightly concerned and he very gently said, once again, "I'm not withholding anything from you. I asked that question because it was something I was curious about. I really don't know what else to say."

Biting back my tears, I left the building, walked to the bus stop, and caught the bus across London to my friend's house where I was staying. I was sitting on the top of a double-decker bus in a window seat and as I watched London go by I started crying uncontrollably, quietly, with my face pressed against the glass hoping no one would notice. Why was I so upset? I really wanted to learn how to do solution focused therapy. It had resonated so strongly with me in the training but I felt there was something I hadn't "got" about it and if I didn't get it then I wouldn't be able to do it. I felt really angry with Evan. What did he mean by saying he was "just curious"? That was ridiculous! I had learned psychology at college during my occupational therapy training. I had learned counseling skills based on psychotherapeutic principles. I had worked at the Maudsley Hospital, the world-renowned center of excellence in psychiatry, and had always been highly praised for my work. I kept up to date, I read loads, I had a phenomenal memory, and I knew lots of things about people and therapy. I knew that there must be some underlying pattern or theory that Evan was drawing upon or else what he was doing wouldn't be so effective. He was applying some sort of knowledge and I desperately wanted to have the same command of it as he appeared to have.

And then the thought struck me, what if he *really* was just curious? What would that mean? As my raging thoughts subsided I began to reflect on the last three days of training. Right from the beginning it was evident that a primary underlying assumption of solution focused therapy was that the client had strengths, qualities, and resources and was able to create workable solutions for him/herself when given the opportunity through the interview. How would Evan's curiosity fit in with that? Very quickly I realized that, of course, if the clients really are the experts in their own lives, then curiosity is the only sensible stance to take on the part of the therapist. But why hadn't I got that before? Why did I have such a strong emotional reaction?

I don't know where thoughts come from. In the West, we associate them with the head. Buddhists have a more holistic view that includes all emotions, sensations, and thoughts as phenomena arising in a space that is vast and limitless. I had been a Buddhist for some years and practiced sitting meditation and was therefore much attuned to my experiences. Therefore, when I say that a thought came up from deep in my stomach and spread through my entire body in dull waves, you will perhaps understand how much it shook me to finally realize what I had to do in order to learn solution focused therapy. I had to give up being the expert. I had to give up knowing better.

For me this was not a trivial matter, a mere shift in attitude. As a child I was very clever and a quick learner. I was also rather odd (nowadays I suppose I would have been dubbed a geek) and found it hard to make friends. I was foreign, culturally different to my British companions, and at secondary school I was bullied in my early years. My only weapons were my intelligence and knowledge and it was the way I had learned to survive. Both my parents were refugees; my father from Palestine and my mother from Silesia. My father was a brilliant man, a professor and leading scholar in his field. When I begged for some material good such as pretty shoes or a toy I just *had* to have, he would smile and tap his head and say, "Things can always be taken away from you, but they can't take what you have in here." Knowing facts, techniques, theories, and technologies better than others had kept me sane and were the greatest riches one could own. This was what I was going to have to sacrifice in order to do solution focused therapy.

When I returned to the final day of the training, it felt as though the whole world had changed. I could see that the questions were just really good questions. I was no longer trying to work out the underlying theory in psychological terms. The feeling of desperation had left me, and my mind felt clearer and more open. I found that when I was listening to my partners in the exercises, I could relax and hear what they were saying without wondering about their underlying motives or hidden agendas.

This "one-down" (versus one-up) stance toward the person is what most drew me to practice solution focused therapy. When I returned to work I found myself relating quite differently to my clients. I was curious about them, how they led their lives, how they had coped, and where their strengths lay. Gradually I saw that everyone is an expert in his or her own life; as therapists we only enter their lives for a short period and cannot hope to know all the intricate details of their inner and outer worlds. I found that asking solution focused questions allowed my clients to discover and rediscover their own strengths and solutions. I didn't have to hold all the responsibility for their lives as they gradually took control. What a relief! After a few weeks I couldn't believe how much my stress levels had reduced and how much I looked forward to seeing my clients.

I quickly became aware of how compatible the solution focused approach was with occupational therapy. Occupational therapists help people regain their ability to participate in daily living activities. This includes all the activities that encompass self-care, leisure, and productive occupations—not just work. To do this we are trained in activity analysis. This is the process of analyzing everything that goes into doing things! And we do it in enormous detail. For example, making a cup of tea might seem like a fairly simple task: Put water into the kettle, turn the kettle on, put a tea bag into a cup and pour the boiling water over it, add milk and sugar if you want. However, just putting the water in the kettle involves a huge amount of cognitive processing—from having the idea of making tea, the knowledge and memory of the sequences and the perceptual processing required to know when the kettle is full enough, to orienting yourself in the kitchen. Physical strength is required to lift the kettle, turn the tap while holding the kettle, and then transport it. And there are lots of smaller stages such as opening the kettle lid, turning the tap, regulating the water flow, turning off the tap, and so on.

Because we work with people with any type of impairment, this knowledge is invaluable. For example, someone with an amputation of an arm will need a different strategy to fill the kettle; someone who has become blind needs to know when the kettle is filled; a person who has a learning disability might need help to remember the sequences and safety aspects. As I worked in community mental health services, my clients did not usually need this type of microanalysis, but I would spend time analyzing the patterns and habits of their daily lives, how they spent their day, and organized their week. People with mental health problems often lead chaotic or limited daily lives because of the effects of their difficulties with things like motivation, decision making, and lack of structure (many people with mental health problems are unemployed and don't have the ready-made timetable that work provides).

As you can imagine, analysis on this micro level is quite difficult and requires a lot of engagement in a person's life. However, when I starting asking my clients the miracle question, a solution focused question that asks people to describe in detail what they would be doing when their lives are on track, I found the clients were doing their own activity analysis. Instead of having to painstakingly map their week, they were coming up with their own plans. After asking the miracle question, one finds out what part of the miracle is already happening and this proves invaluable in identifying parts of the client's daily life that are more satisfying and supportive. Subsequently one asks for a "next small step" and I was amazed at how sensible and insightful my clients were into their needs. For example, a woman with severe depression identified getting up at a regular time in the morning and getting dressed for three days out of seven as her small step. Very quickly she built on this and in a few weeks not only was back to a more regular daily routine but saw her mood improve rapidly with each small success. Of course, this was the exact same small step that I would have recommended as an occupational therapist, but without the preceding solution focused conversation I am sure it would have been met with the usual apathy: "What's the point?"

Other times, I found that clients came up with solutions that were so random I could never have hoped to come up with them, however much analysis I had done. I had a client, a middle-aged woman with two teenage sons and a husband who she felt didn't pay her much attention or give her support. She was depressed and frustrated with what she saw as a life of drudgery and servitude. She had described her miracle but felt it was so unattainable she could not come up with a next small step. I remembered the two basic tenets of solution focused therapy: If it's not broke, don't fix it. If it's not working, do something different (de Shazer, 1985). Therefore I suggested she should go away and when she felt stuck she should "do something different than what you normally do." When she returned in a fortnight I could tell straightaway from her demeanor that something had changed. She was grinning from ear to ear.

She told me that one evening, around 6:00 P.M., she had gone to prepare dinner and was angry to find dirty clothes left on the floor, washing up on the draining board, and general mess left by the men of the house. She remembered her homework and wondered what she could do that was different. She went into the living room and selected one of her son's heavy metal music CDs, put it on extremely loud and started to dance wildly to it! Her sons and husband came in and she ignored them and carried on dancing for half an hour. During this time, all the clothes were cleared away, dinner was started, and apparently from that point on the whole situation at home had changed. I learned how creative people can be from that woman.

For me, this is the most exciting aspect of working in a solution focused way. Apart from the reduction in my own stress levels due to being able to trust my clients to find their own solutions, it became a regular source of amazement and delight to see how resourceful and creative my clients could be when I worked in a solution focused way. People with mental health problems are generally seen as incapacitated and needy, requiring huge amounts of input from a range of professionals. This tends to result in clients being treated in such a way that their sense of capacity is reduced further and their dependence on professional help is increased. This is not deliberate; most people who work in mental health services care deeply about helping people and do what they do out of the best intentions and because they are trained that way. Although as an occupational therapist I had been trained to be an enabler rather than a helper, I also subscribed to the view of the mental health client as needing considerable help. After working in a solution focused way for some time I realized that this is a limited and *limiting* view.

As I gained confidence in using the solution focused approach, my belief in my clients grew. Rather than simply asking a question as I had been doing initially, I think my whole stance probably changed and the clients could sense that I was regarding them as resourceful and capable right from the beginning. I never forgot Evan's lesson about curiosity and have come to realize that a genuine interest in people's lives allows them to feel they are experts in their own world and experience. In that sense I came to think of myself more as a consultant or coach than a therapist.

WORKING WITH CLIENTS: THE PROFESSIONAL IMPACT OF SFT

As an occupational therapist, I was already working to enable my clients to become more independent and develop their own coping strategies for daily living, but the language and communication skills I used reflected my original training. I had been taught to focus on clients' feelings when talking to them, to paraphrase what they said to me, and to reflect it back. I listened hard for underlying issues, wondered if they were in denial about something, and thought that therapy was going well if my clients cried because this meant they were in touch with their feelings. If they didn't want to talk, or became oppositional in some way, I would describe this as resistance. However, I was also able to talk to clients about their daily lives and take them out into the community, into cafes and bowling alleys, swimming pools and workplaces, where I would chat naturally in order to provide a role model and put people at ease. To tell the truth, I had become increasingly suspicious of the need to talk about feelings all the time and to imagine there was always some hidden agenda. I had noticed that whenever I slipped into this more therapeutic type of talk, my clients became more guarded or they would go over and over the same issues and it would be hard to move them forward.

When I started working in a solution focused way I felt liberated. I could have conversations with people about what mattered to them and focus on what they would like to be doing. This fitted in more naturally with occupational therapy practice and I felt that I had found a much better language for my profession. Occupational therapy enables people to get on with their lives through engaging them in everyday activities and by helping people relearn old skills or learn new ones. We help get structure and pattern back so that new, better habits can be formed. Talking to people about what they would be doing differently meant I could quickly prioritize goals for intervention with my clients. Better still, they often came up with their own solutions. At first I wasn't sure which questions to ask so I would lay out my prompt sheets on the floor in front of me and look through them before deciding which question to ask. One day, a client said, "Don't ask me that question, ask me that one instead," pointing to a different sheet of paper.

I was reminded recently that Steve de Shazer made a distinction between goal-focused and solution focused therapy (de Shazer, 1994). Occupational therapy is very goal-focused and is very good at working out small steps to reach goals. However, clients often seemed lacking in motivation to engage in working toward goals or they would lose momentum or their progress would be halted when some life event got in the way. This seemed to change when I started using solution focused questions. Being solution focused is much more than simply goal setting. It is about getting people to describe the life they want to live so their goals are set in the rich complexity of a human life. A goal is a single point toward which someone works in a linear fashion. A solution is one of many possibilities that could help someone move toward his or her idea of a preferred future. The clients I worked with got excited about solutions where before they had felt oppressed by goals. Goals are often therapist or agency led whereas solutions are generated by the clients out of their own experience and expertise.

Rather than getting different results when using solution focused therapy it was almost as though I started getting completely different clients. All my clients were resourceful, talented, and able to take control of their lives. They were able to come up with creative and successful solutions and found the motivation to work toward them. They were able to deal better with unexpected events or setbacks and they recovered more quickly than before.

I was referred to more and more difficult clients, some who had previously been in weekly therapy with psychotherapists and cognitive behavioral therapists and were not making progress or were presented to me as untreatable. They would comment on how different it was working with me. One of the main remarks was that they felt understood for the first time. Many said that I really understood how they felt, which was surprising considering I never asked about feelings! Other observations included feeling respected, feeling that I wasn't trying to manipulate them, and feeling that they were listened to. Many clients commented on the amount of laughter in the sessions and also they began to wonder why they had had to talk so much about the past with previous therapists. However, the most common comment I heard was that they were surprised at how much progress they had made in a short time when previously they had been in therapy for months or years without substantial changes taking place.

It's very tempting to try and pin down exactly why solution focused therapy is so effective. I firmly believe that solution focused therapy is radically different to all other forms of therapy because of the nonexpert stance on the part of the therapist that permeates and underpins every question. But does one really have to believe that the clients have their own solutions and capacity to achieve them—is it enough to simply ask the questions? Does one have to ask all parts of the solution focused process; future focus, exceptions/what's working now, and small signs of the solution happening—or is there one part that is more effective than another?

Having worked with many clients I have come to believe that there is often one part of the process that really resonates with clients. For some, creating the rich detailed picture of the future opens up unconsidered possibilities; for others, the possibility that some part of their current situation may not be so terrible provides a glimmer of hope; and for others, the recognition of strengths and resources gives confidence to move forward. The setting of a small step is enormously powerful. This is different from the objectives of a goal-setting approach. Because the goal is a fixed point in the future, objectives are often rigid sequential stages.

If something unexpected happens or an unforeseen event conspires to push one off course, objectives become unattainable or it is difficult to regain direction. In contrast, a next small step is always in relation to where one is now and moving toward a general direction of the preferred future. The beauty of the next small step is that it is flexible and can respond to anything that life throws at you. Of course the "future perfect" is important to establish but it is a compass, rather than a map. While the world is changing around you, the next small step can always be set by the compass of the future perfect, and everyone, regardless of circumstances, can always set one small, achievable step. If the unexpected occurs, then one can still always set a next small step because there is flexibility—it fits better with the messiness of real life. This is an easy technology to reproduce on a daily basis.

I think that solution focused therapy is effective because it does not have anything surplus to requirement; the requirement being a conversation that focuses on helping people clarify the way they would like their life to be, and on helping them develop a way to move toward that utilizing their own expertise, strengths, and resources. There is no theory to distract one from listening to what people are saying. There are no questions that focus on problems, barriers, or distractions from the task in hand. The questions all center on simple realities rather than the exploration of abstract constructs and fleeting emotional states. Its simplicity is its greatest strength.

I found that my clients were also great trainers in solution focused therapy. I learned a lot from them; how creative and resilient people are, how people just need to be given space and time to come up with their own solutions, and how it's often hard to know whether therapy is working until long after the session is ended.

One of my favorite cases was a woman who was referred to me because she was suffering from anxiety and depression, which was beginning to impact on her ability to work and raise her family. She worked as an attendant at the local garage. When she came to see me she revealed that she had suffered sexualized abuse by her father and that memories of this were resurfacing and causing her symptoms. I was quite new to working in a solution focused way but I started as I normally would, by engaging her in some problem-free talk. I found out about her family life and her hobbies, which included creative writing. I then asked her about her preferred future and she described it in great detail and was able to identify times in the present where parts of her aspiration were already happening. I had attended a workshop with Yvonne Dolan (Dolan, 2000) and one with Allan Wade (Wade, 1997) and used some of their questions to elicit strengths and signs of resistance. This session fell just before the Christmas break, so I wasn't able to see her again for about four weeks.

At this time, it was more common to give clients homework (de Shazer, 1985) so on an impulse I suggested a task to her. As she loved creative writing, I suggested she write me a short story about herself and the theme would be that she was on her way to see me for the last time, when her miracle had happened, and she was reflecting on how she had achieved that miracle. To be honest, I didn't expect her to write the story, but I thought, as a writer, it would probably go round her head and perhaps help to form some solutions that she could put into effect.

At our next appointment four weeks later, she came in grinning, sat down, and handed me a notebook in which she had written the story. It was written in perfect handwriting with no crossings out. I started reading it and quickly realized this was an exceptional piece of writing, but it was too long for me to read in the session so I said I would read it later. As is customary in a second session, I asked her what was better. "Everything," she said, beaming at me. I was really shocked and frankly disbelieving but I hid it well and asked her to tell me more. She described how writing the story had cleared her mind, and helped her make some important decisions about herself, her relationship with her husband, and her children. Furthermore, she had decided to go back to college to train to become a hairdresser and would eventually set up her own hairdressing business!

Now, I hadn't been using solution focused therapy for very long and I was a bit stunned by all of this. Inwardly I wondered if she had become a little manic—some habits die hard. However, I congratulated her and complimented her and asked for her next small step. She told me she was going to investigate hairdressing courses.

After the session I sat down and read her story and before long I was alternating between laughing out loud and crying. She was a brilliant writer and the story was an incredible description of her recovery, step by step, interspersing her memories of the past abuse with hopes and dreams of the future. It was rooted in the realities of her present life and contained clear solutions to practical issues. When I finished the story I decided to, in a sense, publish it. I know all writers secretly want to see themselves in print. I typed up the story using software that turned it into book pages and printed a cover on a card. I then sewed the cover and pages together as I had learned in bookbinding classes as a child at school. At the next session two weeks later I presented her with her book and told her how impressed I was with what she had done. It was her turn to be stunned and she cried, saying she couldn't believe I had gone to all that trouble and it was the best sign she had that she was ready to get on with her life on her own.

After she was discharged, Sharon would send me regular updates and I know that she did train as a hairdresser and set up her own business. The story that she wrote, "One Day" by Sharon Carter (Carter, 1994), has become a solution focused resource and traveled round the world. Sharon gave permission for it to be given to other survivors of abuse in the hope that it might help them. Working with Sharon was a humbling experience as it made me realize how easy it would have been for me to pathologize her, assuming that someone with a history of sexualized abuse would need a lot of time to overcome the damage. I think Sharon was very lucky that I had found solution focused therapy because it gave her the freedom to use her own strengths and resources to move forward quickly into her new life. Previously I would probably have spent the first session getting a detailed account of her problems and missed the most important piece of information. Without problem-free talk, I doubt I would have known that she enjoyed writing so much. This case broke the final niggling concerns that I had about solution focused therapy not really addressing deep-rooted problems always described in psychology as difficult to work with. After one session of solution focused therapy, Sharon literally rewrote her life.

LIFE OUTSIDE THE THERAPY ROOM: PERSONAL EFFECTS OF SFT

I suspect that solution focused therapy has had an impact on my personal life but I don't think I ever actively set out to incorporate it. The more one works in a solution focused way, the more one's perspective changes subtly. I know that the way I approach my children is probably influenced by a solution focused perspective. Instead of assuming that I knew why they were behaving in a certain way I would try to interact directly with what they were doing in the present moment. This is about remaining, as we say, on the surface. For example, if I came into the room and found them engaged in a destructive activity—pulling all the leaves off my plant, for example—I would ask them what they were doing rather than shouting at them that they were being naughty. Usually they had a perfectly logical explanation that had evolved from an initial play idea. I could then point out my perspective and the plant's. They rarely repeated the behavior and became quite considerate at a young age.

I also used the "do something different" principle quite a lot. It wasn't uncommon for my younger daughter to storm into the room and make some demand in a rude manner. I would tell her in a friendly way that I was happy to listen to her but the way she was addressing me wouldn't work very well, so I sent her out of the room and told her to think up a better way and then come back in. Unfortunately she is now, at 14, a very skilled negotiator and master at getting me to buy her things!

I find it very hard to generate ideas of a preferred future so I haven't found that particular aspect useful for myself. I want too much and too many different things. I want the world and I want it now! If I encounter some block or have an issue, I will then use solution focused strategies such as looking at what's worked in the past, being confident that exploring many possibilities is worthwhile, and focusing on what I can do right now. Recently when I found myself very overworked this was invaluable because I could focus on what I needed to do without getting overwhelmed by my feelings. It was tough, but just by reminding myself of my personal signs and strategies for coping, I got through this difficult period.

One of the things I love about meeting other solution focused practitioners is seeing how different we all are! However, if I had to focus on some key similarities, I would say that we all tend to be quite relaxed about status and don't take ourselves too seriously. I guess when one is practicing a therapy that relies on taking a "one-down" position, one doesn't feel the need to show off or be important quite so much. I always seem to laugh a lot around solution focused people and find them very welcoming and collaborative.

TRAINING AND REFLECTION

Since 1998 I have been running training courses in solution focused therapy, primarily for people working in mental health services in the United Kingdom. For the most part the approach has been received enthusiastically, although some people wonder about its effectiveness with so-called difficult cases given the simplicity of the method. As most of the cases I have dealt with could be considered complex or difficult I tend to think that it is precisely its simplicity that helps to untangle them. Nonetheless when people first encounter the approach it is natural that they try to fit it within their own experience and prior training. I know from my own experience that the shift from expert to nonexpert is a hard one to make and professions with accountability for high-risk cases are wary of ways of working that might put them or their clients at increased risk. I often invite people just to try out one question here and there in order to build up confidence in the approach.

I'm not sure that I can identify the students who will end up wanting to do SFT and feel it fits with their way of working. People learn in different ways and some students get very excited about the method while others take more time to think it through and reflect on how it fits with their work. Some of those who are initially very enthusiastic will go on and make huge changes to their work and their organizations but many also seem to run out of steam quite quickly and are unwilling to do the practice required to build up solid solution focused skills. I have found some people who were very negative and challenging in the classroom are, two years later, working in an exclusively solution focused way; and others who appear quite untouched by their exposure to solution focus. I guess I am reluctant to make assumptions or hypotheses about my students in the same way I am reluctant to do that with clients.

All students take some time to make the shift to solution focused working and there are some common mistakes I have observed people make. Probably the most common mistake is to try to do solution focused therapy too rigidly and invest too much importance in doing it a certain way. This tends to lead to being solution forced rather than solution focused. In this instance I would recommend that the therapist slow down and give plenty of time for the client to answer. Rather than moving on, the therapist could ask a question that expands the topic such as, "What else?"' or one that elicits more detail such as, "What would you be doing?" or "Can you tell me a little more about what you do when you are feeling confident?"

Novice practitioners are often too eager to ask the questions but then don't know what to do if the answers are not quite what they expected. I think this is strongly related to holding on to the expert stance. If you believe that solution focused therapy has to be done in a certain order or that certain questions have to be asked, you are still imagining that the therapist is more important than the client and that you know better than the client. Otherwise you would not be so concerned about the answer of the client being right or wrong or disconcerting. The questions are powerful in their own right, but the real power of solution focused therapy is in being able to listen and accept what the client is saying and respond to that rather than worrying about whether the answer will lead on to the next question you want to ask. It takes a lot of practice to get over the tendency to hypothesize about the client and to be genuinely open, but a good first step is to start to notice what happens when you allow yourself to be genuinely curious about what your client is saying rather than thinking about what your next question should be.

I use a variety of strategies to train people in solution focused therapy. The main thing that I do nowadays is to try to get people to get the difference between solution focused therapy and problem-solving techniques. This is because most people who encounter solution focused therapy initially regard it as a form of problem-solving. This is similar to thinking it is a goal-focused therapy. While solution focused therapy does help to solve problems and set and reach goals, it does not do so through conventional means.

My most recent strategy is to get students to work in pairs and choose a real-life problem to work on. I then ask them to do it in a problem-solving way; finding out as much detail as possible about the problem, and discussing some ways of solving it and giving each other advice based on what they've heard. I ask them to set a goal and to scale their confidence in attaining the goal on a scale of 0–10. I then elicit some feedback about how they found the process and what was useful. I have found people mostly report positive experiences.

After this I talk a little about solution focused therapy, its underpinning assumptions, principles of practice, and stance toward clients. I follow this by asking them to take the same problem they have already discussed and I take them step by step through the solution focused process. First they ask the miracle question with some additional questions to elicit detail such as, "What difference would that make?" or "What would make other people notice you doing this?" The next step is to get them to rate where they are in relation to the miracle on a scale of 0–10 and to ask, "How do you know you are at X?" which elicits exceptions and signs the miracle is already happening. I then ask them to form a next small step. Finally I ask them to look again at the goal they formed using the problem-solving approach and I ask them to rate their confidence in attaining it now.

After this I host a discussion around the differences in the two approaches. This is fascinating because most people feel much more confident in reaching their goals while others feel less confident. However, the reduction in confidence is not regarded as a negative—the participants report that using the solution focused approach made them realize their situation is more complex than they had previously appreciated or that the goal they had set before was unlikely to succeed. Overall the response so far has been incredibly positive with the participants saying that when involved in the solution focused approach they felt that the "therapist" was listening much better, that they felt much more engaged with the process, that it felt more grounded in reality, and that they felt more capable of managing their situations.

I also really like to use some visual representations for students and Figure 11.1 is a very simple slide that I use to show how the underlying assumptions are translated into what the therapist asks.

Another strategy I use is to link to the metaphorical side of the brain and I use a slide with a small quotation from Antoine de Saint Exupery: "If you want to build a ship, don't drum up the men to gather wood, divide the work and give orders. Instead, teach them to yearn for the vast and endless sea" (quoted in goodreads.com).

I think this sums up perfectly why solution focused therapy is so good at motivating people to change even when their lives are very challenging.

Figure 11.1 Spoken and unspoken questions by the solution focused therapist.

INFLUENCES

I have been very lucky to meet many talented solution focused therapists who have been unfailingly generous in sharing their knowledge and encouraging my skills. To have to choose one person who has impacted in my work is virtually impossible. Some of the people who have inspired me are Evan George from BRIEF who patiently allowed me to be confused and come to my own path to solution focus; Yvonne Dolan who helped me to develop my work with survivors of sexualized abuse; Linda Metcalf who inspired me to work with excluded teenagers; Charlie Johnson who helped me to develop a service for people with chronic pain; and Mark McKergow and Paul Z. Jackson who inspired me to be more creative in applying a solution focus to my own profession.

However, I would have to say the biggest impact has come from Steve de Shazer, whose books I constantly referred to as I was trying to become solution focused. In particular, I relied on *Words Were Originally Magic,* which helped me to understand the importance of staying on the surface. Chapter 2 on "Language & Structure and Structure & Language" is to my mind one of the most important pieces of writing in the solution focused canon as it is the key to understanding why solution focused therapy is so radically different to all other forms of therapy.

I joined the SFT-L listserv in 1996 and found that to be an invaluable resource. It is the main reason I ended up meeting so many other solution focused therapists. When I did my training I was the only person in my area doing solution focused work and I felt very isolated. An unfortunate by-product of becoming solution focused is that one becomes more and more averse to problem-focused thinking and one can come into conflict with one's colleagues due to the differing perspectives. Knowing that there was a space where I could feel safe to discuss issues that were arising was a lifesaver in my early years as a solution focused practitioner. I was overwhelmed by the welcome I received on the SFT-L list and this eventually gave me the confidence to attend my first European Brief Therapy Association conference in Bruges in 1998. This was a fantastic experience as I met many people with whom I had been corresponding and found that they were very willing to help me and encourage me. There didn't seem to be the same sort of professional rivalry or hierarchy I had encountered at other therapy conferences. On the contrary, the atmosphere was one of interest in and celebration of each others' work regardless of any particular status.

Over the past 10 years there has been a blossoming of research and literature on solution focused working and the approach is becoming more recognized and sought after. One of the exciting things is the way solution focused working is being adopted into preexisting professions rather than simply being practiced as a therapy. There are nurses, social workers, psychologists, teachers, care workers, doctors, speech and language therapists, musicians, and organizational consultants all applying a solution focus to their work with wonderful results. In my own profession of occupational therapy I would very much like to see solution focus adopted as the primary language for engaging with clients. Occupational therapists already focus on ability rather than disability and are concerned with identifying what people can do, rather than what they cannot. We are holistic practitioners, looking at people's participation in systemic and contextual ways rather than simply as a function of the person. This all fits in very well with solution focus, which also gets people talking about what they will be doing differently when all the parts of their life are in place.

I would love to see solution focus filtering into the public consciousness and replacing the current medico-psychological paradigm that most lay people draw upon to explain their actions or solve personal problems. I have this fantasy about opening a women's magazine and seeing an article about how solution focus can help you talk to a friend who is having a hard time. You know the sort of article where it starts something like, "Do you find it hard to think of what to say when your best friend comes round to moan about her husband yet again, or if a colleague at work bursts into tears at the water cooler? A new approach called solution focus can equip you with some simple but effective ways of guiding the conversation to practical solutions and steps to improve the situation." I think it would be great if teenagers instinctively thought, "This isn't working; what could I do differently?" I think it could change the world if teachers looked at pupils in school and thought, "What are their particular strengths and resources? What can I do differently to enhance their performance?" Perhaps more marriages would survive if couples took the time to talk about what is going on when their partnership is working well and how they could do more of it.

I genuinely believe that solution focused therapy is unique among talking therapies because of its lack of the need to define some kind of pathology or problem in order to be effective. This is a radical idea because it challenges years of received wisdom since psychology became the dominant way of describing a person. Ideas such as personality, inner drives, the unconscious, the ego, and denial are so deeply entrenched in our vocabularies we rarely stop to question their validity. We are blinded by the huge body of empirical evidence that purports to prove these objects are real, having lost sight that they are objects created in the first place by the disciplines that study them. We therefore tend to think that the language of psychology describes real structures in the human psyche comparable to the organs of the body, but Steve de Shazer refutes this and suggests instead that it is language that *creates* reality rather than describing it (de Shazer, 1994).

Take a moment to think about that statement. What are the implications of adopting such a stance? If language has the power to create reality, then in each therapeutic conversation, a person and his or her life are being created and re-created. If the conversation focuses on problems and pathologies, then what is being created? If, on the other hand, the conversation focuses on possibilities, options, choices, strengths, and evidence of potential for change, how might people's view of themselves be transformed? It's an interesting thought, possibly a daunting one, but if we believe that what we talk about and how we talk about it makes a difference, it's hard to think of a better way to bring about positive change than to use solution focused therapy.

My favorite quotation that encapsulates this idea that a life can be transformed in the space of a conversation is from a wonderful solution focused therapist and poet called Dvorah Simon. This is a solution focused haiku that she posted one day on the SFT-L mailing list:

> Life is working now,
> Given the right conditions.
> Now: what can they be?

EDITOR'S COMMENT

This chapter is one of my favorites. Rayya's enthusiasm for the model, both when she was learning as well as the way she writes about it now, is so clear. When Rayya agreed to contribute to this book, I had only heard of her by reputation; I had never been exposed to any of her work. So when her chapter arrived I became an instant fan. It is this type of passion and enthusiasm that Dr. Metcalf and I hoped to capture in this project. This passion is what attracts me to this approach and the people that use it. I can just imagine her in tears as she rode the bus home from the workshop where she saw SFT in action; she was already unknowingly demonstrating key traits that allow this model to flow: curiosity and passion.

—Elliott Connie

REFERENCES

Carter, S. (1994). *One day.* Unpublished: available on request from rayya.ghul@gmail.com.
de Shazer, S. (1985). *Keys to solution in brief therapy.* New York: Norton.
de Shazer, S. (1994). *Words were originally magic.* New York: Norton.
Dolan, Y. (2000). *Beyond survival: Living well is the best revenge.* London: BT Press.
George, E., Iveson, C., & Ratner, H. (1998). *Problem to solution: Brief therapy with individuals and families* (Rev. ed.). London: BT Press.
Wade, A. (1997). Small acts of living: Everyday resistance to violence and other forms of oppression. *Contemporary Family Therapy, 19*(1), 23–39.

12 My Encounter With the Solution Focused Therapy Model

DEBBIE HOGAN

If you want others to be happy, practice compassion: If you want to be happy, practice compassion.

—Dalai Lama

A NEW DISCOVERY

In the early 1980s, I worked as a therapist in a mental health center in the United States with the chronically mentally ill who were mostly schizophrenic patients. I was trained to believe that pathology resided within a person and medication was disseminated like candy. Side effects were common and more medication was given to offset them. I also worked in psychiatric hospitals for a few years with an interdisciplinary team of psychiatrists, psychologists, social workers, and therapists and we would discuss which diagnosis and treatment plan seemed appropriate for each patient. We discussed maintenance but rarely recovery. There was a belief that people didn't recover from mental illness. I learned a lot about pathology and grew more and more disillusioned by a system that didn't seem to be making a significant difference. The revolving-door syndrome was common, with our patients repeatedly going in and out of the hospital. I had a belief that treating people with respect and dignity was important. What I often witnessed was quite the opposite. Professional burnout was common in this setting and I began searching for ideas that would keep me engaged in my work.

My brother, who was also a therapist at that time, suggested I read *The Tao of Physics* by Fritjof Capra. It was mostly over my head but the few ideas I did understand were quite radical to me at that time. I was challenged and stretched such that it had a profound effect on the way I saw the world and the way I do therapy. I began to be aware of the predominant worldviews that shape how we view life and how the medical model and classical physics influence our way of doing therapy.

The enormous success of Newton's mechanistic model lasted until Albert Einstein's revolutionary ideas and quantum theory radically shifted our view of reality (Fisch, Weakland, & Segal, 1982). Quantum theory reveals that there is a basic oneness and interconnection of the universe, and that by our mere observation (even life at its smallest component like the atom) we, in effect, influence it. Life at its bare component is not static or linear but interactional. This revelation was very significant to me as a clinician since many clients would come for therapy wanting to know *the* definitive reason and cause of their problem, as if this could be accomplished.

Around the same time I read *The Tactics of Change* by Fisch, Weakland, and Segal (1982) and *Change* by Watzlawick, Weakland, and Fisch (1974) and was influenced a great deal by the team at the Mental Research Institute (MRI) in Palo Alto, California. They studied the phenomenon of change, not only how change occurs but how change can be promoted. The ideas of the MRI group gave me some hope. They proposed that rather than pathology residing within a person or system, difficulties arose out of an interactional pattern. I was drawn to this view that depathologized human difficulties and saw them more as a function of an interactional pattern. So, when I learned solution focused therapy, it seemed to integrate the key ideas I had found so helpful. I realized this was what I had been looking for.

I later learned that the MRI group often consulted with Milton Erickson. Being a big fan of Erickson, I studied Ericksonian hypnotherapy and psychotherapy and I learned hypnosis. I know that Erickson had a great influence on Steve de Shazer's and Insoo Kim Berg's work. I'm told that they spent part of the early years at the Brief Family Therapy Center studying and observing his work and exploring what actually helped people to change. Erickson did not have a theory of pathology but was known for his innovative and unconventional approaches to working with people.

Milton Erickson is one of my favorite human beings and he was a remarkable person. He was struck by polio at age 17 and paralyzed from the neck down. I was deeply moved by his determination and keen powers of observation, which enabled him to learn to walk again and eventually become a doctor who specialized in psychiatry. Erickson's work taught me about people's "forgotten learnings." He believed that people were walking resources and possessed a storehouse of ideas and experiences. Solution focused therapy is about tapping into people's competencies and reservoirs of stored experiences. That richness of experiences is often forgotten or unrealized. This has become one of the areas that I enjoy the most in working with clients—looking for our client's competencies and experiences to draw from, and the belief that they are capable.

One of my favorite Erickson examples is from *My Voice Will Go With You* (Rosen, 1991). On the spur of the moment he was asked to give a speech at a conference and he was not prepared. He got through it by reminding himself that he had all the knowledge and ability that he needed for just that moment and to trust what he knew. This has become an important part of my repertoire in moments when I feel anxious or insecure—to trust what I know and what I have learned. It has helped me in many situations where I have been momentarily immobilized by fear or anxiety. I think it has been a tremendous gift.

After seven years of working in a psychiatric setting, I decided to move to Singapore with my family and I started a private practice there. I specialized in marriage and family therapy and dealt with a variety of issues. Into my 17th year as a therapist, I started experiencing burnout. I worked really hard to be prepared for each session and tried to stay current on the latest treatment modalities and tried to come up with creative treatment interventions. I started to feel burdened and ineffective.

I began to meet regularly with a group of private practitioners and we shared cases and networked. That was where I first heard of solution focused therapy. Someone showed a video of Insoo Kim Berg working with an alcoholic. I was baffled that Insoo did not address the alcoholism (the "real" problem) but instead asked what he wanted, which was to find a job. In the second session he had gone for a job interview and had been alcohol-free for two weeks. I was intrigued by what I saw and wanted to learn more.

I called myself an eclectic because I borrowed ideas from several models but was not very satisfied with what I was doing with my clients.

I felt I was the proverbial jack of all trades, but master of none. I started gathering books and resources on solution focused therapy and was eager to learn more.

When Insoo Kim Berg and Steve De Shazer came to Singapore in October 1999, I couldn't believe my good fortune. It was the opportunity I was looking for. They conducted an introductory course and I believe over two hundred people attended. It was fascinating watching Insoo and Steve running the workshop together. I enjoyed watching them deal so expertly with the Singapore audience and handling the questions with such respect.

In 2000, I signed up for the first Graduate Diploma in SFT in Singapore conducted by Insoo, Brian Cade, Terese Steiner, Ariel Aambo, Wolfang Eberling, and others from Europe. The great value of this training was learning from so many different practitioners who specialized in different areas. Each module became an expansion of the model in a different setting.

Brian Cade came from a brief therapy perspective and came several times to conduct supervision sessions for us. I especially appreciated his work with adolescents and his use of humor in his therapy. Over many lunches and dinners we listened with great relish as he told us stories about Insoo, Steve, John Weakland, and other key people in the therapeutic community. I loved the fact that he had personally known John Weakland and some of the key people at the MRI. Brian added an invaluable dimension to our training because of his roots with the MRI and brief therapy. Terese demonstrated the solution building process with children using different tools such as blocks, puppets, stories, and other means of engaging children. For those of us working with children, it gave us some creative ways to do this. I had always been a little hesitant to work with adolescents and children in my practice. But after these workshops I began to accept more work with children. I'm glad I did because it has become one of my favorite areas. I was touched by the work Ariel was doing with the immigrant population in Norway and how he was able to help them identify their own resources and contribute meaningfully and with such dignity. Wolfing came from an organizational perspective and helped us learn how to use the ideas with teams and in a corporate setting.

It was about a 1.5-year study and it was the beginning of a radical change in my private practice. It felt like a roller coaster ride. After each workshop, I found new energy and resolved to try different things. However, after a while, it became very hard again. Insoo made it look so easy.

It was as if Insoo was a little parrot on my shoulder, saying, "It's easy to learn but hard to do!! Easy to learn but hard to do!"

There were also some pivotal learning moments during this training. One of those moments was her statement that, "If you are working harder than your client, then something is wrong." I had never heard that before. I thought it was my job to work harder and come up with clever interventions. Learning about the core assumptions helped to shape my understanding of the foundations of this approach. The shift from viewing difficulties from a problem-focused to a solution focused paradigm was another pivotal moment. I learned that being solution focused isn't the same as being a problem solver. I guess I had tried to be the "problem buster." I think I spent that year unlearning much of what I had learned about being a good therapist.

A few of us during this training would meet in between sessions and talk about what we were learning. We were excited about it and what we were doing with our clients. I think this enthusiasm made a huge difference. We were able to provide ongoing peer supervision and support.

My last face-to-face encounter with Insoo was in August of 2006 in Singapore at our First Asia Pacific Solution-Focused Approach Conference, in which she was our keynote speaker. During a break we had a few moments to chat. She pointed her finger at me and said jokingly, "You were the difficult one in class." I had to agree with her because I really struggled with some of the ideas she had taught us, which were such a far cry from what I had been trained to practice. I told her that now, in fact, I was her biggest fan and commented how much her work had impacted me both professionally and personally. She looked puzzled, cocked her head and said, "No, I had no idea. Tell me more." I was touched by her humbleness and unassuming nature. Insoo listened with keen interest. I don't think she really knew how much she affected people and how much of a presence she was.

Insoo and I began working on our next conference, scheduled for July 2007. We were in regular contact through e-mails up until the night before she died on January 10, 2007. Even at that point, there was no indication of illness, but excitement as she shared the news of what she had been doing in Europe. It was always amazing to me how she kept in touch with so many people, in various countries and continents, working on so many different projects, all at once. During one visit to Singapore I asked Insoo how she enjoyed spending her time when she was not working. She said, "I write." It is evident by the numerous books and articles she wrote that she loved what she was doing and had what seemed to be a never-ending desire to keep contributing, shaping, influencing, and mentoring.

THE PROFESSIONAL IMPACT OF SOLUTION FOCUSED THERAPY

Over the next few years I began noticing a shift in my practice. My sessions shortened from six to eight sessions to around four sessions, and sometimes only one or two sessions. It affected my pocketbook, but I decided to stay with the model because of the impact it was having on my clients.

I often got clients who came because they heard I worked differently from other therapists and they were ready to move on instead of talking about their problems all the time. One such client came after being in psychoanalysis for seven years, several times a week. He claimed he had an obsessive-compulsive disorder and was ready for something different. I asked him how the seven years of therapy had helped and he said, "It didn't." I was tempted to ask him when he realized that the therapy wasn't helpful. He was an expert on the problem and had a lot of speculation about why he had it and what kept it going, but didn't have a clear view of what he wanted instead. So we began to explore what he wanted and the times he could have given in to the problem but didn't. His countenance started to change. I think he began to see a small glimpse of himself as competent and capable. He left smiling, saying he had never thought of it like that before. A lot of what we do is to help reframe and offer a different way of looking at things.

Insoo taught me to have belief and trust that my clients would come up with their own solutions. She said the real learning happened outside of the therapy room. I've often been amazed at what clients say in a follow-up session about what they have done. Sometimes they want to give me credit and tell me they followed my advice when I actually didn't give them any. I really like the idea of staying curious and being amazed by their brilliance.

One thing I heard from clients that I had not heard before was that they started to feel some hope. This seemed to really resonate with couples who had been stuck for many years and were finally able to find something that made a difference. I think part of that difference was their shift from demonizing each other and playing the blame game to looking for small signs that things were already moving in the right direction. Building a picture of a preferred future and clarity around what they wanted, instead of what they didn't want, made a huge difference. Their energy and focus shifted. I've learned that getting details around the preferred picture is a type of mental rehearsing.

As I tried different things, it was exciting to see the impact it had on my clients. It was a more efficient way of working and change occurred much more quickly and with fewer sessions. I think I was learning to be a better therapist as a result and therefore more confident in the way I did therapy. I relied less on my own ability to be clever. I started listening differently. I was no longer looking for pathology and dysfunctional patterns but instead was listening for areas of competence and strengths.

During this learning curve, I started to experience some personal shifts. The solution focused ideas started helping me to deal differently with my own skeletons in my closet and to feel some hope and energy. This is a theme I hear from my students as well. They start to realize that their own perceptions and behavior are changing.

I do some executive coaching in my practice and worked with an executive who came in a suit and briefcase. He was all hunched over and had a deep frown on his face. He came saying his boss was going to fire him and his wife was going to divorce him if he didn't get help. He had been to several other therapists and was getting nowhere. He had been told he had a "shopping addiction" and he was wearing the label as if it was branded on his forehead. He had run up thousands of dollars on his credit card. It was a huge amount. He especially liked expensive art pieces and going to art auctions. I began to explore his "shopping addiction" asked if he had ever gone to an art auction and not bought anything. He looked puzzled and said he actually had done that recently. He was tempted to buy an expensive painting but resisted. I told him I was really baffled by that because everyone knows that a "shopping addict" cannot resist the temptation to buy things. I asked him if he had ever bought anything and then returned it. He looked puzzled and said he had actually purchased something recently and returned it. I told him I was really quite baffled by this because anyone knows that a real "shopping addict" never returns anything. They just stack things up in a room, whether they need it or not. I told him he was not a very good "shopping addict." His face changed after that and he started to think. He started to smile and said, "I know what to do!!" He left standing tall, shook my hand vigorously, and said he knew what he needed to do to face his marriage and job with some new energy and resolve.

I also get referrals from teachers and school counselors and some of them began to be curious about my approach. They noticed the improvements their students were making and they started making more referrals, including some of their difficult cases. One of the major things I learned about working with students was the importance of developing a useful goal—one the student was interested in working on. The model taught me about being respectful and honoring what the client wants. In the past I think I was more invested in what the referring person wanted and maybe tried to bully the student into working on someone else's goal. As a result, some teachers and school counselors started attending our training programs to learn the approach themselves. I think that is what convinced me even more to keep to the model.

CASE STORY: THE OVERWEIGHT WOMAN WHO WAS AN EXPERT IN LOSING WEIGHT

I think one of the cases that impacted me the most was early in my training and practice in this model. I saw a woman who was a teacher who worked with children with learning difficulties. She loved her work and the children. She was an innovative and creative teacher and had won several awards for her teaching methods. She was, however, very overweight and discouraged. She had tried to lose weight all her life and had gained and lost hundreds of pounds. She came seeking help because she was depressed and withdrawn and had become somewhat isolated from her peers at work. Her weight problem now had escalated out of control and she desperately wanted to get pregnant but the doctor told her she would not be able to carry a baby safely unless she lost weight. She felt embarrassed and angry. She didn't seem to be able to get what she most desired in her life—to have a child and be happy.

It occurred to me that this lady was actually an expert on losing weight, so we began to explore what she knew about it. She said she had been on every fad diet known to man and none of them worked. So I started writing this down and came up with her list of "Do's and Don'ts for Successful Weight Loss." She dictated things like: "Diets don't work. Don't deprive yourself." She had successfully lost weight in the past when she didn't deprive herself. Keeping certain foods "taboo" only made them more desirable. Eating breakfast helped. Eating often but smaller amounts helped. Being careful during the week and rewarding herself on the weekend helped. I gave her the list and suggested she really did know a lot about losing weight. She was almost ecstatic as she had never thought of herself as being competent in losing weight.

I asked her the miracle question and she began to describe a day where she was engaged with her colleagues at school, accepting invitations for lunch or on the weekends. She described herself as being her "old self" when she wasn't so concerned about her weight but more social and outgoing. I suggested she choose one day and pretend the miracle had happened. Two weeks later she returned and had lost about 10 pounds. She was ecstatic. She described her life as "living the miracle and not having to pretend anymore." I cautioned her on not being discouraged if she didn't lose as much weight the next time. She assured me that she was now sure of what seemed to work and that she was not going to worry about it. She was the happiest she had been in a long time. She had gone out for dinner with her husband on the weekend, and this time, ate all she wanted to but didn't overeat like before. She had, in fact, even ordered dessert and enjoyed every bite. And she had still managed to lose 10 pounds.

By the third session, she was still losing weight and had found a new burst of energy by exercising; she had started taking walks with her husband and friends in her neighborhood. I again cautioned her on not being discouraged if she didn't lose as much weight as before. She was already three dress sizes smaller and still going. After the third session, she decided she could manage on her own. She said she had been to several therapists before seeing me and had almost completely given up on therapy.

About a year later, I got a card from her with a picture of her new baby. She looked radiant and had lost even more weight. About a year and a half later, I received another card with a picture of her second child. She had lost more weight. I ran into her some time later and she had still kept the weight off and was a very different person. She thanked me for helping her but the truth was, I merely reminded her of what she already knew.

LIFE OUTSIDE THE THERAPY ROOM: PERSONAL EFFECTS OF SFT

One of my favorite personal solution focused skills that I find very helpful is the "do something different" idea. It has become my favorite mantra and something I remind myself to do when I'm faced with a person (my daughter or otherwise) with whom I am having a head-on collision. As soon as the familiar "here we go again" pattern starts, my mantra reminds me to look for something different to do or say in hopes it will make a difference.

A couple of months back, I had a little sun bird that pecked all day long on the sliding glass door of my office. Every day, like clockwork, the bird came for about six weeks. It pecked nonstop. It fluttered from one side of the door to the other. I guess it saw its reflection and thought it was trying to communicate with the other bird. Sun birds are very small, sort of like humming birds, and they mate for life. I guess this little guy was looking for a mate and thought it had found one. My clients and I would amuse ourselves by wondering how long it would take for this little bird to finally get the point: What you are doing isn't working!

Well, one day, he stopped. Just like that. I have not seen him since. He finally learned that doing the same thing over and over again was not going to get him what he hoped for. I think some of us are like that. We keep doing the same thing over and over and hoping for a different result. So, my clients and I really had a blast learning from that little guy and we hope he found his mate some other way!

SFT has widened my professional community to include practitioners from all over the world. Training is a major aspect of what I do and it has been a real joy to invite speakers from other countries to conduct training for our SFT programs. As a result I have met and become friends with some key people who have helped to shape the SFT community here in Singapore. I have found them to be very collaborative, humble, and generous, and they have often conducted training at reduced fees. Mark McKergow and Jenny Clarke have come on numerous occasions and helped us envision our miracle picture for our training company. Much of what we are doing now came out of those early meetings. Mark has been a key player in our corporate programs and serves as our corporate consultant. Peter Szabo, Mark, and Jenny are a regular part of our Solution-Focused Coaching program. Brian Cade with his unique wit and humor teaches every year in our Graduate Diploma in SFT, as does Terese Steiner, who conducts training in our work with SF and children. Linda Metcalf has come several times to do training with schools. Ron Warner has been very pivotal in helping us become accredited to offer certification through the CCPC. And most recently, Harry and Yvonne came to be our keynote speakers at our conference in June 2008. Later this year, Chris Iveson will do training for our SFT and coach programs.

The bonus for me in working with external trainers has been the little gems I've picked up here and there. Peter did a preview for our coach training program with a group of about 60 corporate people. In a coaching demonstration he worked with someone who was very confused and made no sense to the audience! None of us had a clue what he was talking about. Later, Peter said he also had no idea what he was talking about. What was pretty amazing is that the "client" said he had experienced something powerful and wanted to sign up to learn about solution focused coaching. What we learned from this amazing demonstration is that the clinician doesn't need to know anything about the problem in order to be helpful. What we need to know is something about what the clients want to be different in their lives.

TRAINING AND REFLECTION

In 2004, two associates and I started the Academy of Solution-Focused Training in Singapore. The other two have moved on and I have continued as a director. I work with a team of locally and internationally based SFT practitioners who help with the training. Our main purpose is to continue to teach and develop other practitioners who want to learn this approach in Singapore and the region.

We now conduct training along three tracks: therapy, education, and coaching. For those who want it, we offer certification through the Canadian Council of Professional Certification. In Singapore, this has become a very important drawing card, as practitioners want to know that their training hours will lead to something. We attract participants from all over the Asia Pacific Rim. This is an encouraging sign that SF is gaining more interest and opportunities for training have opened up in other countries.

It has been my desire to develop and build a solution focused community of like-minded practitioners who want to network, offer support, and spread the great ideas of the solution focused approach in this region. There are some encouraging signs that this is happening. One of the recent graduates started an SFT chat list and there are over 65 people registered on this list from Singapore and the region. There have been some very impressive posts on this list. There have been beginning solution focused therapists who returned to their workplace very excited about what they learned and realized that they are all alone locally in using this approach. What seemed to make a difference was having a support network.

It has been fascinating to observe the learning process and how different people take to the model. To borrow from Mark McKergow's analogy of the traffic lights, I have witnessed people shifting from various positions in terms of their acceptance level to the SFT model: from red to amber to green. Some remain skeptical and perhaps are not interested in changing a mind-set but merely adding to their toolbox of therapeutic skills. Some start cautiously, trying different things, and then somehow become "hooked" and want to learn more. Some are eager from the beginning and are like sponges that take to the ideas and learn them very quickly.

One student, after going through an SFT exercise of comparing the difference between the problem-focused and solution focused approaches, immediately saw the paradigm shift. He sat in his chair almost in a trance and kept saying, "Wow! Wow! Wow!" Another student remarked on coming to the training to learn a skill and ending up learning a "philosophy of life."

One of my favorite things I do as a trainer is to see students for supervision. That is where I hear some very powerful personal stories. I'm learning from students all the time and am amazed by what they do. One student who was not in our SFT program asked to see me for supervision during his practicum. He had heard about SFT and wanted to learn how to use it with his clients. He told me of a case of a juvenile offender who believed he was fated to be bad and there was no hope of changing. He had seen this juvenile for six sessions with little change. I suggested he use the scaling question. He said it had not gone well. I realized that he had used a problem-focused scaling question so I suggested he change it. When he did, it made all the difference. He came to the next supervision with big eyes and was amazed by his client. He first asked his client to rate himself as "10" being totally bad and no hope for change and "1" as able to change. The client rated himself at a "9" and any higher meant he would have committed murder. The next time the student asked the client to rate himself as "10" being he has the ability to change and "1" no hope. To his surprise the client said "6" and then a very different discussion followed. I think the client was even more surprised. There was at last some hope that the client did have something to say about his life and it was not all fate. I was excited and surprised by this student who had no other training in SFT and seemed to capture what was most important. Once he realized the importance of how to scale, he used it much more effectively. I think this misuse of scaling is a common mistake beginners make.

I taught the WOWW (Working on What Works) program to a group of teachers and each session I began by asking them, "What have you tried and what has been working?" In training, I think this is a productive question to begin with. It is similar to the follow-up counseling session when we ask, "What's been better?" One teacher of a Mandarin Chinese language class told us of a problem student who was failing, never turned in his assignments, and was disruptive in class. The teacher's way of dealing with him was punitive and she employed shaming. She realized it wasn't getting anywhere so one day she remembered some of the skills she was learning and decided to try them. She noticed the student had been working on his worksheet for 30 minutes and decided to compliment him. He looked up, stunned. His comment was that it wasn't that hard. She asked, "How did you do that?" and had one of many positive discussions that week. By the end of the week, he had turned in all his assignments and his grades had improved. And he no longer was disruptive. He told her that he used to hate Mandarin and now she was his favorite teacher and it was his favorite class.

Each time I teach the SFT skills I notice there are some common questions that come up and some very similar stages of learning that take place. I think it helps to be reminded that it takes time to learn to trust that others will get it, but in their own way and in their own time. I think part of the learning curve is the time factor. I remember Insoo did not try to convince me of anything but let me come to my realizations on my own.

It has been a privilege to be associated with students and colleagues whose interest is in helping other people be their better selves. I think in many ways, the solution focused model is a spiritual model because it helps people to ask some very important questions and search for important answers. It helps people to see beyond their "stuckness" and catch a glimpse of a more hopeful future. That is where energy can be found again and the beginning of small steps toward a better place can occur.

I think one of the participants in the course captured the essence of the solution focused model. During supervision I was informed that the day before, the student had tried to commit suicide. I was stunned. I began to explore the student's journey through this traumatic experience. I asked how the student was able to keep going to work, attend training, and attend our supervision despite a painful situation. The student talked about having learned from the model and experienced its life impact. I think the student's response epitomizes the model: "SFT is a constant reminder to live well."

EDITOR'S COMMENT

While I was in graduate school, taking a course taught by Dr. Metcalf, she often spoke about her trips to Singapore to visit Debbie Hogan and do a presentation for the Solution-Focused Training Academy. So when Dr. Metcalf and I compiled a list of people we would ask to contribute to this book, Debbie Hogan was at the top of the list.

When we contacted her, she immediately demonstrated one of the key traits to being solution focused: the nonexpert stance. She stated she would be happy to contribute but could not understand why we would be interested in her. I was thinking of all of her accomplishments in the field, but to her none of that mattered. Debbie did not see herself as the "expert." That response alone highlights why this chapter is an indispensable addition to this volume. The chapter also explores something that many students experience when first learning about this theory; the difficulties encountered when one comes from a heavily pathological background. I enjoyed the honesty with which Debbie discussed this topic.

—Elliott Connie

REFERENCES

Fisch, R., Weakland, J. H., & Segal, L. (1982). *The tactics of change.* San Francisco: Jossey-Bass.

Rosen, S. (Ed.). (1991). *My voice will go with you: The teaching tales of Milton H. Erickson, M.D.* New York: Norton.

Watzlawick, P., Weakland, J. H, & Fisch, R. (1974). *Change.* New York: Norton.

13 Learning to Pay Attention

HARRY KORMAN

If at first, the idea is not absurd, then there is no hope for it.

—Albert Einstein

Q. How did you first learn about solution focused therapy (SFT)?

A. It is the late 1980s, perhaps early 1990s. I have just seen a family for their second session and I have filmed it. I go up to the coffee room for a break and perhaps to find someone to watch the film with. That's always useful. Two interns, social workers in training, are there chatting so I ask them if they want to join me to review the tape with the family. They agree, so we go down to the studio and I start the tape.

When you don't have a team or someone handling the equipment, the film starts with the family waiting for the therapist, who is in the control room starting the recording. So, on the tape we see the family waiting for me. They look relaxed as I walk into the room and sit down. I always have a moment in the beginning of a session when I prepare with my papers and my pen and my notes from the previous sessions, and so forth. They notice that too, and for a little while, they are patiently waiting for me to settle in until it looks as if I'm ready. Well, it only looks like it. I can see that I'm not, but the family thinks I'm ready and they start telling me something about what has become better since I met them one week earlier. I see myself on the tape not hearing what they are saying. Some seconds pass and then I ask my first question, which is something around how the problem has been this last week. I see the family somewhat surprised by my question, I see myself not noticing it, and then they make an earnest effort to answer my question. I guess that they think that it is important information so they tell me. I am a child psychiatrist and a family therapist and think that most of the problems are the same from either viewpoint, and of course the family confirms that.

I'm embarrassed with the two interns sitting there watching me, as I am not listening to what the family tries to tell me about what's been better. I know enough about solution focused therapy to see what I missed so I get even more embarrassed as I see myself move into a typical structural/strategic family therapy session with enactment, unbalancing, and so on, working on the problematic, interactional sequences in the family that I had "diagnosed" in the first session. It is a great session in many ways. Structural family therapy has a particular flavor to it and is exciting and entertaining to watch. The only problem I can see with the session from a technical point of view is that it is extremely similar to the first session I had with that family one week earlier.

As I sit there watching, I think about what I missed. What were those things that were better? How did those changes come about? Who did what that made things slightly better? The most worrying thought in my head is: "How many times did I do this? How many times in my career have I missed people trying to describe changes they've made since we last met? How many times have I missed an opportunity to talk about change and growth and success and build on that?" As these thoughts run through my head I curse myself for not knowing solution focused therapy better and I make this definitive decision: I am going to learn and acquire some real depth in solution focused therapy.

Q. How did you discover that SFT was the model that seemed to fit with your way of working with clients?

A. My first encounter with solution focused therapy was a couple of years earlier. I and seven colleagues (Lars Dannerup, Sonja Edvardson, Kristina Engman, Jehoshua Kaufman, Jocelyne Lopez-Korman, Barbro Persson (now Jacobson), and Aviva Suskin-Holmquist) were doing a controlled, randomized trial trying to replicate Stanton and Todd's study from 1978 where they had treated heroin addicts with family therapy in their families of origin (Stanton & Todd, 1982). In 1988 we invited Steve de Shazer and Insoo Kim Berg to Malmö to do a workshop and to work with us. We had read most of Steve's peer-reviewed journal articles in the 1970s and we had read his first book on ecosystemic brief therapy. Based on those writings we thought Steve was a brief strategic therapist. Steve started the workshop with the cocaine case. It took me about 30 minutes to understand that this was not strategic therapy. It contained exceptions, goals, client therapist relationships, interventions. It was radically different and beautifully elegant and too simple to be true.

Q. What characteristics of this model drew you toward it?

A. In 1989 we (the team from the heroin addiction project) went to BFTC in Milwaukee and sat behind the one-way screen for a week. The therapists in Milwaukee were seeing cases that made most of our child psychiatric work in Malmö seem trivial. In itself this was no surprise since we had already been told that a lot of the clients at BFTC came from poor neighborhoods. What was surprising was that almost every client and family came in talking about what had been better, either since the last session or since they decided to seek help. The clinical impression was overwhelming, and the contrast with the work we were doing in Malmö was scary. The therapists at BFTC truly believed that people would get better. They expected people to tell them about what had been better and truly believed that this was the way things would go in every case. I couldn't say that I truly believed that to be the case for my clients in Malmö and I could sense the power of such a belief. So I asked myself over and over again during that week what difference it would make doing child psychiatry this way.

Moving from structural/strategic therapy to solution focus was a choice and for many years I have tried to explain the many reasons I had for doing it apart from my simple clinical impressions of it being such an efficient method. I always run into the same problem. Everybody uses the same million-dollar words to describe what they are doing even though therapists are clearly interested in different things and the dialogues in different therapy models are vastly different.

Q. How has utilizing SFT impacted your work with clients? (Please mention if you utilized a previous model and the difference you noticed in clients and yourself after switching to SFT.)

A. I have no words to describe the particular relationship developing in most solution focused interviews, one where I am admiring the client's imagination and ways of dealing with things that happen in life. This relationship is very different from the kind of relationships I developed with clients first during my psychodynamic days and then in my family therapy days but I cannot describe this difference in a way that makes sense. I can show it on videotapes, though, and sometimes I can hint at it.

When I was a young doctor working with alcohol problems and had never heard of solution focused therapy, I worked in traditional ways and a case has haunted me ever since. A woman in her 40s came to the alcohol clinic and when I asked her how I could be helpful, she answered that the problem was that her husband was an alcoholic. At the time I thought that the first task of the doctor was to evaluate and assess the situation so consequently my first question was: "What tells you he is an alcoholic?" and she answered: "He drinks a light beer every day and he is dependent on it."

Being the all-knowing doctor I immediately knew what was wrong. This woman suffered from a lack of information. One light beer a day does not make anyone alcoholic and is not a symptom of alcoholism. I immediately proceeded to solve the problem that I had diagnosed. Not difficult at all. I informed her about what quantities of alcohol are needed to make someone an alcoholic. After less than 5 minutes she got up from the chair and walked out of the room in a way that showed clearly that she was very dissatisfied with the professional help she had gotten.

Q. Has the use of SFT impacted you in your personal life? If so, please explain.

A. Since becoming a solution focused therapist, I have wondered many times over the years what that patient wanted. I have developed curiosities that I did not have before. That woman certainly didn't seek information on alcohol or alcoholism, so I have let my imagination run wild. One of my wildest fantasies is that this was a woman who loved sex and couldn't stand the smell of beer. I have thought a lot about what an interesting and funny conversation we could have had. I talked with Steve de Shazer about this case once and he laughed and started speculating about possible problem definitions and solutions and the funniest one he came up with was that she actually had a nose problem and that the number of possible solutions were infinite, among them a nose-clasp for use in bed.

Learning solution focused therapy was hard work for me. Every time I was in a workshop or seminar with Steve de Shazer or Insoo

Kim Berg, I could do parts of it for a week or two, and then I reverted back to problem-solving techniques I had learnt before.

In the early 1990s I was getting better at it but it wasn't stable. I had entire weeks when I had solution focused dialogues with all the families I saw and then I had entire weeks when I had problem-solving dialogues with every family. I knew enough about solution focus to be able to tell when I was in a solution focused dialogue and when I wasn't. I had no idea how it happened, though. I speculated, like I've heard so many people do since, that perhaps some families just needed to spend more time on their problem. It was a lousy argument, though. Why would all those families come the same week? Eventually—and this is a bit embarrassing—I realized that I had more problem-focused interviews when I had young, bright (and often good-looking) interns or trainees that I was trying to impress with my skills as a therapist. I believe that at the time it was much easier for me to appear brilliant while figuring out what caused a problem and what needed to be different, rather than appear brilliant around what the family wanted to get out of therapy and how they would notice it happened. Someone once said that watching a good solution focused session is about as entertaining as watching grass grow. Eventually I discovered a pattern that made a difference for my own learning and I have tried teaching it ever since.

In almost every conversation we have with clients, they will at some point and most often early in the interview present a complaint. A complaint has the general form of:

- "I feel something I don't want to feel" or
- "I think thoughts I don't want to think" or
- "I behave in ways I don't want to behave" or
- "Other people behave toward me in ways I don't like"

The first thing all therapists do, regardless of their theoretical orientation, is to acknowledge "the problem" with some variation of "that's tough." The problem-solving therapist will then start interviewing around the details of the problematic feeling, cognition, behavior or interaction, its history, its potential causes (internal, external, systemic, biological), and so forth. Once the therapist has developed a hypothesis, he (or she) will start intervening to solve the problem. These interventions will most often be suggestions about what the client could do differently, think differently, or behave differently.

The suggestions will be disguised as questions with the general form, "Have you thought of . . . " "Have you tried to . . . " Most often these suggestions are useful if the client accepts them. Steve de Shazer used to say that it is not difficult to know what someone needs to do to solve a problem. The difficulty lies in how to get the client to do it.

Therapeutic suggestions of this form will generally start appearing within just a few minutes of the interview and very many clients will "resist" these ideas. I used to be completely unaware of this. I noticed on tapes that when I was interviewing I would often get stuck when the client started to say "Yes, but . . . ," and I noticed that I would often answer this by saying, "Yes, but if you thought/tried this . . . " and the client would regularly answer, "Yes, but . . . " to that, too. Thus we would get into something that I call a "yes-but dialogue." I also noticed that when the client said "yes but" it was always because I had had a suggestion of some kind, some attempt to solve the problem. When tracking that backwards in the conversation, I noticed that there would always be a complaint stated by the client, followed by my questions on the details of that complaint/problem, then leading me on to ideas about what the client could do that would solve it.

Q. How would your clients describe your work with them? Have any of your clients who might have experienced another model of therapy commented on the difference (if any) that they perceived when working with you?

A. The solution focused therapist only acknowledges the complaint with some kind of empathic statement instead of advising people, and that's different. Steve would often say, "I can imagine." I will often say, "Oh, shit." The therapist will generally not ask about the details about the complaint. The therapist will then ask some variation of:

- "How do you want to feel instead?"
- "How do you want to think instead?"
- "How do you want to behave instead?"
- "How do you want those people to behave differently toward you?"

The exact phrasing will depend on the client's wording of the complaint.

The answers to these questions will then lead into how the client and other people will notice when this happens, what difference it will make, and so forth.

Once you're stuck in a "yes-but" conversation it's impossible to jump directly to "how do you want it to be different?" For the question to perform its function, it needs to be connected to the complaint that started the sequence. What I started doing was to learn to apologize for my stupid ideas and then say: "You said you didn't want to feel this—so what do you want to be feeling/thinking/doing instead?"

Once I had learnt this, all my sessions became solution focused.

We learnt solution focus by learning questions and for many years I taught solution focused therapy the same way. For the last couple of years I have been doing microanalysis (Bavelas, McGee, Phillips, & Routledge, 2000) of sessions and it is changing my focus in teaching. What I have learned is that about one-third of the therapist's utterances in solution focused therapy sessions are questions. About a third are variations of "Aha, uhum, good, great, wow" which all seem to perform different functions in the dialogue (Clark & Fox Tree, 2002). Some utterances are sympathetic, acknowledging pain and difficulties, others more encouraging, like shorthand for "say more about that," while others are just marking a pause—like saying, "Wait, I haven't finished yet."

The last third of the utterances are echoing, paraphrasing, summarizing, and generally commenting on what the client said, or checking understanding. We put them together and call them formulations because they function similarly in dialogues. They pinpoint or hammer out what we want to talk more about and then questions are asked to get into the details of what we want to know more about.

Q. What is it about SFT that makes it so effective?

A. A client comes in. As she sits down she says, "I want to be a good mother but I'm such a worthless, worthless person." She then starts crying. The therapist has a choice after the client's first utterance. The therapist makes a choice. He thinks, "Are we going to talk more about feeling worthless or are we going to talk more about being a better mother?" These conversations are vastly different. The solution focused therapist may begin: "That must be awful," says the therapist. She nods. "So you want to be a better mother?" She nods again. "So what would be a sign to you—in the days to come—that you were becoming a better mother?"

"That must be awful" preserves and acknowledges the feeling of despair (or whatever) she is expressing while deleting the details of the complaint (being a worthless person). The "So you want to be a better mother" preserves the words that are connected to what she wants. The solution focused therapist will listen for anything that could be connected to what she wants to have happen as a result of therapy and as she nods, the dialogical space opens up for questions around details of that. Often, as in the example above, the formulation is then repeated again inside the question: "So what would be a sign to you—in the days to come—that you were *becoming a better mother?*" This process is repeated over and over in the session and the hammering out of what we want to know more about seems necessary to get a flow in the session.

Q. Describe one of your favorite cases and how it impacted your work as a therapist.

A. At the time I was working 10 hours a week with the heroin project and 30 hours a week as a pediatrician. The week after Steve and Insoo had done their workshop a mother came with her 5-year-old daughter to pediatrics, referred from a general practitioner because of hematuria (a small amount of blood in the girl's urine). As I walked into the consultation room I asked how I could be helpful and this young mother, shoulders sloping and a sad tired look on her face, answered: "The problem is that she is not dry. She pees and poops in her pants every day." I was surprised—after all the referral was for blood in the urine, not for urine and feces in her pants. Then I thought, I'm training to become a child psychiatrist and this is probably a case for a child psychiatrist anyway, so let's move on.

I had just come from the course with Steve and Insoo and even if a lot of the details had already started fading, I still remembered the idea of exceptions. So I asked: "Are there days when she is dry?" Mother answered, "Excuse me?" so I repeated the question. She thought about it for a couple of seconds and then said in a somewhat hesitant voice, "Yes." So I asked: "When was the most recent day you remember that she was dry?" She thought long and hard about that before answering: "Last Tuesday." "So what do you think was different about last Tuesday?"

The mother was still hesitant as she lifted her right hand toward her left shoulder and answered thoughtfully, "Maybe my shoulder wasn't aching as much and . . ." She looked thoughtfully at me before continuing, "Maybe I wasn't thinking so much about the divorce."

I was amazed. There was such an obvious and clear connection for her between how she felt and her daughter's symptoms. What a responsible parent. I asked: "So when your shoulder doesn't ache and you're not thinking so much about the divorce how do you think you're different toward your daughter then?" She talked for several minutes about how she was more attentive, more patient, more caring and loving and simply doing more things with her daughter when she felt better, and some days she did feel better and she didn't really know why, but she could clearly see the difference in her daughter, who on those days was calmer and generally more happy.

I finished off with a physical examination of the girl. Mother dressed the girl. I wrote up the paperwork for the tests needed to exclude any serious cause of the hematuria and then summarized the consultation. I told her I was impressed by how clearly she was able to describe how she functioned as a mother on the days when things were more like the way she wanted them, and how insightful she was. I was also very impressed that she had days when things were going the way she wanted them to and I then suggested that she define when she was functioning the way she wanted, pay attention to the differences it made with her child then, and set up an appointment 3 weeks later.

When I came into the examination room 3 weeks later the girl and mother were sitting calmly doing a puzzle together. Both mother and girl smiling and the girl had been dry since the first visit. This last case was one of a series of cases where small pieces of solution focused techniques seemed to make a huge difference and perhaps the most important difference was in making me more interested in solution focused therapy.

Q. What are some common mistakes that therapists trying on the model make most often? If you had a chance to guide them differently, how would you do so?

A. Today I think that we need to improve our understanding of how language works in the therapeutic dialogue. I believe that microanalysis shows promise as a method of both describing what happens in solution focused therapy sessions, what is distinctive and specific, and learning ways to teach the specifics of it more easily. It is apparent as I watch tapes of Steve and Insoo and myself and my colleagues that we do a lot of the things we thought we did, but we also do a lot of things that we had no idea that we were doing. Some of those things are things that we see (at this point) only happen in solution focused dialogues.

If you were training therapists in the SFT model, what strategies would you use to train them and how would you present the material?

Microanalysis.

Q. What developments would you like to see in the future of this model?

A. My hope is that the more specifically we will be able to describe the specifics of this the easier it will be to teach solution focused therapy and be clear about the results of that teaching. It remains to be shown if this will be of benefit to our clients. The fact that we are convinced through our clinical impressions is worthless evidence these days. Unless we are able to show both the specifics and the benefits of this way of working, I worry that solution focused therapy will water down to a mindless attitude of being positive and optimistic, which to me is a grave misunderstanding and threatens the survival of solution focused therapy as a model

EDITOR'S COMMENT

I appreciate Dr. Harry Korman's journey very much. It was similar to mine. I began my work as a strategic family therapist, paving the way (I thought) for clients to change. To take on the solution focused model, I had to put my tools of change aside and literally sit on my hands. When a practitioner moves from one model of therapy to another, the experience is one of excitement yet uncertainty. People tend to gravitate back toward what they know and feel comfortable in. Yet Harry is candid about what happened when he finally saw the helpfulness in using the solution focused approach, and his explanation of looking back over cases where it would have been helpful is reassuring.

What I learned from Harry too, was the importance of experiencing the "aha" moment when exploring solution focused therapy. His obvious excitement when experiencing for the first time the light in the eyes of a client who solved her own dilemma happens often to those of us who have tried out the model. Once we see that light, we never go back. For many practitioners reviewing the model, the solution focused approach at first seems too simple. They almost feel guilty for working so little! Yet clients view the same experience differently. As the mother and daughter showed Harry, the solutions were not the obvious sort to the mother at first, but once she discovered them, her adherence to the solution was definitive. To assist clients in this discovery is more than exciting; it is respectful, noteworthy, and almost always emotionally rewarding to both client and therapist. When clients walk out of our offices smiling, feeling as if they have discovered a new trait within themselves, they are never the same. And when a solution focused therapist experiences that vignette for the first time, neither are they.

—Linda Metcalf

REFERENCES

Bavelas, J., McGee, D., Phillips, B., & Routledge, R. (2000). Microanalysis of communication in psychotherapy. *Human Systems, 11,* 3–22.

Clark, H. H., & Fox Tree, J. E. (2002). Using uh and um in spontaneous speaking. *Cognition, 84,* 73–111.

Stanton, M., & Todd, T. (1982). *The family therapy of drug abuse and addiction.* New York: Guilford Press.

14 Believing With a Curious Mind

LINDA METCALF

> If you can dream it, you can do it.
>
> —Walt Disney

Q. How did you first learn about solution focused therapy (SFT)?

A. I remember the time well. I was a graduate student at Texas Woman's University. I had just returned from Rockville, Maryland, where I had attended a week-long intensive on strategic family therapy with Jay Haley and Cloe Madanes. I had become quite enamored with their work as a student, particularly favoring the creativity that strategic family therapy employed to help clients get on track with their lives. I was puzzled, too, as the metaphorical strategies used by strategic family therapy were complicated. I recall going to class the week after the workshop and writing on the use of metaphors. The paper was a disaster. I only earned a B on the paper and my professor, Frank Thomas, agreed that it was not my best work. As a strategic family therapist, I had struggled to understand how my interventions would influence people, mostly because I noticed that after studying and preparing for a session, my clients often came back better anyway. I began to realize (although reluctantly) that life somehow interrupted the sequences of events that kept their problems viable and they didn't always need my magical interventions after all.

The year was 1990 and in my "Communication in Family Therapy" class, Dr. Thomas began talking about Michele Weiner-Davis and Bill O'Hanlon's new book, *In Search of Solutions* (O'Hanlon & Weiner-Davis, 2003). He also introduced Michael White and David Epston's book, *Narrative Means to Therapeutic Ends* (Epston & White, 1990). Of the solution focused book, he told the class that the solution focused approach was "exciting." Of the narrative therapy book, he said, "I have never read such elegant questions." I was intrigued with the new approaches and bought both books immediately. Once I began reading *In Search of Solutions,* I felt validated on many levels, particularly that of recognizing that clients did have strengths. I also loved the creative questions and the manner in which the material was presented to the reader. I had read too many family therapy books that were too hooked on theory. Not that theory wasn't important; I just wanted to know more on how to actually *do* therapy.

The narrative therapy book was a journey into language that I had never experienced. The authors were obviously in love with their work and it showed. What also showed was a respect for people that I had never seen. The strategic family therapy approach had me doing therapy *to* people. The solution focused and narrative therapy approaches had me observe the strengths first, then work side by side with people. I began feeling like a field guide. I still use that metaphor to this day when I teach the approach. As a field guide, I ask my clients to show me their world and as we walk into it together, I get to remark on the sidelines what I see and they have forgotten to see.

I began reading more books on solution focused therapy by authors such as John Walter and Jane Peller, Scot Miller, Insoo Berg, Steve de Shazer, Michael Durrant, and Brian Cade (Cade & O'Hanlon, 1993; de Shazer, 1985, 1991; Durrant, 1990; Miller & Berg, 1992; Walter & Peller, 1992) and began watching all of the videotapes of the model that I could find. I took notes and began formulating my own process from questions that I read in case studies, trying to put together steps that made sense to me. I was an educator, so process, steps, and formulaic ideas always gave me a sort of traction and I needed that since my mind tended to wander with clients who had much to tell me. I wanted to stay on track while using the approach.

I was also fortunate in that my professor, Dr. Thomas, was also quite intrigued with the model and sought out workshops and speakers to bring to our campus to talk with his students. Among those was Michael Durrant, who I am indebted to for publishing my first article in his journal, *Case Studies* (Metcalf, 1991). I remember the day I picked him up from the airport for Dr. Thomas (who was teaching a class). I had never met anyone from Australia, so his charming accent and his simplistic way of thinking about clients was almost musical. I was also able to meet Bill O'Hanlon and Pat Hudson, when they both spoke for the Texas Association for Marriage and Family Therapy. I found Bill's work to be fascinating. I noticed how both he and Michael Durrant had personalities that were positive and hopeful about people. This was different than strategic family therapy, where clients were seen as burdened with problems and the therapist's job was to understand what function the problem had. I liked the spirit of those who embraced solution focused therapy. I wanted to become one of them.

Q. How did you discover that SFT was the model that seemed to fit with your way of working with clients?

A. My first attempt was with clients in a psychiatric hospital where Dr. Thomas and I worked with groups and individuals. We began training others at that time, although we were still learning ourselves as we went along. The group we worked with consisted of women who were codependent and the hospital program leaned toward convincing the women that they were victims. They grasped that idea and soon got more depressed. We came in with some new, solution focused ideas and began drawing genograms for the women and talking about survivorship. Soon, the staff became upset with us because the women preferred our groups to theirs. I typically left sessions feeling better and lighter. I didn't have to study and present strategies to help people change anymore. I merely had to show up, listen to them, and relate to them about their abilities and strengths. It felt good to me and to them.

Once I started working in this way with groups, I did the same with individuals, couples, and families. I kept a clipboard of the process and steps that I was developing in front of me at all times, and used it religiously for about three years. It was too easy to float back into "problem talk" so the clipboard kept me in "solution talk." I noticed that professionally I was getting better at the model because my clients did not have to stay in therapy as long as before. I found joy in working with them, even when the subjects were difficult, mostly because my clients kept saying, "You work differently than other therapists . . . and I like it." So did I.

Q. What characteristics of this model drew you toward it?

A. Hands down, it was the creative angle that I saw in it and in the narrative approach. I have to admit that I incorporate narrative with solution focused therapy often. I simply loved the language of narrative therapy and the exception-seeking questions of solution focused therapy. Together, I could use them to talk to people who came in with depressing diagnoses and before the session was over, the person was sad rather than depressed, moody instead of bipolar, and energetic instead of hyperactive.

I remember one lady who came in with about five diagnoses. She was depressed that she had so many things wrong with her. I was quite respectful of the diagnoses and the psychiatrist who had given them to her, but asked her politely if we could leave the diagnoses out in the hallway so that I could speak to just her. She was rather surprised but said yes. We then began to talk about times when the diagnoses were not as intrusive in her life and we gave them different descriptions. When the session was over she looked at me and said, "Thank you. I really thought things were hopeless."

After hearing this type of feedback from people, problem talk began sounding like the wrong note that one hits on a piano. I decided to do my dissertation on change, and to study how both clients and therapists perceive change happening in solution focused therapy. I was lucky enough to get approval to do that study at the Brief Family Therapy Center in Milwaukee. The lessons I learned from the dissertation still remain with me each time I see clients. From my research, I learned to always ask, "What did we do in here today if anything, that might have made a difference for you?" The answers have all been different . . . as different as my clients.

Q. How has utilizing SFT impacted your work with clients? (Please mention if you utilized a previous model and the difference you noticed in clients and yourself after switching to SFT.)

A. As I mentioned, I was a born-again strategic family therapist early in graduate school. I switched to the solution focused approach prior to graduation. My practice at that time was at my husband's dental office, where I saw a variety of clients, including school-related cases involving adolescents and children. Being a former educator, I was amazed at how quickly the school-related issues resolved using the approach. My practice grew with school referrals and soon, I found myself going back into the school system for four years where I used the approach with every student, faculty member, parent, and staff person I encountered. I noticed that I would leave school each day with little stress . . . seriously. Once, a vice principal cornered me after a busy week and asked me how I coped with the issues I dealt with each week. She went on to lament how much she worried about students over the weekend and remarked how she actually feared Mondays because of what she had to deal with again. I answered, "I don't worry about them. They have the tools they need." She looked rather disappointed in my response. I walked away feeling awful for a few seconds for saying that and then started smiling. I did believe that the students had the tools that they needed. Because of this belief, I leave my practice with fewer concerns and many more satisfying moments from the therapy room.

One more thing that this model has done for me professionally is to convince me that if a client doesn't change right away, it's not the client's fault. This was a dramatic discovery for me. I had worked with psychiatrists who had confronted me when I was trying harder than the clients and had told me to work less until the clients wanted to change. Meeting Michael Durrant changed all of that. I remember him telling me that if a client doesn't change, it is me who has not found a way to cooperate yet. I got the same feedback from Steve de Shazer too, when he visited Texas Woman's University. What a relief it was for me to learn to say to a client, "I don't think I listened to you well enough last time . . . tell me what I missed." Then they would tell me.

Q. How would your clients describe your work with them? Have any of your clients who might have experienced another model of therapy commented on the difference (if any) that they perceived when working with you?

A. Yes, they have. I recall specifically a lady who had been attending sexual abuse support groups where the facilitator made each woman recall the events of the abuse to each other. She found it very painful. When she came the first time, she cried that she did not want to go through the events and when I told her she did not have to, and that I wanted her to only tell me what she wanted me to know, she cried harder. After the session, she said she was never going to go back to the support group. She stayed in individual therapy and did well as she began thinking of herself as a survivor, which she was.

Most of my practice over the years often centered on school-related issues, and it became pretty common for children and adolescents to come to therapy and then remark on how differently

I worked. This was particularly true when I went to school with my clients to visit with their teachers after the first session. Parents were rather surprised that I would take the time to go to their child's school. To me, there wasn't a choice. I needed to understand how the system worked at the child's school and I also wanted to give the teachers, parent, and student another look at who the student was or could become. I learned a lot during the first few visits. I learned to never present myself as an expert, which wasn't hard for me, but was easy for the school to see me as; and I learned to always listen. I listened to lots of complaints and slowly began to get more skillful at changing the sessions into solution focused ones by asking for additional information such as times when the student turned in work, behaved, was slightly more respectful, and so forth. When the session got on that track, the student came in with my invitation and I shared what his/her teachers discovered. After the next session, I rarely saw the client again. Things got better very quickly.

Q. What is it about SFT that makes it so effective?

A. I could go on about the process but I think what makes solution focused therapy the most effective is the respectful, accepting relationship that develops between therapist and client. In many traditional therapies, clients attend therapy to have therapy done to them. Too often if the therapist thinks the client needs to do certain things to work through issues, clients drop out when the pain becomes too intense. In solution focused therapy, the therapist only goes where the client wants to go. This is sometimes criticized heavily by therapists who embrace other models, and is called Band-Aid therapy. What those therapists don't realize (yet) is that by respecting where the client wants to go first, the relationship becomes so strong between client and therapist that the client allows the therapist into the deeper issues later.

A second factor that makes the model effective is that it is completely client driven: the client picks the goal, discovers exceptions (sometimes with the therapist's assistance) about when the goal occurred even slightly, and those discoveries become tasks. The client is more likely to follow through because it is his goal and the tasks develop from his exceptions. This sounds so simple but is actually quite complicated in that it requires the therapist to sit back and wait. For some therapists, waiting can be the breaking point. They assume that the client is resistant so they must push harder. But a therapist who learns to wait and listen to clients patiently, asking exception questions with the Columbo stance, will be rewarded when a client discovers things about himself that mesmerize even him. It is that true discovery of past successes that gives confidence to the client that he can succeed again.

Q. Describe one of your favorite cases and how it impacted your work as a therapist.

A. I have had the fortune of working in public schools for many years and coming in contact with students that were often referred to as impossible. No one else wanted to talk to them because of poor behavior and school performance. Fairly often, those students were written off as having no real futures. I seemed to hear a reoccurring chant of "until he tries hard, I'm not doing anything" or "until she respects me, I won't respect her" throughout the hallways. I have to admit that I have always taken the side of the underdog, especially when it comes to school clients. It didn't always win me glowing feedback from those the underdog burned, but I wasn't after glowing feedback anyway. I merely wanted the students to see themselves differently than the way others described them. I had beliefs that when the student did that, he would succeed.

Tyler was such a student. At 16, he was two years behind in high school credits, had a standing appointment with a psychiatrist who gave him medication for anxiety and depression, and lived with his grandparents because he did not get along with his father. His parents had divorced years ago and his mother had been cited with drug possession charges so often that Tyler's friends found out and teased him unmercifully. This resulted in Tyler dropping out of a promising athletic career in high school and working at a lumber yard after school until 11:30 every night. With all of these distractions, Tyler was distant to people at school and would often sit in his pickup truck and drink after attending only one class.

One morning, the associate principal caught up with Tyler before he exited the school. She liked him, yet had to hold her boundaries in regard to his truancy. She asked him to step into her office and called his father about the truancy. His father came to the school and the associate principal called me in to visit with all of them. I had not met Tyler before.

I was struck with his hopelessness. He stared at the floor during our initial contact. I inquired about the possibility of meeting with Tyler, his father and mother, since I am a family therapist. I was immediately shut down by his father, who said Tyler was to have nothing to do with his mother. Tyler's head just bobbed at this remark, while he continued to stare at the floor. The associate principal went on about his truancy issues, except in one class, psychology. That got my attention and I asked him what it was about the class that helped him to attend. He quickly replied that it was psychology class where the teacher always greeted him. Besides, he said, in psychology he had a chance to try and figure himself out. He said he knew he had psychiatric issues; why else would he be sent to a psychiatrist so often? I asked him the miracle question because I felt he needed a miracle and geared it toward a miracle day at school.

"Suppose you went to sleep tonight and a miracle occurred. When you woke up tomorrow, you thought, 'Hey, I don't mind going to school today.' What would be different that would tell you a miracle had occurred?"

He looked up for the first time and told me he would be in classes with students his own age. Seeing some movement and some light in his eyes, I asked what else would be happening in the miracle school day and he continued with, "I would feel a part of this school . . . I don't have friends," and "I would have more teachers like the psychology teacher who actually cares when I walk into the classroom." With these ideas, I asked him to go to my office where together, he and I redesigned his schedule for the next semester.

In January, when Tyler returned from winter break, I asked him to stop by my office before going to class. While he thought that request was a bit odd, he showed up at my door on the first day. We walked together to his first class. I had picked teachers on his schedule that I knew would give him the emotional support he needed. He was also assigned as an office aide, to help a secretary where he would meet other office aide students. Routinely throughout the semester when I saw him in the hallways, I sent him a short note just stating how glad I was that he was at school. At the end of the semester he had missed one day. His grades were A's and B's. He had made some friends. He requested admission to the accelerated high school program and got in.

He attended the accelerated high school program the next fall and within nine months he gained all of his credits to get a high school diploma. On his graduation day, he received an award for creative writing. After the ceremony, he told me he had applied to a local university to major in psychology. He asked if I would be a reference.

I was quite excited with his decision and asked him what he thinks made the difference that helped him make a difference in his own life. He told me: "Teachers—when they care that a kid is in their classroom it helps so much. Some kids never get anyone to care. People should build relationships with kids that need them. That's the difference for me."

At my last contact, Tyler had completed his undergraduate degree and begun his master's degree in . . . you guessed it, psychology.

The field of education is in trouble. The traditional methods of dealing with students are failing because the students are no longer responding, yet the field of education continues to operate in the same way. The results are not pretty. Working in schools and in private practice with school clients using the solution focused model has brought to my attention the increased need for new approaches in schools everywhere. I have had the luxury of traveling to many places around the world and visiting all kinds of schools. In each place, the same events occur. Teachers get frustrated when their students do not receive openly and readily their instruction or directions. Instead of seeking alternative ways, they utilize the same methods and when those don't work either, they criticize and ostracize their students. No one wins. It is this purpose that I continue to have professionally that drives me to keep talking and writing and working with schools on this approach.

Q. Has the use of SFT impacted you in your personal life? If so, please explain.

A. One memorable experience comes to mind of my youngest son, Ryan, who was about 6 years old when we all went skiing the first time in Colorado. Ryan tended to be fearful of new experiences, even though once he tried something new and gained confidence, he just soared. We took the ski lift up to a mountain that was a beginner slope and as soon as we dropped off the lift, he fell. Crying, he wanted to go back to the lodge. Normally, I might have told him, "No, we are going to do this. You said you wanted to learn to ski." Instead, I took a more cooperative approach (out of desperation) and said, "Sure, let's do that. How are we going to get back? We can't go down the lift." He looked around and found a very easy slope and together we started down. When he got a little ahead of me, I yelled, "Hey, don't go so fast, you are going to beat me!" which made him smile and go faster. He did beat me, of course, and when we got to the bottom of the slope, he said, "Mom, let's do it again."

I think over the years, I have become so much more accepting, appreciative, and understanding of my family and spouse. Maybe this has occurred because I am older, and there *have* to be some positive aspects of that, but I also think it is because the solution focused approach, now in my blood, keeps the problems that come along from taking over my thinking and prompts me to look for the exceptions.

With my children, learning the solution focused approach was a blessing as it taught me to notice not only their differences in talents and abilities, but their responses to parenting. Once in adolescence, I began noticing that each of them responded quite differently to the expectations and boundaries that we set. On the occasions when we had to discipline or consequence them, I would often think more about times when they did stay on track versus the very occasional mishap, and this probably lessened the harshness of their consequence and led me to talk to them more. Our older son could be talked to seriously and would become completely remorseful within minutes, practically making up his own punishment. Our daughter took time. If she was upset about something we had confronted her with, but was allowed two to three hours of time, she would eventually come around, admit she had erred, and vow to do better. Our youngest needed some space too, and silence, as he was quite distractible as a young boy. He needed more boundaries and short-term consequences so that he could see the light of day after his issue. They each turned out spectacularly, earning college degrees and becoming hardworking people. They also stay in communication with us on a weekly basis, now that they live away from home.

With colleagues, I try to use the model when I am frustrated with others and ask myself, "What am I really the most frustrated about and what do I need to make that frustration less?" I also have learned to ask myself, "How do I want to respond so that months from now, I am proud of my response and the effect it had on someone?" These tools, which I stumbled onto after some rather difficult times recently, have given me a peace that I needed to achieve.

Q. What are some key personality traits that you think are shared among solution focused practitioners?

A. I mused to Elliott when we were in the beginning stages of this book that every solution focused practitioner I had ever met that was really invested in the model was hyperactive, or, as I would rather describe them and myself, full of energy. There seems to be a sense of impatience with pathology and an incredible patience with seeking hope. They also smile a lot. The key personality traits I see in therapists that choose the solution focused model and follow its tenets completely are those of being modest, humble, creative, curious, and having acute perception skills and a belief that people have what it takes to get better. They don't seem to need others to say that they do a good job. They get joy when they see clients rediscover themselves and that's enough to make them work harder. They also never represent themselves as knowing the model completely. They see themselves as perpetual learners . . . and the clients are their teachers.

When people try out the model and say *it didn't work with that client* it is usually because the therapist tried too hard to impose the questions on the client and didn't allow the client breathing room. The questions are different than those in other therapies, so clients often are taken aback when the solution focused therapist gives so much confidence to the client. There is also a real need to be "unknowing" and that's tough for some therapists to grasp, since the client pays them to help them. When I teach school counselors and teachers the approach, I encourage them to learn to say to a student who answers "I don't know" to their questions, "I don't know either. Take a day to explore and come back to tell me what you find that you want different." Not everyone can see this unknowing approach as helpful, yet it is.

Q. What are some common mistakes that therapists trying on the model make most often? If you had a chance to guide them differently, how would you do so?

A. The most common mistake is that therapists think that using the miracle question or searching for exceptions makes them a solution focused therapist. The solution focused approach is more than questions and it is not about techniques, it is about a belief that going back into the past to figure out why people hurt will get them nothing but more understanding of their pain. It is about looking at a person and believing that they are competent and hearing their competence in their stories.

When I do supervision with therapists who are learning the model, I try my best to not give them suggestions, but to listen to what they are doing that they think is working and what is not. I give them lots of compliments on what they do well with the client and when I feel a little instruction is necessary, I say, "I wonder what might happen, in your opinion, if you said this . . ." That way they can accept or deny the idea, which I present as just that, an idea.

Another way that I have come to train therapists in this model is to respect where they come from completely. If they argue or confront me on the model, which happens less now that I have taken on this stance, I agree with them and then ask them what I can do to help them understand better. The model itself guides me in the training and I make sure to mention that the solution focused approach is just another idea. Try it on and see what happens.

Q. What are some things you notice students doing while trying on this model that lets you know this model may fit them?

A. When students come back from a session, excited to tell me what the client did in response to something they said and you can see the passion on their face and the pride that they did something that might have helped the client to make a change, I know that the solution focused model is one they should study. Some students like to think that their therapeutic language or strategies pushed a client to change and they like to talk about how they "dealt with the client" and how they moved the client toward change and to "deal with issues." They will make great therapists, but their focus and their need to be experts will inhibit them from being successful solution focused therapists. These students often tell me, "I used a solution focused question with strategic family therapy or CBT today and I think it worked." Using a solution focused therapy "question" with a model that is worlds apart theoretically means they are experimenting with models to see how they work. The solution focused therapist is more concerned about the impact that words have on the client so that the client recognizes his or her own competency.

Q. If you were training therapists in the SFT model, what strategies would you use to train them and how would you present the material?

A. Currently, when I do training, I present a variety of cases to the trainees and ask them to tell me what they heard that I did that might be different from other models of therapy. I write their answers down and tell them that they are brilliant. I keep this up throughout the training. I add theoretical tenets of the model such as, "It takes a nonpathological approach, encourages people to do what works, doesn't need insight to be helpful, encourages the client to define the goal, looks for different contexts" and ask them to tell me what that might look like. I do lots of role plays between trainees where they use a problem-focused approach and then a solution focused approach. I talk about descriptions of issues and how changing descriptions changes meaning, which changes language and then gives a new perception to the client.

It is the application of the work in their own life and in their own cases that seems to help them visualize how the model works. I do give them scripts that I developed from reading many case studies, since many people need some guidelines to develop a new skill. But, I also tell them that it is merely a template to get started with, not a template to apply to a person.

Q. If you could pick a pioneer solution focused therapist who impacted your work, who would you name and why?

A. It would be Bill O'Hanlon. He was the first solution focused therapist I ever met in person and heard present on the model. I loved reading each of his books because of his candid, down-to-earth way of writing. He always wrote of cases as if you could see him working with a client, which made the process simple for me. He also took risks when he presented, of working with people from the audience on the spur of the moment, and that was impressive. It told me that he believed enough in himself to take a risk with an unknown issue and that gave me confidence.

When I wrote my first book, I needed someone to write an introduction. I contacted another solution focused therapist who had a good reputation, whom I had met and talked with at a conference during that time. He wrote back and said he would not endorse a book that blended some narrative therapy with solution focused therapy. I admit to having utilized Michael White's narrative approach to redescription and writing letters to clients, but the inclusion of his work was minimal. I was devastated. For some reason, I called Bill O'Hanlon, hoping that he remembered that I had met him briefly with Dr. Thomas at the Texas Association for Marriage and Family Therapy conference in Austin. He did. I told him my dilemma and he said, "Send me the manuscript. I will write one for you. There is always room at the top and I want you to have a chance to get there." I will never forget his words and to this day, I do the same for students as often as I can.

Q. What developments would you like to see in the future of this model?

A. I would like to see more applications of the model in business, medicine, schools, and community agencies. At the time of this writing, the economy and world situation seems full of problematic explanations, which leave communities and people feeling hopeless. I would like to see legislators learn more about the impact that the model can have on school retention, and on increased motivation for schoolchildren who fail subjects with traditional teaching methods. I would like to encourage psychotherapists to be hired to work with students in schools. I would like to see physicians learn more about the model so that they can talk to their acutely ill patients with hope, and help them to recognize how they have dealt with crises before. I would like community agencies that deal with people on welfare or the homeless to learn how to talk with their clients about past successes, no matter how small. They can tailor those to seeking new jobs and feeling hope.

EDITOR'S COMMENT

Every student should have a teacher like Dr. Metcalf—not just because she is a skilled teacher and not because she cares about her students, but because she lives what she teaches. This can be seen throughout her chapter. Notice the way she described the interaction with her family members; those interactions allow for a high level of empowerment for the children. Also, notice the way she describes her students and clients. There is great respect present. Treating people with respect is key to SFT and Dr. Metcalf does it in session, in her case examples in class, and in this chapter. People, not just clients, feel empowered when they are treated in this way. This allows for the SFT approach to flow through her when she is talking about it, practicing it, or skiing with her children.

—Elliott Connie

REFERENCES

Cade, B., & O'Hanlon, W. (1993). *A brief guide to brief therapy.* New York: Norton.
de Shazer, S. (1985). *Keys to solutions in brief therapy.* New York: Norton.
de Shazer, S. (1991). *Putting difference to work.* New York: Norton.
Durrant, M. (1990). *Creative strategies for school problems.* New York: Norton.
Epston, D., & White, M. (1990). *Narrative means to therapeutic ends.* New York: Norton.

Metcalf, L. (1991). Therapy with parent-adolescent conflict: Creating a climate in which clients can figure what to do differently. *Family Therapy Case Studies, 6*(2), 25–34.

Miller, S., & Berg, I. (1992). *Working with the problem drinker.* New York: Norton.

O'Hanlon, W., & Weiner-Davis, M. (2003). *In search of solutions.* New York: Norton.

Walter, J., & Peller, J. (1992). *Becoming solution focused.* New York: Bruner-Mazel.

15 Trust Client Strengths

TERESE STEINER

The client is the expert.

—Steve de Shazer

Q. How did you first learn about solution focused therapy (SFT)?

A. In 1991 I participated in a workshop with about a hundred participants in Heidelberg, Germany. In this workshop Steve de Shazer showed us the most amazing tape of one of his interviews with two persons diagnosed with schizophrenia. The topic was, as usual in a solution focused interview, about personal strength, small successes, and a concrete description about how life will look like once things improved one step. I forgot about the diagnosis. It was this tape which changed my professional life. I thought this was the best therapeutic work I had ever seen. Although the way Steve de Shazer presented his ideas was puzzling me, I decided I wanted to know more about this way of doing therapy and enrolled in an intensive training with Steve de Shazer at Gunther Schmidt's office in Heidelberg.

Q. How did you discover that SFT was the model that seemed to fit with your way of working with clients?

A. Originally I was trained as a couples and family therapist. I liked to see a problem within the context of the whole family, explore the interactions, and ask circular questions. However I was not at ease digging in the past, formulating hypotheses, and elaborating on sophisticated interventions. I was looking for another way of doing therapy. On my search for something different I first encountered hypnotherapy. I attended trainings in hypnotherapy in Phoenix. What I liked about hypnotherapy was its utilizing of the problem and its focus on the present and the future. Hypnotherapy already came close to what I was looking for and SFT then really seemed to be my choice of doing therapy. The following two assumptions of SFT really fascinated me:

- the clients are the experts of their life
- clients have the resources to create a better future

These assumptions implied that I did not have to be the expert on the client's life anymore. I felt such a relief from not having to carry the responsibility of knowing which intervention suited the client the best and was going to be most successful. I never felt comfortable with the expert position of having to know what was right and wrong for clients; it was something I felt I could never succeed in. With SFT, all of a sudden, I did not have to know anymore what was best for the client. My responsibility shifted to having to ask helpful questions in order for the clients to find out what *they* wanted to achieve and do. It was only when I got to know SFT that I could imagine practicing therapy for many years to come without burning out.

Q. What characteristics of this model drew you toward it?

A. Beside the above-mentioned assumptions I was thrilled by the core characteristics that there are always exceptions and that the future is both created and negotiable; also the fact that the language required for solution development is different from that needed to describe the problem. I have a passion for language and precise wording. The careful use of language is a strength of mine and it is crucial in SFT. So SFT and I were a good match. I enjoyed developing this skill further. Another characteristic of SFT I liked was the flat hierarchy: The client is the expert of her/his life and the therapist is the expert in helpful interviewing.

Q. How has utilizing SFT impacted your work with clients? (Please mention if you utilized a previous model and the difference you noticed in clients and yourself after switching to SFT.)

A. The first thing that crosses my mind is, there is much more laughter in the therapy room! The most important impact is that even very heavy cases never seem to be hopeless anymore because the clients are formulating concrete goals and are working with their strengths. To work with the resources and the strengths the clients have, instead of trying to compensate deficits, encourages both my clients and me as therapist. It is much easier to add on to something that is already here, rather than start something from scratch!

I started to ask lots and lots of questions and stopped giving advice. When clients complain about a problem, I now ask questions that invite them to describe what they want to see happen in their life instead and I pay attention when they use verbs rather than nouns and adjectives. If a client answers, "I would like to be happy," I want to know what she is *doing* when she is happy. This procedure results in a perception of being able to do something and implies the possibility of change.

I am leading my interviews much more than before. I interrupt my clients more often, I ask the same question in different variations, and am very persistent in focusing the client on the next little step in the future. I give my clients only little (maybe sometimes too little) time for complaining.

It took me several years to internalize the attitude that the client is the expert. While this attitude became more and more natural to me, my clients started to work harder and harder on their preferred future. At the same time, they were somewhat confused that they did not receive advice from me, like they expected to get from a medical doctor. Believing truly that the clients are the experts on their life, I leave it up to them to (for instance) decide what family members will attend the first session. I trust that they can make many more helpful decisions for themselves. This is not how I was trained to conduct sessions as a systemic therapist. However it works and it was again such a relief not having to know what was best or in which constellation the intake session should take place.

As child psychiatrist, I started to make goals, and scales came alive. I had many more activities in the family sessions than before. I invited the families to experience their strength within the session. I trust my clients and myself more to do our best during the session. As a consequence I hardly ever think about my clients after work. Before I used SFT, I often thought about my cases when I was at home. I had them sitting on my sofa or sharing the bed with me!

Q. How would your clients describe your work with them? Have any of your clients who might have experienced another model of therapy commented on the difference (if any) that they perceived when working with you?

A. She makes me work hard! She gives me such a lot of responsibility and it is always me who has to make decisions. A client of mine once said to me at the end of therapy: "With you it was not easy and I could not lean back. Your trust in my strength was challenging and also uncomfortable because I had to realize: I can do better and the only person who can do it is me! I changed things much quicker than I did in a previous therapy. I did not feel pushed because you asked me several times, 'How will you know the time has come to move on?' And then of course I realized again: it is just up to me."

The children and adolescents would say that I take them and their ideas seriously. I keep asking about the "good reasons" they have to do things the way they do it. I inquire a lot of details about certain things other grownups disapprove of and therefore would never discuss. My clients say that I inform them about the consequences they will most likely have to face if they continue to do certain things and at the same time I am always leaving the decision up to them how to go on. Finally, particularly the adolescents would say that it is kind of hard to work with me "because you cannot fight with her."

Q. What is it about SFT that makes it so effective?

A. Since the clients are assumed to be the experts of their life, they decide what the goal of therapy is. No energy and time are lost on finding out what the problem is and on imposing the therapist's point of view on the client. I am convinced that hope, the sense of having control, a goal in the future, and the freedom to make choices is crucial for therapeutic change. SFT fosters all four of them. We give the clients the choice of what and how to achieve the goal they want to reach, and then we search for exceptions and estimate progress—as little as it might be.

Focusing on how an exception is realized helps random exceptions to become deliberate and gives the client the sense of having control. That is what is needed to be motivated and keep going. An adolescent once told me at the end of a first session: "I was always told I am a very bad-tempered, impulsive, and aggressive creature, and in the end I was silly enough to believe it. After having talked with you I just realize there *are* moments I can keep control. Now I feel encouraged and I will train myself to be able to make my choice on when and where to stay calm and when and where to lose my temper. You know I always felt awful when I was told I should become a calm person. I like my temperament, I have a wonderful fire inside, but I agree it makes sense to do no harm. My goal will be to become a responsible fast driver of my character. By the way, my character looks like a red Ferrari!"

Q. Describe one of your favorite cases and how it impacted your work as a therapist.

A. Once, an 8-year-old boy was brought into my office because of severe sleeping problems. He had been examined by several physicians and even stayed several days at the children's hospital to change his sleeping pattern. Unfortunately the sleeping disorder could not be solved.

I first explored what the boy's strengths were, as I always do when I see a child for the first time. Then I gave the mother time to tell me about her perception of the situation. The boy had a very hard time falling asleep in the evening. When he eventually did fall asleep, he would wake up again within two or three hours and wake up his parents. This had been going on for months and the parents were exhausted. The sister of this boy was mentally and physically disabled and taking care of her demanded a lot of attention and energy from the parents. Previous therapists understood the boy's sleeping problem as an expression of the little boy's jealousy and advised the parents to have their disabled child taken care of by a professional institution. However the parents could not bear the thought and they refused to even look at any specialized institutions for disabled children.

The parent's goal was clear: They wanted to take care of *both* children and give both of them a chance to develop well. The boy's goal was to be fit for soccer practice and more alert and energized in school.

I wanted to know about all the different recommendations the family had received concerning the sleeping issue thus far and asked for exceptions to the problem. Unfortunately nothing seemed to have worked up to now.

The assumption that the clients are the experts—and that this holds true for children as well—was key to the solution that we developed. Of course I had to ask the boy for his ideas in a child-appropriate manner. I asked: "Suppose you were allowed to do whatever you think is helpful for you to sleep well, what would you suggest?" He looked at me in a very astonished way and then said, "No one has ever asked me this, but this is very easy: Mom has to tie me down as she does it with my sister." The mother had told me that the disabled sister was very hyperactive and therefore had to be tied down to her bed in order to find sleep.

The boy's answer made his mother look very anxious. I ignored the mother's reaction in this moment and asked the boy to tell me a little bit more about his suggestion. He explained that this would keep him in bed and that he was convinced that it would calm him down because he would not have to think whether he should get up or not. With a twinkle in his eyes he said, "And should it be very urgent, I am sure I could manage to open the straps." I wondered if he knew how long he would need this procedure and he said, "I think a fortnight will do."

I then discussed with the mother whether or not she could imagine doing what the boy suggested. We had a long talk about the ethical issue of the procedure and at the end the mother agreed to give it a try. And it worked! After 10 days the boy told his parents that he would no longer need the straps in order to fall asleep and he became a fairly good sleeper. Only occasionally would he still get up in the night and wake up his parents.

About six months later, I had a phone call from the boy's mother telling me that they had decided to place their daughter in a specialized institution during the weekdays. They did what many professionals were telling them to do, except for myself. The mother explained to me that it had been extremely important to them that they could make this decision deliberately and not because they had failed as parents. The solution of this family had a great impact on me because it proved to me that it is worthwhile asking the children what they think and taking their and the parents' ideas seriously. Of course not all children will have such an impressive solution to their family's problems if asked. However, over the years I've seen that almost all children can contribute to a good solution with their ideas.

Q. Has the use of SFT impacted you in your personal life? If so, please explain.

A. I think my husband and my children should answer this question. I would say I became more determined and in many ways more focused. It helped me to deal much better with my own ADD because I started to do things step by step. As a child I was often blamed for my curiosity and my slowness. I discovered that both were virtues and that made me think differently about my character. By learning and using SFT I met many fascinating people and some of them became very dear friends who enrich my personal life far beyond my professional life.

Q. What are some key personal traits that you think are shared among solution focused practitioners?

A. I am not sure. If I think of Steve de Shazer and Insoo Kim Berg and how different they were, it makes me wonder if there is such a thing as key personal traits among SFT therapists. Steve de Shazer was a man of few words and Insoo Kim Berg was very empathetic and emotional; and yet both of them were doing SFT. I believe as long as the therapist focuses on what the client wants, and is able to go with that, listens to what the clients says and respects the client's ideas, it works.

If there is a personal trait that is helpful I would say it is the ability to be able to deal with uncertainty and cope well with the fact that as a therapist you only have control over the procedure in the session and not the content. It also makes your life easier as an SFT therapist if you are fascinated by thinking out loud.

Q. What are some common mistakes that therapists trying on the model make most often? If you had a chance to guide them differently, how would you do so?

A. A person who starts to use SFT needs a lot of encouragement. We should not forget that most of the therapists who had been trained in a different approach were educated often over years to find out what is wrong and dysfunctional. I think it is hard to make the shift to focusing on little exceptions and little moments when things are better. Therefore I think the trainer should do the same with the student as the student is asked to do with the clients: namely focus on what is working for the beginner and highlight the helpful questions they ask and build on that. I would not talk about mistakes, but instead about helpful and maybe less helpful questions.

I would suggest that learners should tape their session. Then they should review the session and look for the part of the session which went particularly well, and pay careful attention to what question they asked. The beginner therapists should ask themselves how they can find out whether they asked a helpful question or not. What are the clues telling the students that they are on track from the client's point of view?

It is important that the students understand that SFT is, first of all, a mind-set. No doubt there are some very helpful tools; and yet I am convinced that you are only able to apply the approach successfully if you trust in the client's strength and believe that your clients always cooperate with you the best they can in the given moment. How do I communicate this mind-set? In workshops and professional trainings, the students are my clients. If they experience during the training how it feels to be encouraged, respected, and taken seriously they will get the idea.

Beginners in SFT working in the educational and pedagogical fields sometimes hesitate to set boundaries for children. To confuse SFT with not setting boundaries is a large misunderstanding. Children have to learn how to function in our society, which means following a lot of rules. Working with children requires that the adults around them demand things of them, react when the children go beyond the limits, and set up rules that cannot be negotiated. This stays unchanged when one works from a solution focused perspective. The difference is that the SFT professional in an educational or pedagogical setting will conduct solution focused conversations with the child on a regular basis. This means that the professional listens very carefully to understand the children's point of view, to understand the reasons for their behaviors, the advantages the children see in breaking the rules and so on. Furthermore, the SFT professional will interview a child in how the professional can help the child stick to the rules. In my workshop, I call this conversation "cooperative information development." It takes beginners some time to navigate between the role of the professional who is demanding and setting boundaries and the professional who develops information (in a solution focused manner) with the child. It is not only difficult to switch forth and back between different roles, but also a challenge to find out when what reaction is appropriate.

Q. What are some things you notice students doing while trying on this model that lets you know this model may fit them?

A. I doubt that I can actually tell whether the model fits a student or not. What I observe is that the students who are more confused than others at the beginning of their training and who are asking a lot of critical questions seem to be the ones who want to go on and learn more about SFT. To my observation the "not knowing position" is easier to handle for young students, therapists who feel that their way of doing therapy was not helpful enough, or very experienced therapists. The advantage the young students have is that they do not have to get rid of lots of theory they learnt about figuring out the problem. The advantage of therapists who are somewhat frustrated with the therapy they have been doing are usually fascinated by the simplicity (which is not the same as being easy!) of SFT and its effectiveness, which motivates them to learn about it. Finally, experienced therapists tend to have fewer problems letting go of the control over the content of therapy. I assume this is because they have experienced over and over again that clients can achieve amazing results that are not linked to their therapy.

There is a saying that describes well one of the strengths needed to be a good SFT therapist: "You have to be able to hear the grass grow." So, if I watch a beginner who already notices a very small change a client is talking about, and is able to pick up on it and amplify it, this may be an indicator that SFT would be a good fit for this person. Often these are also the students who find it easier to give the credit for success entirely to the client by showing curiosity and interest for the change and new ideas the client comes up with. They can go along well with the wisdom Insoo Kim Berg used to teach: "A therapist should not leave footprints behind."

Q. If you were training therapists in the SFT model, what strategies would you use to train them and how would you present the material?

A. I use the same procedure that I use in therapy sessions. I ask the students what they want, how they will know that the training has been useful for them, and how the clients of the students will find out that the student therapist learnt something helpful in this training.

Steve de Shazer told us: "Practice, practice, practice and be disciplined! These are the ingredients for success." According to my opinion it is important that we make students practice already during the workshop. Native American wisdom says: "Show me and I will forget, tell me and I will not be able to remember, involve me and I will understand." It is this involvement during the workshop that has an impact.

Each exercise my students do in a workshop is processed; that means that in the plenum, I ask what worked well during the exercise and whether there is additional information they need. Usually it is during this processing that important questions are raised. It seems that it is through trying it out that students start to get the essentials of SFT.

There are different settings for exercises I use. For instance, I form little groups (3–5) with one person in the role of an observer. In larger groups (8–10), I will have one part of the group role-play an interview while the other part acts as the reflecting team. At the end, every participant on the reflecting team mentions what was outstanding to him or her, which strengths she/he observed. The observers may also raise questions that crossed their minds.

Another way is to watch a tape with the whole group. To formulate feedback, the participants split up in smaller groups and think about what to say. What is important is that the feedback is role-played. It makes quite a difference whether I just offer my feedback, or whether I actually deliver the feedback to the "client." The person who role-plays the client gives feedback by telling the "therapist" what was an especially good fit.

The role of the observer is crucial. The observer's task is to write down the helpful questions the trainee asked and to focus on the interaction. This helps to make the client work hard and come up with new ideas. As most of the trainees are not familiar with the role of the observer, it is important to introduce this exercise setting very well. In my workshops on SFT with children, I always have the participants actually do the hand puppet work, simulate a family session by using different materials like painting or clay, or use visualization materials. It is again this involvement and the experience the students make that increases the chance they will apply new ideas in their professional context. Lecturing is a form of teaching I very seldom use. I prefer that the students read a handout or text and formulate questions regarding what they have read.

In an ongoing training I have two approaches. On the one hand, I teach what for me has turned out to be essential. On the other hand, the learning objectives should be formulated by the students. At the beginning of a new module I am interested in the recent success in their professional work. I ask them to scale the progress they made between the last module and now. On this scale, 10 stands for the level of mind-set, knowledge, and skills they want to achieve by the end of the training. I then ask them to find out how they would know, how their clients would know, and how their boss would know if they moved one step up on their personal scale. This procedure results in a list of specific questions we will try to answer during the module and which meets the needs of the students at the given moment.

In ongoing trainings it is also helpful to have participants practice in the same group for a certain time. Once they are familiar with one another the observations they make and the feedback they give seem to be more precise and helpful than in groups that change all the time.

I would like to share a memory with you I have of a workshop on training trainers I attended in Bremen with Steve de Shazer: We were a group of about 20 people, all coming from different parts of Germany and Switzerland. Steve de Shazer started the workshop by greeting us very warmly, and then he kept silent. He neither started lecturing nor did he suggest an activity. He just waited and waited and waited. Some participants were wondering what was going on, why he did not start the training and some got increasingly irritated and after about an hour the first started to leave. It became clear that there was no program.

It took us a very long time to find out that we were supposed to ask questions on topics that we thought would be important in order to improve our skills. Once we presented our well-reflected questions, Steve immediately started to work with us. I think this procedure had a strong impact on me as a trainer and I am ever so grateful he had the courage to expose himself in this way in order to give us the opportunity to make the experience of what our roles as trainers should be. When I think of this memory a sentence of Wittgenstein, by whom Steve de Shazer was strongly influenced, always comes to my mind: "Never do for your readers what they can do for themselves." To me this translated to: "Never do for your students what they can do for themselves!"

Q. If you could pick a pioneer solution focused therapist who impacted your work, who would you name and why?

A. I had the chance to meet Steve de Shazer and Insoo Kim Berg in 1991 and soon our families became close friends. Through our friendship I often had the opportunity to watch them teach. After a few years I started teaching with them. It was definitely Steve de Shazer and Insoo Kim Berg who had the greatest impact on my work. The two of them had very different personalities and therapy styles. To observe this big difference gave me the freedom from the start to develop my own very personal style in doing SFT. It is the mind-set that counts and it is perfectly all right to express your attitude the way it fits your personality best. To me that was an important message.

Among many other things, I learnt from Steve de Shazer that it is possible to not use one word after work about therapy. We talked about jazz or beer, exchanged recipes, and went for silent walks. From Insoo Kim Berg I learnt to stay hopeful for people even in the seemingly most desperate situations. It was also she who in her very gentle and yet very persistent way made me write down how to apply SFT to children. What a challenging empowerment! It was great and at the same time there were times I wished I had not said yes. Still while writing the book *Children's Solution Work,* I experienced her wonderful support, her encouragement, and maybe most important, her trust that I could do my part. And it was Steve de Shazer, of course, who asked Insoo Kim Berg and me helpful questions that made us figure out what it actually was that we were doing that was successful.

Q. What developments would you like to see in the future of this model?

A. What is most important to me is that therapists practicing SFT are truly committed to making a (positive) difference in other people's life that they hoped for. In this sense, I would like SFT to stay the same. SFT is very simple. This makes it very attractive but it is also tempting to think that it is easy to practice. SFT requires a lot of discipline from the therapist to keep to the core assumptions. I wish that not anything and everything will be called SFT just because someone once used the miracle questions.

While I have this wish to conserve the core assumptions of SFBT and reserve this name for these core assumptions I would like to see the solution focused thinking applied to other professional fields than therapy and education. It would be great to see more people use solution focused ideas in classical social work settings, working with delinquent populations in and out of prison, homeless people, and so forth.

I am currently engaged in a pilot project called "youth4youth" sponsored by Terre des Hommes, an international federation for children, teaching young local Africans the solution focused approach. The goal is to enable young volunteers to support orphans as well as young people with HIV and AIDS. In the midst of all of this tragedy, it is wonderful to see how these young people are becoming more and more hopeful throughout this 2-year-long training. They start to focus on what works rather than the disaster and the apparently hopeless situation around them. They tell me, "Before we looked at the mud and now we started to look at the stars together with the children and adolescents we support. We have forgotten that there are many stars at the African sky."

Just like this project, I believe that there are many other areas where the proper application of solution focused thinking and acting could make a positive difference. Finally, I would appreciate it if we continued to do more serious research on the effectiveness of SFT as well as on how SFT works linguistically as well as neuropsychologically.

EDITOR'S COMMENT

Dr. Terese Steiner has given us a glimpse into the mind of a psychiatrist that has taken the solution focused approach and given her clients a gift. While many physicians stay in the context of symptoms, Terese has shown how not only her clients improve quickly, but how she has improved her quality of professional life. Don't we all enjoy the fact that as solution focused therapists we are off the hook in regard to creating tasks? I also enjoyed Terese's dialogue about de Shazer and Berg and how different they were, yet how similar they were theoretically. I like Terese's ideas on keeping the model as it is yet expanding on its usefulness in so many areas. Imagine more medical practitioners like Dr. Steiner! I was thrilled to read about the young man who had his own ideas about sleeping. Other therapists might have mused that he just wanted attention like his sister. Yet, Terese acknowledged his bright ideas and it worked. Client strengths can be amazing and fruitful. How fortunate that we can learn from Terese to seek them slowly and carefully, so that they can do the same.

—Linda Metcalf

16 A Journey Toward Solutions

ALASDAIR MACDONALD

> The person who says it cannot be done should not interrupt the person who is doing it.
>
> —Chinese proverb

I have been a consultant psychiatrist in the British National Health Service since 1980. My father was a physician and a psychoanalytic psychotherapist and so I had an interest in the psychotherapies before I entered medical training. I chose the field of mental health intending to work as a psychiatrist and psychodynamic psychotherapist. However, there was waning interest in such therapy within the medical establishment and the workloads provided little opportunity for such training. Trainees were required to conduct once-weekly supervised individual psychodynamic psychotherapy with one case for up to one year as a training requirement, but this was not strictly adhered to. A consultant would have responsibility for a population of some 40,000–50,000 persons, so that the best to hope for was to have one psychotherapy case, or perhaps a weekly outpatient group, simply in order to retain one's skills. I considered child psychiatry; however, individual psychotherapy for children was almost all provided by specialist psychologists and psychotherapists, with the medical role confined to assessments and the management of biological disorders.

My great good fortune during my child psychiatry attachment was to meet a young consultant from the Middle East who had a special interest in family therapy. He was an energetic therapist, so much so that school refusers might find him at their front door on his motorcycle, demanding that they climb aboard to be taken to school. He introduced us to strategic therapy as described by the Mental Research Institute (MRI) in Palo Alto. When I returned to adult psychiatric practice, I retained my interest in family therapy and specifically in the brief therapies.

In the late 1970s, the United Kingdom government wished to reduce the large mental hospitals then in existence and was exploring alternative forms of service. My first independent consultant post was in a novel community service based around a day hospital. For my consultant colleague and myself, our catchment population was 100,000 persons (25% of whom were over 65 years old), spread over an area of 900 square miles, with some beds in a hospital in the next county. My car became my office, as I had no other. After assisting at an emergency childbirth when roads were blocked by a snowstorm, I bought a four-wheel drive vehicle as a precaution against any further such events.

Our team of colleagues had all chosen to work in the new setting and were therefore enthusiastic and enterprising. Our day hospital came to provide long-term support, community nursing and social work services, emergency and routine assessment, and liaison psychiatry. We established a sheltered lodging house and developed an assessment unit for the elderly. In the psychotherapies, we offered couples work and groups for anxiety and for women's issues. After staff training, we had four family therapy sessions weekly with different personnel in each team. At that time the principal model used was Milan-style family therapy, although the team of which I was a member drew heavily on MRI concepts and methods. We became the training agency for the region in all aspects of family therapy, and I was the psychotherapy advisor to the Regional Medical Training Scheme for psychiatrists (see Macdonald, 1987).

After some years in this post, I returned to Scotland. I took employment in a rural county within a hospital where there was a long tradition of research into the biological aspects of psychiatry. The hospital wanted a consultant who could provide the mandatory training requirements in psychotherapy for their large number of psychiatrists in training. This hospital had a famous residential child psychiatry unit, an outstanding psychology department, and an innovative community-based learning disability service, but these services were not perceived as relevant to "real psychiatry." Throughout my professional career I have held posts that included traditional psychiatric responsibilities, in order to demonstrate that talking treatments are of use in the real world of daily mental health. The hospital had a long-standing rivalry with the hospital in the next county, which had a worldwide reputation for therapeutic community skills. On my arrival, I was instructed by the director of nursing not to turn all the nursing staff into therapists, so I promised not to do this.

In fact, it soon became clear that many of the nursing staff were therapists already, or wished to become so. In the interests of supporting their practice rather than allowing "wild" therapy, I established a strategic brief therapy clinic for training purposes, once a week and then twice weekly. We had a video link initially and then one-way screens, earbugs for the therapist, and a team behind the mirror. The team included nurses, doctors, occupational therapists, and social workers. Nine months with the team and case management of two families were required to receive our certificate of competence. We took on trainees from other local hospitals (fees being paid to our employing hospital) and delivered training workshops in Scotland and the north of England. Our efforts are described in articles in family therapy and nursing journals (Bowditch, 1991; Macdonald, 1990).

SOLUTION FOCUSED THERAPY ARRIVES!

In 1988 I read the information about BRIEFER II (de Shazer, 1988) because of a current interest in information technology and algorithms for clinical work. I found the work fascinating and read more of de Shazer's publications. Others in the team found these of significance also. We agreed that for a 6-month trial period we would employ solution focused practice instead of our MRI model. At once, we found that sessions became less demanding for the therapist and that the families became more receptive. Our team discussions in the break became shorter because we had already noted strengths and ideas within the family during the conversations. It became more common for our families to attend only once or twice. This was important because they had sometimes driven 100 miles each way to attend the appointment, and had to receive their therapy within the demands of isolated farms with many animals to care for. The practical rural population of the county found solution focused thinking and using their own resources more congenial than the psychodynamic and Rogerian methods that had previously been the main local options.

We had established a regular one-year follow-up program to ascertain the benefits of our work. Results from this program showed no adverse effect on our success rate when we changed to the new solution focused model. (Evidence from this rolling follow-up program has been published: Macdonald, 1994, 1997, 2005.) At the end of the 6-month trial period, every member of the team believed that solution focused therapy (SFT) was a significant improvement on our previous strategic approach and that we should continue to use it instead of returning to our previous MRI methods.

THE PROFESSIONAL IMPACT OF SFT

At first my use of SFT was confined to the training clinic described above. However, over time I found it more and more useful in other settings. My use of the psychodynamic approach declined steadily because I felt that solution focused interventions were more respectful and more effective in a shorter period of time. I continued to use some strategic interventions within the admissions unit because of the diverse nature of the residents. Among other problems, the hospital had closed its secure unit, so that all major disturbances had to be handled in the open ward. Over time, many of our inpatient staff completed the solution focused training, and we were able to contain many problems more effectively.

As a demonstration of this effectiveness, our team's unit served the distant parts of the county. The neighboring team had a near-identical building for an equivalent catchment population from nearby. Our unit was relatively peaceful and always had beds available even though our patients had more difficulty with access to family and home because of the distances involved. The neighboring unit was always full, with a high incidence of disturbance. For some months there was a quiet but sustained campaign pressing for us to exchange buildings with the other team. Eventually we realized that the managers of the other team thought that the magic lay in the building itself. They hoped to emulate our outcomes by exchanging buildings. They had no comprehension of the idea that staff skills might affect the quality of care that we delivered.

I was able to continue supervising trainees in psychodynamic work, which was a requirement of my post. However, I changed the form of the supervision groups toward a solution focused version. Eventually I left that post because I believed that offering training in psychodynamic methods was no longer justified, given the greater value and effectiveness of postmodern techniques such as solution focused working.

In my next hospital post I was in charge of the secure unit for the county as well as providing a consultant service to part of the local area. This unit was purpose-built and had a highly skilled nursing team. I decided not to discuss my ideas with hospital staff unless I was asked to do so. As had become my custom, I used solution focused questions all the time within the secure unit and in prison assessments. Staff became interested and the use of these ideas spread through the unit. About one-third of our staff undertook a full training in solution focused work; another one-third agreed that it was useful and that they might use it in certain cases, but that they already had skills of their own that they would continue to use; and the remainder preferred to continue with their existing approaches. We know that choice and control are helpful in producing better outcomes in psychological therapies. We also know that solution focused approaches, like other psychotherapies, benefit about 70% of our client groups. For these reasons, it is important that teams make more than one approach available. As long as we respect each other's skills, difference offers advantages and not problems.

Violent confrontations within the secure unit and the length of stay in the unit decreased as we became more solution oriented. Similar results have been reported by Vaughn and her colleagues from Denver (Vaughn, Young, Webster, & Thomas, 1996). Our unit became so successful that we were often the only unit in North England with beds available for emergencies. At times we had contracts with other counties because our turnover had become so rapid that the staff complained that the unit was too quiet to be interesting!

All the medical staff in the hospital took part in regular case presentations. After the history had been described, the patient would be asked to come to the room and answer questions from 15 to 20 medical staff, many unknown to them. It was often remarked that I was the only person able to have a conversation with the (usually anxious) patient. In spite of repeated discussions, I was unable to convince my medical colleagues that this was an aspect of the solution focused method in action rather than a personal skill or talent. They seemed to prefer to compliment me rather than to examine their own practice.

In work with individuals and families, many families have had previous experience with other approaches. For the general psychiatric population, many attenders commented on how our conversations seemed more practical and respectful. This helped engagement with treatment, although our outcomes remained similar to those of my colleagues. We found solution focused work to be especially helpful for obsessive-compulsive disorder and for moderate depression. The United Kingdom textbooks state that obsessive-compulsive disorder may not remit for five years, whereas using solution focused methods our patients achieved remission within a year in most cases. The disorder seemed to benefit from longer intervals between sessions, allowing people to change at a slower pace. I was the only psychiatrist in our area who was pleased when additional referrals for obsessive-compulsive disorder were sent to me. I had found strategic therapy very effective for these conditions, but I found that solution focused work was more collaborative as the attenders designed their own tasks and went at their own pace.

Because of local policies, our training clinic in SFT was the only one offering anger management, work with perpetrators of domestic violence, and work with those accused or convicted of stalking offenses. Other disciplines would not work with such people, or could not engage with them, or found their work ineffective. So this showed a clear new benefit arising from the work of the Milwaukee team. The first person to be convicted of stalking in England was pursuing someone in our catchment area, but we did not have the chance to offer him help because the courts barred him from the county.

In work with offenders, I found that solution focused interviewing produced a sense of being understood and respected in many persons, even in a single interview for court reports. I certainly would not have claimed to understand offenders so quickly, but something in the method helped them to perceive these qualities in the interview. This cannot be harmful, even if there is no prospect of an offer of formal treatment processes at that stage.

I remember one lady who was referred urgently and had been seen in the past on three different occasions by psychodynamic workers. She was taken aback to be asked about her goals and next steps instead of a lengthy discourse about the problems (which were significant and affected others in her family, including becoming pregnant by her son-in-law). With a solution focused approach, she moved on within three sessions, and made successful adjustments that allowed her to live without recurrent therapeutic support in the years thereafter.

Another interesting case was a clergyman who had retired to the area. He attended complaining of a number of issues around his retirement and his (reduced) pastoral activities. He had seen a counselor about such issues for over a year in his previous hometown. After three sessions with us, he suddenly said, "You want me to *do* these things to achieve my goals! I don't want to do that; I want to talk to an attractive lady once a week about my troubles!" We respectfully acknowledged this new goal and referred him to another department that might provide this for him.

In my opinion, one strength of SFT is that it has been shown in our studies and others to be equally effective across all socioeconomic groups (De Jong & Hopwood, 1996; de Shazer & Isebaert, 2003). It may not be successful, but it is not social class that affects its success. This is important since all other talking treatments have been shown to be more effective for those of higher social class and those who are better educated and psychologically minded. There are very many people in the world who lack social advantages and so we need therapies that are effective for them. The world's resources are getting less. Especially in socialized health care systems, we urgently need cost-efficiency and cost-effectiveness in our treatments.

Another strength of SFT is that it has been shown to be effective with those for whom traditional therapies have been found ineffective. It is rare for mandated individuals and families, substance misusers and adolescents to enter into effective treatment contracts. However, using SFT it is often possible to achieve a treatment alliance and for useful results to follow. See Milner and Singleton (2008) and Lee, Sebold, and Uken (2003) for examples of such work.

CASE STUDY

The following case is used with permission; names and identifying items are changed.

Don (51 years old) and Pat (48) were brothers who shared a house. They attended therapy together.

Problem

Don reported being anxious, which had been worse since their father died two years before. Pat thought that Don "needed to see someone." Anxiety showed itself by Don not going to work and not sleeping well. Their mother ("Mum") lived with them and was getting frailer. Don worried about her and then did not go to work.

Pat had moved away, returning 4 years ago after being made to feel guilty. He now had a manager's job and a girlfriend; he had plans to move out of the home.

Both had agreed that things needed to change but no decisions had been made about how to change them.

Goals

Pat wanted Don to be happier and to cope better with Mum. This would show itself by Don going out more. Don wanted Pat to talk more with him and to share the care of Mum. When things were going well they agreed that Don would be able to read more, go for walks and to work, and take up social invitations.

Exceptions

Don reported that he was anxious almost every day. He sometimes had moments free from anxiety, more often when Pat was at home, "but Pat is not interested in looking after Mum." Don was less anxious when his Mum was in bed. His tablets (antidepressants) had helped "a bit."

Scaling

Don was at 1 on a scale of 0–10 (on the given scale, a 0 represented problem saturation and a 10 represented complete success over the problem). He expected it to take two years to reach 5. Pat thought that Don could reach 8 in that time. He suggested that at 2, Don would be calm like Pat and not make so many lists to remember things; also Pat would be doing some of the things on the lists. Pat said that at 2 Don would be chatty; Don said that Pat would be listening to him and taking him seriously.

Miracle Question

Don said that after the miracle, Pat would discuss things instead of rushing out to work. Pat said that he would be more organized so he had time to talk with Don and Mum. Don would be calmer. Don hoped to go to work more than at present. Pat suggested a home help and Don discussed the practicalities of this. It emerged that Mum herself would decide if home help was acceptable and that she owned the house. Scaling their confidence 0–10, they reckoned that working together they could be 7–8 sure of getting Mum to agree.

Feedback

Acknowledgment: "You are both anxious and worried about Mum."

Compliments: "Don, you expressed yourself clearly and honestly, especially your concerns about Mum." "Pat, you have been concerned both about Mum and about Don's welfare. You have worked hard together on coming up with ideas and possibilities."

Task: "You will continue to talk together about possible next steps."

(Postsession reflection: Should Pat's management skills have been emphasized as a resource? Or would Don have seen this as devaluing his contribution?)

Return Appointment

Five weeks later, as they had requested, we scheduled a follow-up appointment.

Don attended alone. They had talked about home support together and Mum had eventually agreed. Don reported that all three of them were satisfied with the changes and that he had begun to reduce his tablets. Don did not want a further appointment. He was aware that further sessions were possible if required.

Reflections

This case reminded me that couples work is not always about marriages and that someone not in the room is still important. Solution focused questioning revealed the family structure and power relationships without being directive or confrontational. Surprising new information emerged during the miracle question process about Mum's role and significance in the home. As so often in our practice, one session was enough to move many issues in the right direction.

SOLUTION FOCUSED IDEAS IN MANAGERIAL POSTS

I have been the medical director of two different British hospitals. This directorship is a complex task, requiring one to bridge the gap between clinical staff and managers, to represent fairly the views of each side to the other, and to maintain one's clinical credibility as well. In many cases the medical director is the only person with clinical skills who is present when new policies are being developed. The post usually includes human resources and recruitment responsibilities for medical staff, including disciplinary and health matters. It was not feasible to make use of my previous grounding in crisis intervention and group dynamics because of the size of my workload and the attitudes of nonclinical staff.

I found solution focused skills to be invaluable for crisis management and in goal-setting within meetings. They allowed me to detect quickly when there were no customers present for a given idea or when there were such powerful vested interests involved that no solution would be allowed. Recognizing these situations gave me the chance to avoid profitless confrontations and to spend my time on goals that could be achieved.

Nowadays solution focused management in coaching and consultancy is being used around the world. The SOL World management conference attracts international specialists every year and registering organizations exist in several countries.

SOLUTION FOCUSED IDEAS IN PERSONAL LIFE

In my personal life, my experience of SFT has had various effects. The shift in emphasis toward collaborating with individuals and families and the constant search for strengths and resources has made me much more aware of the difficult lives experienced by those I see in the clinics. At the same time, I have become aware of the heroic and determined attempts of others to deal with their problems and difficulties.

Listening in a solution focused way to the stories told to me has made me aware of the limitations of the medical role and of the parts played by other workers in the health care team. Setting tasks thoughtfully and then seeing how rarely they were useful or relevant has been a good reminder that much medical advice, however skillfully devised, is not going to be followed or is not going to be effective once it is followed. A study in the United Kingdom in the 1990s showed that about one-third of all prescriptions of drugs were written for the wrong dose or for the wrong condition. Luckily the study also found that the public protected themselves by not taking all of the medication, or by not taking any of it.

I used to be concerned when people failed to attend for their appointments. Now I recognize that an appointment is only one thing for a busy person to fit into a day, and that sometimes another task will take priority. Equally, I have become more aware of the chance that every session may be the only one, and that we should hope for some effect in every contact that we have with people. Even if the effect is small, the chance is important.

In my personal life, I often use scaling to deal with anxiety about forthcoming events or to devise plans for tasks. For example, preparation for a family trip can be aided by thinking, "What will this journey be like if it scores 10 out of 10? At a 9, what will be different?" This quickly generates a hierarchy of tasks in a preferred order, which means that you can judge priorities and alternative strategies in case any step does not work out on the day. This process helps to bring large concerns down to a more manageable level.

If SFT had not appeared, then I might have become a practitioner in neurolinguistic programming (NLP). Both use language skills, both achieve quick results by means that do not appear logical, and both focus on the goals of the individual. NLP draws on aspects of hypnotherapy, which many practitioners combine successfully with solution focused methods. However, NLP is less collaborative and it is most useful with individuals. Solution focused approaches can be used with individuals, couples, families, and organizations, so that one does not need many different skills and qualifications.

PERSONALITY TRAITS IN SOLUTION FOCUSED PRACTITIONERS

The European Brief Therapy Association (EBTA) is the leading solution focused organization in the world. I have been to every EBTA conference since 1994 and to many other meetings and events organized by solution focused practitioners. To my mind, the attenders are usually pleasant and friendly people, however gifted and famous they may be. There is very little sign of backbiting or professional rivalry. You are more likely to see a senior therapist delaying lunch in order to explain some interesting point to a new attendee, or pointing out another colleague who may know the answer to their question. The meetings are full of mutual appreciation and shared interests. Of course people bring up problems in various ways, but are likely to find a host of suggestions and ideas about how to address the issues.

When I spoke at the second EBTA meeting in Stockholm in 1994, it was my first international meeting for many years. The supportive attitude of solution focused colleagues was immediately apparent. The airline had lost the bag containing my lecture notes and so I had to speak haltingly from memory. Instead of impatience, I received helpful questions and clarifications from my audience.

I was invited to become the research coordinator to the board of the EBTA. I agreed, because there were then only six published outcome studies of SFT and so it seemed an easy task. This has drawn me into many years of work within the field of psychotherapy research, which I have greatly enjoyed and which I hope has also been of benefit to others. Researchers and therapists often have very different values and mind-sets, so the chance to build bridges between the two groups has been a privilege. Thus my cognitive and research skills have also been improved by my contact with SFT. There are now many hundreds of published studies of all aspects of solution focused work, from word-by-word microanalysis of interviews, up to major long-term follow-up studies of therapy outcomes. There are 77 good outcome studies, following from the original 6 in 1994 (see www.solutionsdoc.co.uk and www.ebta.nu for more information). The EBTA awards grants annually for modest research projects, which has enabled some innovative ideas to see the light of day.

Attempts to study the traits of solution focused therapists have been made. The eminent French anthropologists Michael Houseman and Marika Moisseeff designed a question set to explore these issues. Unfortunately there were not enough replies to draw firm conclusions about theses subtle personal issues. It did appear that once workers learn solution focused techniques then they have less interest in new training programs, perhaps because solution focused work is so widely applicable. However, this was not good news for those of us who earn a living by providing trainings!

Another study by Alison Johnson of California and Tomasz Switek of Poland looked at character traits and problem-solving styles in solution focused workers. Again the numbers were too small for detailed analysis, but it was clear that once workers discovered SFT, then it became a part of their everyday life as well as a work tool. These studies have been presented at conferences but have not yet been published.

In terms of my own personality, since I have been drawn into solution focused work, I believe that I have become more relaxed. I am more optimistic about small and large aspects of life. I am less inclined to try to take over and manage things for other people who may have their own preferences. Like other people, I have encountered difficulties in my personal and professional life. I have found solution focused concepts invaluable in dealing with such issues. I do admit to having a minute or two of gloom or resentment on many occasions before I can start my solution focused thinking!

Because I like to travel, attending conferences and workshops internationally has been a great pleasure to me. Sometimes with support from employers and others, I have been able to share in the development of solution focused ideas in many countries around the world. I see a similar enthusiasm for global developments and helpful collaboration in many of my solution focused colleagues. The proliferation of Web sites and e-mail discussion groups for solution focused practitioners is one sign of this, both at the national and international level.

TRAINING AND REFLECTION

I have been training colleagues in SFT for many years, both in formal programs and more subtly in day-to-day interaction. There are a number of issues that commonly arise in learning to use solution focused approaches.

One common one is the wish to move things forward, to be solution forced. This is seen most in those practitioners who have been working successfully for a few months. They are excited by their successes, and want the positive reinforcement provided by successful cases. Having found these wonderful ideas, they cannot believe that others are so slow to grasp the possibilities. So supervision or work with a team is valuable in keeping their enthusiasm within realistic limits.

A related habit is the urge to give advice and tasks, sometimes before the first session has finished. Some come to this because their previous preferred model was directive in style. Others are inexperienced in therapy and cannot accept that people are autonomous and will work at their own pace whatever is said to them by "experts."

For many in mental health practice, there is the urge to say to trainers, "You can't use SFT for (insert diagnosis here)." Because traditional psychotherapies are contraindicated or ineffective in many mental disorders, staff assume that the same rules apply to solution focused work. In fact, one of the strengths of solution focused work is that you can be successful with many different kinds of problem. There is also no evidence that solution focused questions do any harm. The approach may not be effective but there is no report of any damaging effect from these questions.

A similar problem can arise when trainees with existing therapy skills say, "I know who will benefit from solution focused work." One of the features of solution focused work is that we do not understand why it is effective, nor are there clear factors that predict likely success. So it is not justifiable to say that it will or will not work in any given situation. All we can do is try it out and see what the process brings. Very often the results will surprise us. A related group is those who will start a solution focused dialogue and then suddenly switch to a person-centered or psychodynamic conversation. On questioning they respond that they knew that this was the right approach. It is usually difficult to see any clue in the behavior of the individual and the therapist is usually unable to justify the change by any observed evidence. It is of interest that it is very rare for anyone to switch thus into a behavioral model. The switch is always to a reflective, nondirective, emotion-laden model.

A few students grasp the process of solution focused work immediately. They may not be skilled as yet, but the concept fits their understanding almost at once. Others will move more slowly, adding some new questions to their repertoire. Eventually they will use all the solution focused questions and few others. These students may still be asking questions about underlying models and principles years later, in their wish to accommodate solution focused concepts to their previous learning and values. Another group will be experienced therapists from other styles, who will use the solution focused dialogue competently and well. At the end of training they will tell you that it has been very interesting but they will be returning to their previous skills.

I have provided training in SFT in a wide variety of settings. I use standard lists of questions for each of the main areas of enquiry, and I expect these to be used in the same order for the most part. I use the analogy of learning a musical instrument: At first you must play your scales and simple tunes many, many times. Once you are skilled with the instrument then you become creative and able to apply your own interpretations to the music. The same applies to learning a language; at first there is much repetition and the use of simple rules. Later you can hold conversations or write poems in the language, having become familiar with the building blocks of the language.

I usually ask beginners to suspend their long-held ideas until they know enough about the model to disagree competently. Once they have some knowledge of the model, then they can challenge ideas usefully and learn from the discussion. Much of the credibility of solution focused work comes from doing it and seeing it to be effective. This experiential learning is more convincing than any explanation or theory.

The greatest influence on my understanding of SFT was Steve de Shazer himself. His books and papers began my thinking in these ways. Steve and Insoo Kim Berg were great supporters of the European Brief Therapy Association. Through my involvement with the organization, I had the good fortune to take part in many formal and informal conversations with Steve about therapy and SFT in particular. Sometimes we would pass a delay at an airport talking about therapy and the implications of a particular idea or piece of technique. Steve's style of conversation was much the same socially as it was in therapy: attentive, interested, slightly idiosyncratic, forcing one to pay attention to every detail. He rarely said more than he thought was necessary, and would not be drawn into conflict.

THE FUTURE OF THE SFT MODEL

The stages of change described by Prochaska (1999) are a useful way to think about the application of SFT. These stages are precontemplation (6 months long, or more); contemplation (about 6 months); preparation (within a month); action (usually started in the last 6 months); maintenance (anything from 6 months to 5 years). The final phase, termination of change, is common for acute problems, but for long-term problems such as substance misuse, less than 20% will reach termination and the rest may remain in the maintenance phase indefinitely.

Solution focused therapy is an excellent model for contemplation, preparation, and action. It is acceptable for the precontemplation stage, and a good therapist will soon identify that the person in front of them is collecting ideas but is not yet ready to take action. Some teams, especially those who work with substance misuse, are beginning to develop the uses of solution focused ideas for maintenance and relapse prevention. The model does not have specific questions for these areas yet, but themes are emerging. Luc Isebaert in Belgium is developing question sets for chronic disorders, based on repetitively examining how one will handle relapse in the short, medium, and long term. He hopes that chronic depression and chronic substance misuse will benefit from simple repeated questions about what in life is acceptable or satisfactory, rather than seeking for miracles and permanent changes.

Another area of future development for SFT is the move into organizational and management activities. Not many other techniques have been transferred into industry and made the subject of randomized controlled trials (Green, 2006; Hoffman, 2007; Mussman, 2006), so the scientific credentials of solution focused management are already advancing. Many people believe that coaching is almost identical to therapy, with the only difference being the context in which each occurs, and the social boundaries that therefore apply. For example, a therapist may be able to advise you about risks to your health; a coach faced with the same presentation may ask if you have thought of consulting a health professional.

In conclusion, therefore, SFT has brought about substantial changes in my working life and my personal life. It has brought me many friendships and intellectual challenges and I believe that it has been helpful to many of those who have consulted me.

EDITOR'S COMMENT

I have been a fan of Dr. Macdonald's work for some time and was so pleased when he agreed to contribute to this project. The current shift in the field of psychotherapy to demonstrate efficacy through research is demanding that SFT build its research base. Dr. Macdonald has been adding to and reviewing this research for several years and much of his work has been published. When I read his chapter I was happy to notice that he emphasized both the importance of research and his own role as a researcher in the applications of this model. Hopefully people in the field will pay increased attention to the researchers such as Dr. Macdonald and others adding to the research base of this approach and emphasizing the body of research that already exists.

—Elliott Connie

REFERENCES

Bowditch, B. (1991). Brief encounter. *Nursing Times, 87,* 41–43.

De Jong, P., & Hopwood, L. E. (1996). Outcome research on treatment conducted at the Brief Family Therapy Center 1992–1993. In S. D. Miller, M. A. Hubble, & B. L. Duncan (Eds.), *Handbook of solution-focused brief therapy* (pp. 272–298). San Francisco: Jossey-Bass.

de Shazer, S. (1985). *Keys to solutions in brief therapy.* New York: Norton.

de Shazer, S. (1988). *Clues: Investigating solutions in brief therapy.* New York: Norton.

de Shazer, S., & Isebaert, L. (2003). The Bruges Model: A solution-focused approach to problem drinking. *Journal of Family Psychotherapy, 14,* 43–52.

Lee, M. Y., Sebold, J., & Uken, A. (2003). *Solution-focused treatment of domestic violence offenders.* New York: Oxford University Press.

Macdonald, A. J. (1987). Consultant-based services: One man's experience. *Bulletin of the Royal College of Psychiatrists, 11,* 55–56.

Macdonald, A. J. (1990). Brief therapy in a mental hospital. *Context (Association for Family Therapy Newsletter), 6,* 40–41.

Macdonald, A. J. (1994). Brief therapy in adult psychiatry. *Journal of Family Therapy, 16,* 415–426.

Macdonald, A. J. (1997). Brief therapy in adult psychiatry: Further outcomes. *Journal of Family Therapy, 19,* 213–222.

Macdonald, A. J. (2005). Brief therapy in adult psychiatry: Results from 15 years of practice. *Journal of Family Therapy, 27,* 65–75.

Milner, J., & Singleton, T. (2008). Domestic violence: Solution-focused practice with men and women who are violent. *Journal of Family Therapy, 30,* 27–51.

Mussman, C. (2006). Solution-focused leadership: The range between theory and practical application. In G. Lueger & H-P. Korn (Eds.), *Solution-focused management* (pp. 99–110). Munchen: Rainer Hampp Verlag. Proceedings of the 5th International Conference on Solution Focused Practice in Organizations, Vienna, 2006.

Prochaska, J. O. (1999). How do people change, and how can we change to help many more people? In M. A. Hubble, B. L. Duncan, & S. D. Miller (Eds.)., *The heart and soul of change: What works in therapy* (pp. 227–255). Washington, DC: American Psychological Association..

Vaughn, K., Young, B. C., Webster, D. C., & Thomas, M. R. (1996). A continuum-of-care model for inpatient psychiatric treatment. In S. D. Miller, M. A. Hubble, & B. L. Duncan (Eds.), *Handbook of solution-focused brief therapy.* San Francisco: Jossey-Bass.

17 Using Possibilities to Remove the Box

ELLIOTT CONNIE

> To me every hour of the day and night is an unspeakably perfect miracle.
>
> —Walt Whitman

Q. How did you first learn about solution focused therapy (SFT)?

A. Though I had heard of SFT in a previous "Intro to Counseling" course, the moment when I learned about this approach occurred much later in graduate school at Texas Wesleyan University. I remember this moment as though it occurred yesterday; to this day I think of this incident frequently.

It occurred while taking a course taught by Dr. Linda Metcalf intended to prepare us students for the practicum component of the program. I had taken a course from Dr. Metcalf before and I was well aware that she was a solution focused therapist herself, but I am not sure that I knew quite what that meant at the time. Then one day she did something that changed all that. She informed the class that we would have a chance to serve as a reflection team for her as she worked with a family at the school. This meant that we would observe her session; then, she would take a break, and ask us what we observed about the clients. Instantly I was excited. I had been working with families for some time at a local agency as a bachelor's level caseworker, but this would be the first time I would get to see someone do actual counseling.

I have to digress for a moment and give a bit of a back story about my agency experience before I continue. The agency I was working for exclusively utilized cognitive behavioral therapy (CBT). There were several programs where someone with a bachelor's degree could work with families and provide what was called "skills training" or "psychoeducation." There was even an evidenced-based program called Multi-Systemic Therapy (MST) where people with a bachelor's degree could see clients. Throughout my years with this agency I had served clients in all of those capacities. By the time I reached the practicum course, I was an MST therapist and I enjoyed it thoroughly. As an MST therapist I was gaining valuable experience working with families and my peers. However, something did not fit. MST is a program that utilizes an intense model of treatment (usually 3–5 sessions per week), intense weekly supervision, and intense problem assessments with families (Henggeler, Schoenwald, Borduin, Rowland, & Cunningham, 1998). Even before my exposure to SFT I was beginning to wonder, was all of this intensity necessary? The focus was on therapist conceptualizations and the accurate development of systemic interventions (Henggeler et al., 1998). However, I thought there had to be a more efficient way. People in private practice were effective as were other evidenced-based approaches with this type of intensity and pressure on the therapist. But still, I pressed on. I truly enjoyed the systemic focus of this approach and began to be quite skilled at developing creative interventions with families. However, I continued to struggle with the intense problem-focused nature of the approach, as well as the pressure on the therapist to develop effective interventions.

Now that I had the chance to see therapy being done outside of the agency where I was employed, I was excited. As I observed Dr. Metcalf working with the family I remember clearly thinking, "What the hell is she doing?" I had participated in hours of supervision and had never seen anything like this before. She clearly was not thinking in the same way that the CBT and MST therapist at the agency were. She was having fun; each member of the family was actively participating. What was going on?

I thought I had come to graduate school to learn CBT—after all, that was what everyone at my job was telling me was most effective—but she was doing this SFT stuff and it looked so different. She was so elegant and respectful; she was not teaching the family anything or conceptualizing about the problem. In fact, it sounded like she was learning from the family and being curious about their solutions. Wow! Then, during the break when she was getting feedback from the team, she was respectful of our ideas. She wrote down each idea we had, and subsequently read the notes to the family. I will never forget the look on the mother's face as she sat back and heard Dr. Metcalf read off the list of exceptions both she and the team had noticed. I was simply blown away.

I drove home from class that night gripping the steering wheel tight and wondering aloud, "What was that? Where did she learn to do that?" I thought about it all week. In the CBT world I was increasingly uncomfortable. I wanted to know more about SFT and how it worked. The next week in class someone asked if she had seen that family again. Dr. Metcalf explained that she had received a call from the mother reporting tremendous progress since that session, causing her to believe that the family no longer needed therapy. That was it—I was hooked. I was used to the intensity of MST and now I just saw the most respectful conversation based on the client's exceptions instead of problems. It felt so natural, it made so much sense, and now the client was reporting helpfulness. I was hooked.

Q. How did you discover that SFT was the model that seemed to fit with your way of working with clients?

A. After observing this model in action, I began to have frequent visits with Dr. Metcalf about this approach. She shared with me books by Scott Miller, Insoo Kim Berg, and others. As I read these texts, it felt as though I were rediscovering myself. It was as if the words of these authors were giving me permission to be different. I could be myself, follow clients, and look for exceptions just as I desired. Only now, I could cite a source. Each tenet of the approach and therapist assumptions fit my way of thinking. It was just so new to me.

Prior to this reading, I was under the misguided assumption that CBT was the only effective approach in counseling. That is what I had been taught for several years while working at agencies and embarrassingly, I had begun to believe it. Even though there were things related to CBT that did not fit with me, I thought that if I was going to become a counselor, it would have to be the way. The result was that I tried to force it, but here was an approach that I did not have to force. Instead, it flowed.

One day, while attending supervision at my job, I realized that I was no longer able to utilize an approach where the pressure was on me and belief in the client was not stressed. During this meeting, I was asked to discuss a difficult client. I ruffled through my paperwork and chose one at random (this was normal for me because even then, I did not see my clients as "difficult"). I chose to discuss a family I had been working with for a few weeks; a mother and her teenage daughter. The mother informed me that she and her daughter had not been able to get along for several years. The daughter had been struggling in school, routinely violated household rules, and had recently revealed that she was gay. The mother and daughter spent significant time telling me all that had gone wrong over the years, causing the current problems. I wanted to ask a solution focused question, but I did not know how.

My fear almost got the best of me as I nervously asked them to tell me when their relationship was at its best. They instantly stopped talking about the problem and began to tell me something so simple that it just could not have been true: When the daughter's room was clean, they seemed to get along better. When the room was clean, the mother felt comfortable being in there and would often watch movies with her daughter. When the room was not clean, that did not occur. The family agreed to clean the room and look for signs that things were getting better. Two days later, I returned to the home for a follow-up session (MST is a home-based approach intended to last 3 to 6 months). The daughter was not home. She attended school for two straight days, but the mother reported that those were the best two days they had spent together in several years.

I was excited to share this story with the MST supervisor and team. As I described what had occurred, I could see a look of concern on the supervisor's face. She began asking me questions about the family's problem. Because those were not things that I had discussed with the family, I was unable to answer her questions. My supervisor then stated that since the intervention did not lead to learning more about the problem, it did not work. She began to write the names of models on the board, including Adlerian, CBT, Structural, Strategic, etc., then asked the rest of the team to vote on which model I should use next with this family. None of them noticed that the mother and daughter got along well when the room was cleaned. Who cared what the problems were? They were solved by the presence of a clean room.

After this event, I felt a tremendous sense of relief. Therapy could be simple and it was okay for me to believe in that simplicity. SFT made more and more sense to me as I continued to read and discuss the approach with others. It felt like something I could trust as opposed to something I had to learn to do. It became obvious that I could no longer work for that agency and I resigned within a matter of weeks.

Q. What characteristics of this model drew you toward it?

A. There are so many. I was drawn toward the respectful language, the future focus, and the search for exceptions. However, there is one thing that stands out above the rest. The fun! SFT is an approach that requires a different way of thinking on the part of practitioners and for the practitioner to believe in this way of thinking. It seemed to me that SFT practitioners believed in their approach and believed in their clients. This was so different than what I was used to. It was so different from therapists that were looking for a diagnosis; instead, there was an inherent optimism as this approach simply required the therapist to believe. This allowed for fun to enter into the therapeutic process. Dr. Metcalf seemed to be having fun with her clients. The authors of the books she shared seemed to be having fun with what they wrote. There was a playfulness about the whole approach and I just could not resist.

Q. How has utilizing SFT impacted your work with clients? (Please mention if you utilized a previous model and the difference you noticed in clients and yourself after switching to SFT.)

A. As I mentioned previously, I was originally trained to use CBT approaches. The shift toward a solution focused perspective impacted absolutely everything about my work with clients and what I noticed in my clients was different as well. I recall in the days prior to SFT, feeling the pressure of helping my clients. I was trained to believe that our clients needed us and it was our job to be helpful. Whenever an "intervention" was effective I was relieved and noticed my own creativity. I was relieved that the intervention worked. I always feared letting the client down, so when something worked, I was so happy that I had been helpful. I also gave myself the credit for being creative enough to be helpful with a particular client.

Once I began to utilize SFT, I started to see my clients, and myself, in a completely different way. I began to see that they were the ones doing the work the whole time. They were miracles—and I had the honor of sitting front row and watching them. My task became to shut up and get out of their way so they could work their magic. The pressure I once felt was now replaced with a childlike enthusiasm. I became an enthusiastic believer of people and their abilities to create a new future. Due to this belief, my approach in therapy changed. Instead of trying to develop creative and effective tasks for my clients, I was now trying to cooperate with their worldview, allowing them to discover their own solutions. I just asked questions and pointed out things that perhaps they had not noticed. If therapy was not helpful, I no longer believed it was the client's fault. I must not have been curious enough about them; I must not have worked hard enough to cooperate with them.

Q. How would your clients describe your work with them? Have any of your clients who might have experienced another model of therapy commented on the difference (if any) that they perceived when working with you?

A. "You talk differently than I expected." I have heard this remark countless times from clients after they experienced a solution focused conversation. Very recently, a young woman made a comment that stood out to me. Throughout our first session I could see her grow more and more comfortable being in therapy. As we discussed her talents and exceptions to the problems that led to her seeking therapy, she grew more and more excited. At the end of the session, the young lady asked me where I learned to do therapy in this way. I was a bit stunned by this question and explained my graduate training. I discussed with her what SFT was and how it was different from traditional forms of psychotherapy. After hearing my brief and simple explanation, the young woman looked at me and said, "I think this is going to go much quicker." She was right; we met three times before she noticed all of her goals were accomplished.

Q. What is it about SFT that makes it so effective?

A. One of my favorite hobbies is cooking; I love it. I have enjoyed cooking since my days of growing up in southeastern Massachusetts where I learned to make my favorite food, lasagna. Recently, a close friend of mine called to ask for my lasagna recipe, because he wanted to make a romantic dinner for his girlfriend. I admit I was a bit reluctant; after all, it's my secret recipe. However, he was one of my closest friends, so I swore him to secrecy and began explaining exactly how to make the delicious dish. I told him how to mix the ingredients so that when they baked together, it would taste just right. I told him which stores have the best meats and cheeses that will make the dish all the more succulent. For almost 30 minutes I divulged my greatest culinary secrets; then I wished him luck and got off the phone. Then, I noticed something strange. I began to realize that I had a strong desire to make and eat my lasagna. This was unusual, because before the phone call, I was not hungry; in fact, I had just eaten dinner. Now, after having a conversation in which I described the details of one of my favorite meals, I was desirous of that food. To me this is what makes solution focused therapy so effective.

A solution focused conversation is, at its very core, a conversation based on the details of the client's desired future. Just as I became desirous of the lasagna after having a conversation about the details of the dish, I believe people become desirous of their desired future when they have a conversation about the details of that future. This desire is so helpful because when people experience a problem there is a tendency to spend more time focused on the problem or thinking about the absence of the problem. (Focusing on the absence of the problem is very different from focusing on the presence of the solution.) This focus on the details of what is desired is what makes SFT both effective and unique.

Q. Describe one of your favorite cases and how it impacted your work as a therapist.

A. I have had the pleasure of working with many remarkable clients in many extraordinary circumstances, but one in particular stands out in my development with this approach. I was amazed then, and even now, thinking about this client, I am still amazed.

I received a call from a social worker in a local agency asking me if I saw Asperger's clients. After I informed him that I do see people with Asperger's, she explained to me that the person had been struggling with this diagnosis for most of his life. This included interactions with several therapists and multiple hospital stays. As a result, this social worker had a thick file on the client and would be willing to share it with me. According to the social worker, I needed the file in order to work successfully with this client. Shortly after the conversation, the client contacted me and scheduled an appointment. I was nervous! After all, he was described to me as a difficult client who had had several previous therapists.

My office is located in Texas and during the warm summer months the temperature often surpasses 100 degrees. This usually mandates that people travel in vehicles with functional air conditioning systems. So when the client, a man in his mid-40s, arrived at my office breathing deeply and covered in sweat, I became immediately curious about him instead of nervous. He informed me that he had to take several buses to arrive at my office and ran from the last bus stop to ensure he would make it to the session on time. Wow! I remember being amazed at how much this person wanted to attend the session and was instantly impressed by his effort. In addition to sweating and breathing heavily, he was carrying a sketch with him and asked if he could show me the picture.

The picture depicted a hand reaching out of a body of water and another hand in the sky horizontal to the surface of the water. The client informed me that the hand in the water represented him and the other represented God. He stated that God would not help him due to his diagnosis and this allowed others to not help him as well.

I asked him what we would need to do with our time together that would have the hand in the sky reach down toward his just a little bit. The client seemed surprised by my question and responded by saying he would need to learn to deal with the 3 I's. He informed me that the 3 I's were impotence, isolation, and inferiority. I asked him the miracle question about what would be different if he woke up without the 3 I's and he paused for a moment and said, "I would have the 3 P's." He told me the 3 P's were potency, popularity, and power. We talked about times in his life when the 3 P's were present already. It turns out that this amazing man had graduated from college despite several negative life events that occurred during his college years. We discussed the determination it took to get to my office on time despite the scorching heat and long bus trip. We also located other times when the 3 P's were present. He had a cat he took care of, a neighbor he was always sure to say hello to whenever their paths crossed, and a few others. He was amazed with how often the 3 P's were already present.

As the session ended, the client explained that he had never been asked questions like those before and he really enjoyed it. Before I could respond, he asked if it would be okay if he spent the next week looking for more times when he'd had the 3 P's in his life. After I fell out of my chair, I said of course and that I would be sure to ask him about how many of the 3 P's he'd found the next time we met. The client told me how helpful it was to speak with someone who did not mention a diagnosis. He then scheduled a session for the following week.

That was the only time I ever saw this client. He did not call or attend the second session. Several months later, the social worker that originally contacted me about him called me again to inform me that her agency had acquired a car that they wanted to donate to the client. I told her that I'd only seen him once, but would be happy to call him. I called the number he provided me and discovered it was no longer in service. Since it had been several months since I had heard from this client, I began to wonder about him. What was he up to? Did he decide to see another therapist? Perhaps he did not find our session helpful. Since I had no way to contact him, I was left just to wonder.

Then, almost eight months after our first and only session, he called me. He wanted me to know that his life was now completely different. He had acquired a job, a car, and the neighbor he always said hello to was now his girlfriend. I was blown away! I learned a lot from this gentleman and to this day think about the lessons he taught me. I remember that even when the diagnosis is "severe," the client can still discover solutions. Even when the past is bleak, the future can be better, and most of all, a lot can happen in just one session if we believe in our clients.

Q. Has the use of SFT impacted you in your personal life? If so, please explain.

A. The use of SFT in my work has impacted all aspects of my life. It has impacted my overall level of enthusiasm and happiness. In the past, when I was using another approach, I was very negative and it impacted my life satisfaction. I began to wonder if I could practice for the rest of my career. Back then, I saw limitations and pathology even in my own personal life. It was not a fun existence. It all changed when I began exploring solutions and learning about the power of a future focus. I often describe it as if I were surrounded by an invisible box that was limiting my options. The presence of SFT removed that box. It became the lens that I viewed the world with, not just clients.

Once, while on a plane, I began talking to the person in the seat next to me about our careers. I usually do not inform people on planes that I am a therapist to avoid causing them to feel uncomfortable for the duration of the trip, but this time I did. When I told the gentlemen I was a therapist he replied by sighing and remarking, "I could never do that job." I found that comment strange, so I asked him why. He explained that he could not sit and listen to people complain about their problems all day. I silently smiled as I realized,

I don't listen to people complain about problems at all. I listen as people describe the details of their solutions and I love it!

Q. What are some key personality traits that you think are shared among solution focused practitioners?

A. This past year, I attended the Solution-Focused Brief Therapy Association (SFBTA) conference for the first time and had the opportunity to meet many practitioners from around the world that utilize this approach. I noticed several themes that seemed to run through the community of these practitioners and seemed unique to this group. The first was the extreme openness of the group. I have never felt so welcomed and accepted among a group of professionals. I was able to engage in conversations with everyone from students to the keynote speaker, each making me feel special and welcome. What trait would I call this? Respectfulness.

Next would have to be optimism. In order to effectively utilize an approach that relies on the strengths and assets of the client, a therapist must have the ability to believe in the future of others. I truly believe that if someone possesses this trait, then this approach can be a good fit for them. Without this trait, then it may not fit as well.

Q. What are some common mistakes that therapists trying on the model make most often? If you had a chance to guide them differently, how would you do so?

A. While I do not see it as a mistake, I often see students doing one thing that I think leads to a misunderstanding of this approach: Students often focus on only the techniques, believing that asking the miracle question, scaling questions, and so forth, is equivalent to practicing this approach. I do not call it a mistake because it can, and often does, lead to an ultimate understanding that allows for high levels of efficacy with the solution focused approach.

I believe that the tenets and assumptions are more important to becoming effective than the questions or techniques that the approach became famous for. Whenever I have the chance to teach this model, I always focus on the tenets and assumptions instead of the techniques because having an understanding of the tenets and assumptions and allowing those things to guide you in session will lead to your becoming a solution focused person.

Q. What are some things you notice students doing while trying on this model that lets you know this model may fit them?

A. For me, it is in the language. When I hear a student describing an experience with a client with enthusiasm and a focus on the client, I see this model working well for them. When a student lacks enthusiasm, I wonder if perhaps a theory with a more expert stance would be a better fit. I also notice when the students' description of what they do matches the theory. For example, I once was given a resume by someone who claimed to be a solution focused practitioner. As I looked at the resume, I began to wonder. It was littered with phrases such as, "I do solution focused therapy with the chronically mentally ill" and "I am an expert diagnostician." Someone that was truly solution focused would not refer to people as "chronically mentally ill" nor would they refer to themselves as an expert, especially an expert diagnostician.

Q. If you were training therapists in the SFT model, what strategies would you use to train them and how would you present the material?

A. When I am conducting trainings, I always do a few things. First, I always ask what attendees hope to learn from the training. This requires that I be as flexible in trainings as I am in session. It also means that I never really know what will be covered in my trainings until I ask the group what they hope to learn, and together we set the day's agenda. I always show videotapes of myself working with clients. I do this because I think it is important to demonstrate that I do what I teach about and because I want to give attendees the chance to ask me about why I asked a particular question at a particular time. I also use a lot of stories from my experiences. I have had the pleasure of working with clients that have done brilliant and remarkable things, and sharing these experiences helps me to illustrate key components of this approach. I also utilize demonstration and group activities so that attendees can be involved in the training as we learn together about SFT. I hope to provide information about the tenets, assumptions, and practices to this approach in a way that allows attendees to observe and experience it as active participants.

Q. If you could pick a pioneer solution focused therapist who impacted your work, who would you name and why?

A. From the moment she entered into my life, Dr. Linda Metcalf has had a positive influence on my work and my personal life. She was the first solution focused therapist I met and was gracious enough to share her experiences with me and fan the fire I began to show for this approach. Without her early encouragement I honestly do not know what I would be doing right now. Those early conversations about this approach meant the world to me and set the stage for all that has happened since.

While I was in graduate school, and first learning this approach, it was Dr. Metcalf that I leaned on for guidance. That was a difficult time for me. I was working for an agency, and had been invited to do my practicum there as a result of my successful work experience. I enjoyed the job immensely and was openly referred to for a number of promotions once my graduate degree was completed. When I began talking about solution focused therapy with agency staff, however, I noticed a change. Once I began to express an interest in incorporating this approach in my work, my employers informed me that I was no longer being considered for promotions. These same employers also discouraged my curiosity about SFT in other ways, including forbidding use of the term *solution focused.* I later learned that I was targeted so that others would also be discouraged from using this approach. To say I was crushed is not an understatement. I had dreams of working for this agency long-term and was passionate about becoming a skilled practitioner. I had once looked up to the people that were now actively and openly discouraging me.

I eventually went to meet with Dr. Metcalf about what I was experiencing. Even though I was being discouraged about learning SFT by my employers, my curiosity about the approach continued to grow. As we met, she shared with me some of her experiences as a solution focused professional and offered to be my practicum supervisor; I was touched. This ultimately led to the mentor/protégé relationship that exists to this day. This relationship led to my first publication in one of her books, and to my becoming a presenter/trainer, and an author. Her kindness and generosity with her knowledge and experience have been amazing and I am forever grateful.

Q. What developments would you like to see in the future of this model?

A. My true hope for the future of this approach is that social service agencies begin to understand and implement it. Many social service agencies are nonprofit and driven by government contracts and grants for income. This means these agencies are limited to providing services through programs that are endorsed by the funding source. These are usually heavily CBT evidence-based approaches, despite the large body of research supporting other approaches, including SFT. I hope that one day SFT is accepted by these agencies and people understand that this approach is effective and that efficacy can be and has been demonstrated through research.

EDITOR'S COMMENT

I have found the most joy as a professional when I look into the eyes of a student and see the candle light up. Elliott Connie has, in his chapter, conveyed what many of us probably felt when discovering solution focused therapy, yet he identifies the "fun" aspect that many of us feel yet forget to verbalize. In his account, he focuses primarily on his clients and his newness (although he is immensely talented) comes through in his excitement for his clients. To say that Elliott is nothing short of a cheerleader for SFT would be a mild description of his enthusiasm. That enthusiasm is apparent in the videotapes I have watched and in the way he trains new therapists. This book is an example. Once, we casually discussed the common traits of solution focused therapists. The next day, Elliott was in my office ready to write a book proposal. Writing a proposal was new territory for him, in the same way that solution focused therapy was a new approach. Yet, unnervingly, he wrote the proposal with the same determination and excitement that he approached learning the new model. That worked and obviously, so did the book proposal.

I think living in solution focused land (happily ever after) happens when one's personality meshes with the theory. How fortunate this field is to have such a sharp, up-and-coming therapist with such enthusiasm, talent, and charm. May we all capture just a small flavor of his excitement in our work. It will make most of our days exceptional.

—Linda Metcalf

REFERENCE

Henggeler, S., Schoenwald, S., Borduin, C., Rowland, M., & Cunningham, P. (1998). *Multisystemic treatment of antisocial behavior in children and adolescents.* New York: Guilford Press.

18 Go Where the Clients Lead

THORANA NELSON

Where you stand determines what you see and what you do not see; it determines also the angle you see it from; a change in where you stand changes everything.

—Steve de Shazer (1991)

Q. How did you first learn about solution focused therapy (SFT)?

A. I was in a doctoral program in counselor education at the University of Iowa, focusing on family therapy. My supervisor (David Rosenthal) brought in Steve de Shazer's book *Patterns of Brief Family Therapy* in late 1982 or early 1983. We experimented with the formula first-session task in practicum with results similar to those described in the book, which was quite intriguing to me. In 1984, Steve came to UI for a workshop sponsored by the Iowa division of the American Association for Marriage and Family Therapy (AAMFT). I chaired that conference and read more of Steve's works in preparation. The notion of binocular vision really helped me catch on to notions of constructivism and multiple realities or different meanings that two or more people make of the same situation.

Q. How did you discover that SFT was the model that seemed to fit with your way of working with clients?

A. I had been trained in graduate school mostly in a structural/strategic/Bowen model that was developed by some folks who had trained at the Menninger in Topeka, Kansas, but we experimented with some solution focused ideas along the way. In my first academic position, some colleagues and I developed a structural/strategic/Bowen/behavioral model for treating women with substance abuse. All of us had been exposed in one way or another to SFT and began noticing that each of us was adding ideas to the work we were doing in the research grant, particularly noticing in each session what the client was saying about progress as opposed to what had not worked or had not worked sufficiently. By the time we finished the project, most of us were having a hard time sticking to the original model of the research and not adding in too much solution focus. We were learning more by valuing the client's perspective more than our own.

I was very attracted to systemic and postmodern ways of thinking including SFT and Narrative (from Dickerson & Zimmerman, 1996; Epston & White, 1990; Freedman & Combs, 1996). However, in 2001, I was invited to participate in a series of seminars with Steve and Insoo Kim Berg that Steve, Yvonne Dolan, and Terry Trepper put together in Hammond, Indiana. Over the course of the seminars, I became more and more enamored of the ideas and philosophy and not merely the techniques or practices. I wouldn't say that Steve was charismatic because he had a rather laid-back and introverted manner, but he had a way of rubbing off on me. I liked his thinking, particularly the simplicity and elegance of it. It also got me reading more in postmodern and poststructural philosophies.

Q. What characteristics of this model drew you toward it?

A. I was never happy with models of therapy that required digging into people's pasts as though that were the only way to help them overcome adversity or to develop change in troublesome aspects of their lives. One of my early practicum clients came to me in tears one evening because she had been told in her support group that she was in denial because she didn't want to talk about her past abuse, she wanted to move on with her life. The work with her for moving toward what she wanted rather than what she didn't want was so much more rewarding and fun than rehashing old stuff that couldn't change. We did not assume that we needed to talk about the abuse for her to heal. I never liked the ideas of healing and scars that the medical model promotes. I couldn't understand what *working through* meant. And that was before I knew about SFT! So when I learned about SFT and began to explore it more, there was a natural fit for me.

I think the "let's get moving" aspect as well as the total paradigm shift that suggests that solutions don't have to be related to problems was very attractive to me, intellectually and pragmatically. Even my structural/strategic/Bowen work tended to be more oriented toward finding solutions than analyzing problems. Talking about problems or the past was in the service of finding clues for solutions, not for supposedly resolving past issues. Those clues, for me, lie in the imagined future picture that clients develop through SFT questioning.

What draws me now is the interesting and systemic idea that what's happening when troubles (as Lance Taylor refers to them) are no longer around or no longer troubling is a legitimate area for therapy conversation. I usually feel pretty helpless around problems, but more useful when asking people questions about their lives when whatever is bothering them is no longer as bothersome.

Q. How has utilizing SFT impacted your work with clients? (Please mention if you utilized a previous model and the difference you noticed in clients and yourself after switching to SFT.)

A. When I used primarily structural, strategic, and Bowen ways of thinking, I usually focused on analyzing the structure or sequences or family history of triangles of the client system in order to figure out what *I* needed to do to help the family change, what specified intervention would be *the* trick to turn things around. After adopting more of the SFBT approach, I find that my questions have more to do with what *the client system* does that is helpful or what emerges from conversations about nonproblem or less-problem life in terms of what they are doing. I know that *my* way of fixing things is successful for me, but it took me a while to figure out that it wasn't always helpful to clients because their situations are different from mine. It's very tempting for me to share solutions, but it seldom is very helpful unless it gives the client an idea about what they are doing that works or will work—usually with differences—for them.

In a nutshell, I would say that I give much less advice and focus more on clients' experiences in a curious way, making many fewer assumptions about them and what will be helpful for them. I also enjoy learning from clients much more than I did several years ago.

Q. How would your clients describe your work with them? Have any of your clients who might have experienced another model of therapy commented on the difference (if any) that they perceived when working with you?

A. A few of my clients who have been in therapy before have commented that work with me is less stressful, more interesting, and more fun. I have a professional disclosure/informed consent packet that explains how I work and few people comment on it except to say they like the idea of not being in therapy for a long time. One current client, who had been in therapy with a psychologist for seven years, sometimes twice a week, said she really liked it that I was helping her learn about making decisions rather than telling her what to do. Others say they like the pragmatic approach and not digging around in problems—they feel less like they have to blame someone, whether themselves or someone else, and can just move on.

Clients who call for appointments months or even years after stopping have said that it's easier to call when they need to, they don't feel as much like failures. But they also say that there were times when they didn't need to call because they just asked themselves noticing, exception, miracle, or relationship questions. They have said they were amused when I asked, "What did you forget that you remembered to do before?"

Finally, I think my clients say that they seldom leave my office feeling tired from weeping or feeling as though they have been wrung out. I sometimes ask what people expect from therapy and note when they say that we will talk about problems and figure out why things are so bad. When I then ask whether the first session has been helpful, they usually say that they are relieved that we didn't have hard talk and that they are much more hopeful than they expected, and relieved that perhaps therapy won't be as difficult as they thought it would be.

Q. What is it about SFT that makes it so effective?

A. I don't know and that's exactly what Steve would say. He also would say he didn't really care. On the other hand, he was very interested in Wittgenstein's notions of language and how it shapes experience; therefore, I think we can infer that he thought that different language reshapes people's experiences from problematic to hopeful and pleasant. Personally, I believe that one perspective is that it's effective because it gives people a concrete, future vision or idea of a life without the problem. Once something is envisioned, it's possible; if it's *my* vision rather than the client's (e.g., different family structure, different ways of thinking), it's not effective. I also believe that questions around these kinds of ideas reduce anxiety, which allows people to think in detail rather than be flooded by emotion, which prevents cortical processes related to thinking (Bowen and neurobiology). I also think that SFT is more able to honor the *client's* ideas about how change occurs rather than the therapist's. However, a practitioner does not have to have an idea of why something works in order to be able to learn *how* it works.

Q. Describe one of your favorite cases and how it impacted your work as a therapist.

A. I worked with a single mom and her two sons, ages 13 and 15. She called wanting "anger management," which meant that everyone was fighting too much. She was particularly worried about one son, who tended to display anger by stomping around and hitting things. I started to buy into the notion that the son was influenced by his poor relationship with his dad, his developmental stage as a teen, and other things that the mom explained to me. That's a bad sign for me, so I asked all three what would be different when they didn't need anger management any more—I wanted to know more about what was happening, exceptions to that, and what they thought would be different when therapy was no longer needed. Each had different details for the picture, but all agreed that things would be quieter in the house, they'd be talking with each other rather than yelling so much, and they'd be doing more fun things together. I asked about details of what they'd be doing and what difference that would make. The mom learned that the boys really wanted to do things with her like kick a soccer ball around the yard or go to movies, "not like at Dad's, where all we do is watch TV." They came for two more sessions, the last one being a checkup.

Not all of my cases go that quickly or easily, but that one particularly impressed on me the need to be persistent in getting details, details, details about the solution picture, getting them from all angles, and getting them in relationship terms—who would notice, what difference that would make to them and to the client, and so forth. Then, I trusted that the family members got the messages they needed to help them make changes that would be effective for them. I also was impressed with how I didn't have to buy into prevalent notions about anger or correct ways of how to manage it.

Q. Has the use of SFT impacted you in your personal life? If so, please explain.

A. SFT has impacted me personally in at least a couple of different ways. First, I use the questions for myself when I'm feeling stuck. Who would notice if I weren't stuck? What difference would that make to them? To me? What would we be doing together that would be different? What difference would that make to me? What else?

I recently went through a down time and had a good chat with myself on my way to work one morning because I really didn't want to go. I like my work, so I really felt stuck. I started with what I'd be doing if I didn't go to work. There was some comfort in that, but more discouragement because I couldn't do those things. So I switched to, "What would be different if I wanted to go to work, not going to work being an unrealistic goal, therefore not well-formed?" That led to "looking forward to something" and I just continued to ask myself detail questions around that. I started thinking of the parts of work that I would enjoy and the people who would notice and what difference that would make. I realized I needed to do more things that some of those people would notice, and I needed to talk with myself more about what I enjoyed about my work rather than what I didn't like. I also needed to think about the larger context of my work and I realized that I felt out of balance, not having enough personal time or pleasure. I realized that I needed more balance in my life so that I enjoyed more about my work. That led to a decision to spend more time with friends, especially lunch dates and a book club, which led, of course, to a desire to spend more time reading and doing things other than work that would add to lunch and book club discussions. I asked myself about what would be different when I felt a little better about these things, what I would be doing differently as well as what I'd be noticing. I'm now writing in a book journal, which seems to help.

The second area where I have noticed a difference is in interactions with friends or family when they are telling me about the hard things that are going on in their lives. I'm much more able to not get caught up in fixing their problems and commenting more on what I perceive as exceptions to their feelings of failure. However, I also notice that I sometimes move toward solution talk rather quickly, as I would in a therapy session, rather than simply commiserating.

Q. What are some key personality traits that you think are shared among solution focused practitioners?

A. I don't believe much in personality traits anymore. The things we call personality are behaviors that are situation-specific and therefore I cannot know about them outside of the situations we share. However, an important characteristic of effective SF therapists that I've noticed is intense curiosity and a genuine sense of not knowing what is going on with clients unless and until the clients tell them.

Q. What are some common mistakes that therapists trying on the model make most often? If you had a chance to guide them differently, how would you do so?

A. I hesitate to think of mistakes in using the model because that suggests that there is a theory of therapy that underlies the approach, not simply a set of practices or techniques. That said, I do think that this is not an approach for "anything goes." I will reframe this question as lack of understanding or misunderstandings of the underlying principles and how they can be used.

The biggest issue I see in new therapists is a lack of understanding of the systemic or relational nature of SFBT. Insoo, particularly, was interested in the relationships that clients are involved in and how clients see themselves through their ideas of what those other people are seeing. It's very powerful, seeing yourself through others' ideas, understanding the systemic and recursive nature of relationships and the solution focused approach. Those questions are not about reality, but about how people influence each other, how language and social construction shape our ideas about ourselves, others, problems, and solutions. Linear thinking is very limiting.

Another mistake I see people making is believing that certain SF practices don't work, as though the questions or practices themselves produce change. Change doesn't occur through the questions; I believe it occurs through the interactions among the therapist, the questions, the clients' responses, and the therapist's and clients' abilities to envision details about what's different when change has occurred. Therefore, if something isn't working, it's because of the simplistic use of the practices. Steve and Insoo often said that the approach is simple but not easy. It takes experience with the approach, using it in one's own style and cadence, to make it sing. Watching Steve, Insoo, and Yvonne on tape, for example, as well as Harry Korman and others exemplifies these differences in style, which says to me that imitating the style neglects the important aspects of the therapist's ability to work within a unique client–therapist relationship or conversation.

Q. What are some things you notice students doing while trying on this model that lets you know this model may fit them?

A. Oh, I love this question. I can usually tell when I see students hesitating to use diagnosis or labeling. They seem to instinctively understand that, for them, those practices are limiting, that they are happier when they see each client as unique rather than as a diagnosis or label. Other students do well as therapists in other approaches, but students who are really going to get SFT are able to be really curious about clients' expressions of their experiences rather than the therapist's (or supervisor's) description of the "real" problem or assuming they know anything about the clients' experiences other than what the clients convey. SFT students quickly move into the idea that solutions are not necessarily connected to problems and other assumptions of the approach. They don't simply parrot these principles; they integrate them into their worldviews and it shows in their work.

For example, one student was working with a couple and asking them about how they would know that they had reached a decision about a difficult situation, what would be different between them. He came behind the mirror and another student suggested that he draw up a sheet with problem-solving steps on it, and examine the pros and cons of different decisions, leaning toward the one that she (the other student) thought was most appropriate. This exercise would help them see the so-called right decision, of course. The therapist student looked very confused for a moment and I knew that this idea did not fit his current state of altered consciousness that included absolutely no idea what was best for the clients. He looked at me with an expression I interpreted as, "Oh, is she right? Is that what I should do?" and then beamed when I said, "What do *you* want to do? What do *you* think will help them with this issue? What will be different between you and the clients when they have figured this out?"

Q. If you were training therapists in the SFT model, what strategies would you use to train them and how would you present the material?

A. I've really changed my preferred pedagogy in general in the last several years. I no longer think I have much to teach, but want to help students learn. I typically subscribe to the read, watch, do method of learning, so students first read chapters, articles, or books on the approach, then watch videos or watch me, and then try it themselves either in role-play or with clients. I lead lots of discussions along the way, limiting my comments considerably, although I may clarify ideas about concepts and ask questions about what they mean or what they have experienced, how they are putting ideas together. I focus more on the process of the discussion and less on the content except to clarify or correct misconceptions about the approach. Some students, however, are more intrigued by watching therapy and then are interested in reading and practicing.

Supervision in graduate practica focuses on what students are doing that is working for them and their clients plus some comments about assumptions, concepts, and practices. For example, I'll ask before a session if there's something particular they want to focus on or want help with, and then follow up on that as well as commenting on other aspects of their work that fit the approach or helped move the clients toward goals. I also ask them questions that get into their clients' perspectives, such as, "What would the clients say was the most helpful thing that happened in this session?"

Q. If you could pick a pioneer solution focused therapist who impacted your work, who would you name and why?

A. This is not an easy question to answer. Because I've been involved in the Solution-Focused Brief Therapy Association, I have been privileged to work with many outstanding therapists in seminars and summer intensive trainings as well as watching them and learning from them at the SFBTA conferences. I have learned something from each. From Insoo, I learned to allow my humor to flow and resonate with clients, to laugh with clients; and from Steve, I learned to go where clients lead, not where theory might suggest. From Lance Taylor, I have learned that I don't know anything about a client until he or she tells me, and to quiet my brain toward thoughtful and curious listening; from Dan Gallagher, I have learned to pay attention to what the client is telling me I should do next; from Yvonne Dolan, I have learned compassionate listening and persistent solution focused conversation; and so forth.

Q. What developments would you like to see in the future of this model?

A. This is another tough question because I'm not sure what developments are possible, limited only by the people who think about them. I am intrigued by the elegance and simplicity that the folks at BRIEF in London continue to foster and would like to see this direction take on more of its own life within the tradition of SFT. Because the emphasis on evidence-based approaches is not going to change, I would like to see more research using the approach so that more people are using it. We already have a number of publications about using the approach in different settings or with different populations, so I would like to see more microanalysis of session videos that will tell us what it is that therapists do (or not do) that helps clients achieve their goals.

What I would *not* like to see is either stopping the generation of ideas for fear of seeming disloyal to Steve and Insoo *or* the embracing of disparate ideas simply because the approach says to do what works. Clearly, there are therapy approaches and practices that work but that the pioneers would say are not SFT.

Some of us need to get away from the elitist idea that SFT is best for every therapist or that the pioneers think/thought that other approaches are ineffective. That is, we need to integrate ourselves better into the therapy community rather than holding ourselves apart. This is similar to the evolution of family therapy within the field of mental health and I think/hope it's part of our development.

EDITOR'S COMMENT

Elegance, simplicity, respect all seem to be the culture that Dr. Thorana Nelson has conveyed in her chapter, filled with her experiences and applications of the solution focused model in her learning experiences, client experiences, personal renderings, and training. Noted for her excellent training ideas in solution focused therapy, Thorana explains very well how SFT can assist not only therapists, but trainers and instructors in bringing out the best in trainees. When I think of my experiences as a teacher of SFT, I remember most the times when students looked at me for help and I asked them about their ideas in return. Thorana is so accurate in her portrayal of the importance of being solution focused as a trainer, so that new ideas can be created by student and client.

The point I really respect that Thorana makes is the importance of keeping the spirit of solution focused therapy alive and not worrying about new developments taking away from the "original package" presented to us by the solution focused pioneers. The model itself is one of innovation, creation, and nonstop learning. Her ideas of studying the model more intimately through the use of microanalysis resonates with what Harry Korman mentioned as well.

What is a joy is to notice, as I have read through the submitted chapters, the ongoing curiosity of these fine practitioners to seek just how this model works. Perhaps that constant itch of wondering how *and not* why *is the most exciting discovery that Elliott and I have noticed so far. And, it may just be what keeps us alive as therapists and anxious for the next client to walk in the door.*

—Linda Metcalf

REFERENCES

Dickerson, V., & Zimmerman, J. (1996). *If problems talked: Narrative therapy in action.* New York: Guilford Press.

Epston, D., & White, M. (1990). *Narrative means to therapeutic ends.* New York: Norton.

Freedman, J., & Combs, G. (1996). *Narrative therapy: The social construction of preferred realities.* New York: Norton.

19 Becoming a Solution Focused Purist

RON WARNER

If the facts don't fit the theory, change the facts.

—Albert Einstein

Q. How did you first learn about solution focused therapy (SFT)? How did you discover that SFT was the model that seemed to fit with your way of working with clients? What characteristics of this model drew you toward it?

A. Little did I understand almost two decades ago that my pursuit of skills in the SFT therapy model would lead me not only to become a theoretical purist, a position I had strongly opposed for 20 years, but also and more importantly would lead me to abandon one of psychology's central assumptions: I would discard the belief in the assessment and diagnosis of client problems, that there are specific treatments for specific disorders, and that subsequent expert-driven solutions are of critical importance to psychotherapeutic effectiveness.

For the first 20 years I spent as a counseling psychologist at Ryerson University's Centre for Student Development and Counseling, my theoretical orientation was eclectic. This appealed to me because I could choose from the best practices of all theoretical orientations. Using Gestalt techniques, for example, I would encourage clients to "get into their feelings" and although the process was sometimes slow,

I was generally quite satisfied with the results. However, with increasing demands for accountability and the new emphasis on downsizing that began to emerge in the late 1980s, it became apparent to me that I was going to have to make changes to my professional practice. The luxury of offering time-unlimited, humanistic-oriented counseling with my university student clients was becoming out of step with this new reality. Although the mean number of my university counseling sessions was six, I treated some of my student clients for a year or longer. As I look back, I realize that many of these long-term counseling relationships took on a mentoring quality. Although I believe these relationships still had therapeutic value for my clients, and were certainly satisfying to me, the resource utilization left room for improvement.

What also fostered my thinking about the potential to accomplish more in less time was a book that I discovered at an Ontario Psychology Association convention. I was attracted to the book because of its seemly ridiculous title—*Single-Session Therapy: Maximizing the Effect of the First (and Often Only) Therapeutic Encounter,* by Moshe Talmon (1990). Talmon made two compelling points in this book that influenced my research agenda. The first was that there is considerable evidence to show that the single psychotherapeutic session is the most common (modal) length of treatment. The second was that follow-up studies consistently find that the majority of those clients who only attend one session are satisfied and do not return because they got what they wanted.

After reading Talmon's book, I began to explore brief therapy models, including solution focused therapy (SFT). This did not mean that I was ready to give up my favorite intervention ("How does that make you feel?") and my other emotionally intensifying techniques. What it did mean, however, was that I was becoming more convinced of how important a role cognition and behavior play in the therapeutic process.

My first learning experience with SFT occurred in approximately 1990 when I attended a one-day workshop taught by SFT cofounder Steve de Shazer. Although I was not overly impressed by the taped interviews that were shown (little attention was paid to client affect!), I found many of the ideas and techniques presented interesting and practical. Toward the end of the workshop I asked the question: "How can the solution to a problem be independent of that problem?" This concept seemed counterintuitive to all my training and experience.

I remember de Shazer looking at me, scratching his head, and saying, "That's what this whole workshop has been about!" Well, I didn't get it.

For quite some time after the workshop (at least 2 years) I continued to grapple with the question of how the solutions to clients' difficulties could be independent of their presenting problems. In spite of my skepticism I started using some of the techniques of SFT, very timidly at first. But as my clients started talking about the progress they were making between sessions, I became increasingly convinced of the potential of this model. I started extending the interval between client visits from one week to two weeks (with the clear understanding that I was available earlier if necessary). As I continued to take further training in SFT, my skill in applying the model grew. By the early 1990s I would have described myself as eclectic with a preference for SFT—I used it about half the time. When I got stuck, I reverted to the problem-centered approach. This is typical of intermediate skill development in the practice of SFT.

Q. How has utilizing SFT impacted your work with clients? (Please mention if you utilized a previous model and the difference you noticed in clients and yourself after switching to SFT.) How would your clients describe your work with them? Have any of your clients who might have experienced another model of therapy commented on the difference (if any) that they perceived when working with you? What is it about SFT that makes it so effective?

A. One of the things that helped build my confidence that the SFT approach in and of itself was sufficient for my practice and that I did not need to fall back on problem-based interventions was learning to teach the SFT model. At this time I was an adjunct professor in the Counseling Psychology program at OISE/University of Toronto. I taught a variety of psychology courses that helped me keep up to date on theoretical orientations. Because of my interest in brief therapies, I proposed (to the chair of the psychology department, Dr. Mary Alice Guttman) offering a "Brief Counseling Strategies" course that would survey the various brief therapy models including both cognitive behavioral and emotionally based approaches. The chair indicated that she preferred a more practice-oriented course for students. I was not particularly happy with this decision, as it would involve more work than what I had planned. The larger practice component of the course required, I felt, a more in-depth background and so I sought out more training and supervision to enhance my brief therapy skills. I was becoming more immersed in the SFT model.

Here is an example of how far I had changed in my practice: I never asked clients, "How do you feel?" but rather, I would ask, "How are you doing?" This is a subtle but important shift and is reflective of my movement away from emotionally based interventions. Trusting that my clients really did have the answers to their problems permitted me to adopt a nonexpert/not-knowing posture, and this in turn further helped my clients to create their own solutions more quickly. The mean number of my client sessions was eventually reduced by half (from 6 to 3). Although my client load increased, I was no longer as tired by Friday afternoon as I had been when I saw fewer clients but used a problem-centered approach. I became interested in the question of whether, with briefer treatments, students were being well served. This led me to undertake a year-long outcome study of clients who sought personal counseling at Ryerson University. The results of this study indicated that clients were equally satisfied with the service received regardless of the number of sessions they attended, and that more sessions were not associated with improved outcomes (Warner, 1996).

Q. Describe one of your favorite cases and how it impacted your work as a therapist.

A. One of my SFT colleagues, Joanna Uken, had talked about how she found Eye Movement Desensitization and Reprocessing (EMDR) a helpful backup, and this led me to take the EMDR Level 1 training. After the training I had a client, a 21-year-old woman student, who arrived in my office very despondent and disheveled. She appeared to be suffering from posttraumatic stress syndrome (PTSD). For the last two days she had slept very poorly, eaten little, and not attended classes. She had attended a house party a few days ago in which one of the guests ended up in a back bedroom and was assaulted by another guest. My client helped console the victim until an ambulance arrived, and somehow got blood on the sleeve of her jacket. She left the party quickly without speaking to anyone (obviously in a state of shock) and described herself as feeling "numb and empty." After 2 days, mostly staying in her room, she realized she needed help and ended up coming to see me at the Counseling Center. I used several of my solution focused interventions including an outcome question: "How will you know when you are getting over this upsetting experience?" However, nothing seemed to help. I concluded she would be a good candidate for my recent EMDR training, got her permission, and set up the recommended 2-hour session 4 days from then.

Before she arrived for the extended EMDR, I felt reassured that I had a treatment that might be helpful, and was prepared to take her to the hospital emergency room if she failed to respond.

When she arrived I was taken back at her appearance—I didn't recognize her! She was attractively dressed, had color in her face, and spoke with confidence. I asked her what had happened. She replied that when she left my office she did not feel any better, but somehow decided she wanted to walk home, and during that long walk she began to feel a little better, and to think about some of the questions I had asked her. She pointed to the sleeve on the jacket she was wearing, and had a smile on her face. She said she had tossed the stained jacket in the closet when she got home from the party that Saturday night. After our appointment she was able to pick up and wash the jacket, and was now back attending classes. This was the closest I came to utilizing EMDR. I subsequently found the SFT approach sufficient, but with the intention that if a traumatized client did not respond to SFT, my first choice would be the EMDR approach.

Q. Has the use of SFT impacted you in your personal life? If so, please explain.

A. Very much so. I now frequently look for opportunities to remind myself to be grateful for what is working in my life. This philosophy is much more challenging, of course, when things are frustrating and disappointing. What helps me to get back on track is to take time away (long walks or sitting by the lake), and remind myself of the importance of accentuating the positive in my life. These practices have made me more thoughtful, happy, and (I am convinced) more effective in my work and life.

Q. What are some key personality traits that you think are shared among solution focused practitioners?

A. They tend to be more optimistic, thoughtful of others, and more appreciative of their efforts. These traits become more vivid for me when I compare attendance at SF meetings and conferences (e.g., SFBTA) to the colleagues at conventional problem-focused conferences.

Q. What are some things you notice students doing while trying on this model that lets you know this model may fit them?

A. It has to do with experiencing success. The feedback I frequently receive from workshop participants is that this SFT training challenges them to see their clients from a competency perspective and affects not only their professional practice but their personal lives as well.

For example, psychiatric nurses, social workers, and other health care practitioners at two Toronto-area hospitals reported increased levels of job satisfaction and skill development as well as enhanced ability to handle a wide range of patient problems as a result of solution focused training (Warner, 1998). Similar professional development benefits were found with child care workers (Triantafillou, 1997; Warner, 1997), rehabilitation professionals (Warner, 2001), and public health nurses (Bowen, 2003).

One example is how a teacher attending a solution focused training workshop was able to address a serious school-bullying problem that had a national impact. I was privileged to be invited to offer training at the Centre for Studies in Counselling at the University of Durham (UK) a few years ago. At one of these workshops a teacher, Sue Young, came up to me and asked if this approach would work with the problem of bullying in schools. I of course said yes, we had a brief conversation, and I thought no more of it. Sue Young, however, went on to do some outcome studies (Young, 1998) on the topic "The Support Group Approach to Bullying in Schools." Subsequently the support group approach was recommended in the UK government guidance to schools because of her impressive results: over 90% of the students reported the bullying had stopped (De Jong & Berg, 2007). She has published one book, *Solutions to Bullying* (Young, 2002), has a contract to write a second one on this topic, and is now working full time as an independent consultant introducing solution focused practice to teachers on a national level with "astounding results" (personal communication, June, 2008).

Q. What are some common mistakes that therapists trying on the model make most often? If you had a chance to guide them differently, how would you do so? If you were training therapists in the SFT model, what strategies would you use to train them and how would you present the material?

A. During my first decade of teaching the solution focused model, I emphasized the "drivers"—the five primary intervention questions (i.e., exceptions, outcomes, scaling, relationship, and coping). I observed that students and workshop participants frequently experienced two impediments when using these powerful questions. First, there were often difficulties related to the fact that the interviewer did not display adequate understanding of the client's situation—in other words, the interviewer was not sufficiently empathic. The second difficulty related to there being insufficient clarity about what the client wanted—the client-generated goals. As a result of these two difficulties, I began teaching the model using a tri-phase approach that conceptualized the interview as being comprised of three discrete, but interactive, tasks or phases. So, before asking any of the five primary intervention questions (now referred to as strategy phase questions), novices are taught to address two preconditional phases—empathy and goals. This conceptualization provides a template on how to engage the client in a more systematic manner and has resulted in more rapid acquisition of solution-building skills by novices.

Q. If you could pick a pioneer solution focused therapist who impacted your work, who would you name and why?

A. This would clearly be Insoo Kim Berg.

Q. What developments would you like to see in the future of this model?

A. I think one issue that is important is how we are going to define SFT practice. I am not in the camp that requires the presence of specific techniques (e.g., the miracle question) as the defining characteristics of SFT practice. For me what is important is the nature of the therapist-client dialogue; that the dialogue consists primarily of solution-building interventions (see De Jong & Berg, 2007) as opposed to problem-solving interventions. Related to this issue is the practice of "solution-oriented" therapy, which I refer to as eclectic and have labeled as an intermediate level of solution-building skills, wherein solution-building and problem-solving are combined.

To address this issue and improve solution-building skills as developed and taught by Steve and Insoo, I started the Solution-Focused Counseling continuing education program in the Faculty of Social Work at the University of Toronto. This, to my knowledge, was the first university to offer a comprehensive solution focused specialist-level training program that was recognized by the Brief Family Therapy Center, the home of solution focused brief therapy. During the last decade over 150 graduates of this program have been trained in this specialist-level approach. (Four of the graduates are now teaching modules to the new students in the training program.) I am delighted to see the proliferation of other universities, and private training centers offering solution focused specialist-level comprehensive programs. Having the privilege of influencing the next generation of professionals has been one of the most rewarding and satisfying experiences of my career.

EDITOR'S COMMENT

When this project was first conceived, Dr. Warner responded enthusiastically with a "yes" to the request to contribute but went a step further. He asked me to contact him by phone. To say I was nervous was an understatement. I had heard about all of his accomplishments, starting a certification program with this approach, countless publications and presentations, and now he was asking me to call him. I will never forget how quickly my nerves went away as we discussed the project, the SFT approach, practitioners that gravitate toward it, and many other related topics. Two therapists that had never met before now spent almost an hour discussing theory openly. I realized that this is another trait that therapists subscribing to this approach must share: inviting. He later even sent me a copy of the first few chapters of the book he was currently working on. Throughout our phone conversation, Dr. Warner commented on the optimism present in this approach. That same optimism leaps off of the pages.

—Elliott Connie

REFERENCES

Bowen, J. (2003). *Solution-focused interviewing skills for public health nurses and home visitors.* Unpublished manuscript available from this chapter's author (R. Warner).

De Jong, P., & Berg, I. K. (2007). *Interviewing for solutions* (3rd ed.). Florence, Kentucky: Brooks/Cole.

Talmon, M. (1990). *Single-session therapy: Maximizing the effect of the first (and often only) therapeutic encounter.* San Francisco: Jossey-Bass.

Triantafillou, N. (1997). A solution-focused approach to mental health supervision. *Journal of Systemic Therapy, 16*(4), 305–328.

Warner, R. E. (1996). Comparison of client and counsellor satisfaction with treatment duration. *Journal of College Student Psychotherapy, 10*(3), 73–88.

Warner, R. E. (1997). Implementing the solution-focused model: One therapist's experience. *Journal of Collaborative Therapies, 5*(1), 8–14.

Warner, R. E. (1998). Mental health services staff training in hospital settings: A solution-focused approach. *Partners in Psychiatric Health Care, 1*(1), 32–37.

Warner, R. E. (2001, Fall). The solution-focused approach to rehabilitation counselling. *Canadian Rehab Review,* 35–36.

Young, S. (1998). The support group approach to bullying in schools. *Educational Psychology Practice, 14*(1), 32–39.

Young, S. (2002). *Solutions to bullying.* Tamworth, Staffs, United Kingdom: NASEN House.

20 Conclusion

ELLIOTT CONNIE AND LINDA METCALF

> Any intelligent fool can make things bigger, more complex, and more violent. It takes a touch of genius, and a lot of courage, to move in the opposite direction.
>
> —Albert Einstein

In concluding this book, I (Elliott Connie) wanted to share a bit about what the experience was like to embark on this journey. At the beginning of this process neither I nor Dr. Metcalf knew what we would discover. We were simply curious practitioners with a list of questions we desired to ask. We had no idea if the people on our wish list would respond or what those that did respond would think of our questions.

To our amazement we began to get one confirmation after another; almost everyone we asked said yes. I had never experienced such generosity; I had never felt such support. As the stories were sent to us we knew we had something special on our hands, something that had never been accomplished before. We had leaders in the field discussing how they were introduced to this theory and how it had impacted them, both professionally and personally. Some expressed what it was like to shift from being trained in heavily pathological approaches to SFT while others discussed studying the theory as graduate students. Many discussed their interactions with Steve de Shazer and Insoo Kim Berg. We even had Eve Lipchik discussing what it was like to play a role in the development of this approach from the early days.

Writing this book was a great honor. I never had the pleasure of meeting Steve de Shazer or Insoo Kim Berg but Dr. Metcalf and I had frequent discussions about honoring their memory with this project. I sincerely hope we did that.

I also hope that we add to the learning materials for students who are learning to become more solution focused in their lives. Notice that I did not say in their work. One of the things that each practitioner expressed was how this approach is one that they live, not just what they do with their clients. This approach is more than just a collection of techniques; it is truly a way of thinking. I hope that you, the reader, will go forward and practice solution focused thinking, thus adding to the community of people that think in this way and impact many lives. I also hope that perhaps one of the practitioners has a story that resonates with you. Perhaps you are passionate like Rayya Ghul or interested in research like Cynthia Franklin. Maybe you were trained in a pathological approach like Debbie Hogan or felt like this model "is you" like Tracy Todd. Whatever your circumstance I hope you were able to find a theme that fits you in this text and launches you into the land of solutions and possibilities.

—Elliott Connie

Elliott and I (Linda Metcalf) had the good fortune of presenting this work to the Solution-Focused Brief Therapy Association's annual conference in Austin, Texas, in November 2008. We were thrilled to have the opportunity to convey our findings and were honored when some of our participating practitioners attended.

One afternoon prior to our presentation, we sat and brainstormed what we had learned from the chapters *about* the practitioners. We had great fun listing the traits that came across so clearly to us. Below are some of our discoveries. See if they resonate with yours:

- The practitioners always relayed a personal story, a sort of triumph professionally and personally.
- The practitioners noticed that the conversations in SFT reminded them of how others important in their life talked to them.

- SFT connected their lives together . . . sort of made it all make sense.
- They talked of an underlying theme that had been running in their lives before and now they had a name for it.
- They were relieved and thrilled that someone finally gave them permission to do different things in therapy.
- They are quote people.
- There is poetry to their descriptions, narratives, and therapy.
- Everyone in the SFT culture remarks on the openness of the culture.
- The SF therapist lives the model.
- They not only practice SFT, they live it, and their clients are pleased with the results.
- The clients make doing therapy worthwhile.
- The SFT therapists receive pleasure from their work.
- They respond quickly to each other's queries, with questions and not advice.
- They enjoy being part of a project or offering help.
- They are accepting.
- They are trailblazers.
- They are not overconfident. There is no jockeying for positions.
- They are passionate and emotional about the model.
- They don't recognize boundaries of the model. The SF therapist expects the model should go beyond therapy and should be applied everywhere, to occupational therapists, schools, and so forth.
- They are creative.
- They experience a greater sense of quality of living.
- There is less stress, less burnout in SFT.
- There is always a vision and it is never impeded. Where shall we go? Everywhere.
- SFT is a theory for living life.
- SFT is a way to relate to people.

To me, the most heartwarming experience throughout this process was the participation in the project by the practitioners. Not once did anyone worry about whether his or her credentials were noted correctly or whether bios or publications were complete. Instead, everyone was more focused on helping us to produce a quality manuscript and again make a contribution to the field they loved.

We also gleaned information from the individuals about their journey to becoming solution focused therapists:

- Most respondents were trained in other therapeutic approaches prior to discovering SFT; one example is Cynthia Franklin.
- The SFT community has become known for being very accepting of newcomers, as remarked by Alasdair Macdonald.
- Once the therapists made the shift to using SFT in their work, that work became more fun, as is so well expressed by Terese Steiner.
- The theory became a way of life, not just a way of working with clients, as relayed by Ron Warner.
- Once SFT was discovered it was like coming home, putting a name to what "I was already doing," as mentioned by Chris Iveson.
- There is a flow or a poetry to the way the respondents told their stories, humorously related by Brian Cade.
- There is a passion for this model, as written by Rayya Ghul.
- People enjoyed being a part of the project and queries were often responded to quickly by people such as Harry Korman.
- Solution focused therapists constantly search for discovery within uses of the model. They are still students, admitted Alison Johnson.
- Solution focused therapists have a determination to add to the evidence base of this model with different types of research, as mentioned by Sara Smock.
- Most of the questions were hard to answer, according to Tracy Todd, because it took time to remember events. Yet once remembered, the stories flowed.
- Mentors and trainings were very important in the ability to learn this model, as relayed by Debbie Hogan.
- The responding therapists included quotes that resonated with meaning in their work. The therapists chose quotes that conveyed their passion for therapy, so much that Thorana Nelson had several that represented her work.
- Solution focused therapists are creative and energetic, as portrayed by the work of Eve Lipchik.
- Many have been directly impacted by Steve de Shazer and Insoo Kim Berg, which is well told through the descriptive and rich details provided by Yvonne Dolan.

What does the development of solution focused therapy mean? I think that answer will be different for each practitioner who reads this book. For me, it means a sense of community, a professional home of sorts that I can always visit freely and where I can be assured that I will learn something new. Just reading through the chapters supplied to us, I have discovered new ideas to use in training and new ways to think about supervising students learning the model. I have also found a comradeship in the practitioners that is quite refreshing. In this community, there is no hierarchy. Even though I can't help but look up to the people who took the risk to partake in our project and so beautifully cite their work, beliefs, and practices, it is such a comfort to know that they see themselves on the same level with each other. I can only imagine Steve de Shazer nodding at this discovery and Insoo smiling.

One last thought comes to mind as I conclude, and that is that I hope the contents of this book will serve the next group of solution focused practitioners, such as you the reader, in a variety of ways. I hope the book gives you courage to step into a model that will provide you with a wealth of success without working too hard. I hope it gives you hope for the clients whom others see as hopeless when something within you just can't help but be curious about the clients' competencies. I hope that reading the different chapters of the book will give you a renewed respect for those who originated a model that has evolved so much throughout the world yet preserved a core belief: that clients are experts, and we are the learners. I hope you experience the obvious joy that each of the practitioners has alluded to when you encounter those special clients that will one day astound you with their ideas. *When* that happens, I look forward to reading about you in the future.

—Linda Metcalf

Recommended Reading List

Berg, I. K., & DeJong, P. (2007). *Interviewing for solutions.* Belmont, CA: Thompson/ Brooks Cole.

Berg, I. K., Dolan, Y., & Trepper, T. (2007). *More than miracles: The state of the art of solution-focused brief therapy (Haworth Brief Therapy).* New York: Routledge.

Berg, I. K., & Steiner, T. (2003). *Children's Solution Work.* New York: Norton.

Cade, B., & O'Hanlon, B. (1993). *Brief guide to brief therapy.* New York: Norton.

de Shazer, S. (1985). *Keys to solutions in brief therapy.* New York: Norton.

Dolan, Y. (1991). *Resolving sexual abuse: Solution focused therapy and Ericksonian hypnosis for adult survivors.* New York: Norton.

George, E., Ratner, H., & Iveson, C. (1999). *Problem to solution.* London: BT Press.

Kelly, M., Kim, J., & Franklin, C. (2008). *Solution focused brief therapy in schools: A 360 degree view of research and practice.* Oxford Workshop Series. New York: Oxford University Press.

Lipchik, E. (2002). *Beyond technique in solution-focused therapy: Working with emotions and the therapeutic relationship.* New York: Guilford Press.

Macdonald, A. (2007). *Solution-focused therapy: Theory, research & practice.* Thousand Oaks, CA: Sage.

Metcalf, L. (2005). *Solution focused group therapy: Ideas for groups in private practice, agencies and schools.* New York: Free Press.

Metcalf, L. (2007). *The miracle question: Answer it and change your life.* Carmarthen, UK: Crown House Publishing

Metcalf, L. (2008). *Counseling toward solutions.* New York: Wiley.

Todd, T. (2009). *Practice Building 2.0 for mental health professionals: Strategies for success in a Web-based world.* New York: Norton.

Index